GN00832492

SAMUEL FERGUSON:
THE LITERARY ACHIEVEMENT

THE IRISH LITERARY STUDIES SERIES

ISSN 0140–895X

SAMUEL FERGUSON:
THE LITERARY ACHIEVEMENT

Peter Denman

Irish Literary Studies 39

1990
COLIN SMYTHE
Gerrards Cross, Bucks.

First published in 1990 by Colin Smythe Limited,
Gerrards Cross, Buckinghamshire

British Library Cataloguing in Publication Data

Denman, Peter
  Samuel Ferguson: the literary achievement. — (Irish
  literary studies;39).
  1. Poetry in Irish. Translations into English language.
  Ferguson, Sir, Samuel, 1810–1886
  I. Title   II. Series
  891.6213

  ISBN 0–86140–326–6

Produced in Great Britain
Typeset by Textflow Services Ltd., Belfast
and printed and bound by Billing & Sons Ltd., Worcester

For Siobhán

Acknowledgements

I am grateful to the Librarians of the Linen Hall Library, Belfast, the National Library of Ireland, the National Library of Scotland, and the Royal Irish Academy, and to the Deputy Keeper of the Public Record Office of Ireland, for permission to quote from manuscripts in their possession.

A version of Chapter Two was printed as 'Ferguson and *Blackwood's*; the Formative Years' in the *Irish University Review* XVI, 2 (Autumn, 1986), and parts of Chapter Seven appeared as 'Ferguson's *Congal*: Claiming an Epos?' in *Samuel Ferguson: A Centenary Tribute*, eds T. Brown and B. Hayley (Dublin, 1987); I am grateful to the editors and publishers.

I am pleased to acknowledge a generous grant from the Maynooth Scholastic Trust to assist the publication of this book.

My interest in Samuel Ferguson and his writing developed out of my research while on a Fellowship at the Institute for Advanced Study in Humanities at the University of Edinburgh; I am grateful to the Institute for the facilities it afforded me. I want also to record by thanks to Drs Andrew and Wilma Dickson of Edinburgh for their hospitality and friendship, then and ever.

P.D.

Abbreviations and Nomenclature

The following abbreviations occur in the main text or supplementary matter:

DUM	Dublin University Magazine
LHL	Linen Hall Library
Life	*Sir Samuel Ferguson in the Ireland of his Day*
NLI	National Library of Ireland
NLS	National Library of Scotland
PRO	Public Record Office of Ireland
RIA	Royal Irish Academy
SF	Samuel Ferguson

Ferguson himself was exercised about the adaptation of Irish proper names to English usage. In this book I have used the version appropriate to the text being dealt with: thus the character encountered as 'Bealchu' in the context of Keating's *History of Ireland* appears as 'Bealcu' when Ferguson's poem 'The Healing of Conall Carnach' is under discussion; the 'Conaire' of *Togail Bruidne Da Derga* because 'Conary' in the poem of that name; and so on. The variants are not so disparate as to cause confusion.

Contents

1

Introduction

Samuel Ferguson is cited as one of the earliest writers to introduce the word 'boomerang' into English. During the 1830s, when the weapon was still a novelty brought back from the Australian colonies, its peculiar properties made it an academic plaything.[1] The first of the many communications which Ferguson made to the Royal Irish Academy was a paper 'On the Antiquity of the Kiliee, or Boomerang', which was read in 1837. In this paper, arguing mainly on philological grounds, Ferguson set out to show that a weapon similar to the boomerang was known and used in classical times by the Mediterranean peoples. The choice of subject offers an insight into one of its author's most characteristic traits. There is an immediate willingness to set up a negotiation between the ancient and the contemporary, so that a detail of the heroic world of the past is put into a relationship with the latest discovery from overseas. The boomerang is at once a scientific novelty and an exhibit from a distant and unknown culture, and Ferguson attempts to assimilate it into the known tradition; a minor consequence in this instance was that Ferguson's paper was instrumental in assimilating the new word into the English language.

The impulse to assimilate is apparent in other areas of Ferguson's life. It made him an energetic and pioneering Deputy Keeper of the Public Records; one of his tasks was the gathering of parish registers from all parts of Ireland, which he efficiently brought together and stored in one place, with a multitude of other documents, at the Four Courts in Dublin; and so, alas, he unwittingly facilitated the destruction of a great part of them in a single explosion during the civil war thirty-six years after his death. More enduringly, the same assimilative impulse governed his poetry, in which he began to explore the hitherto alien literature of a dissident Irish-speaking Catholic tradition, and to translate it sympathetically into the vernacular of an English Unionist one; later, in his longer poems such as *Congal* and the various 'Lays of the Western Gael', he reached into the lost past

1

of Ireland. This he knew from its archaeological and manuscript remains, but he repeatedly sought for some linkage, stated or implicit, between the remote legendary world and his own age and culture. Where Mangan, his contemporary, rendered material exotic by surrounding it with symbolic suggestion, Ferguson domesticated it, seeking rather to make it known.

Several perceptive assessments of Ferguson work have commented on the apparent contradictions in his work. Even at the simplest of levels, there are multiple facets to his life, each of greater or lesser significance: the move from Belfast to Dublin in early adulthood; the antiquarian and scholarly enthusiasms which ran parallel to his writing; the change of career from barrister to Deputy Keeper of the Public Records. But beyond these biographical details, there is the seeming anomaly of Ferguson, the loyal public servant of Ireland under the Union, being foremost in giving a voice to legendary Gaelic antiquity and so providing a set of images which would eventually help to shape an idea of Irish independence. Such had not been his intention, of course; he sought rather to advance Ireland's claims as a cultural partner to Britain.

For those who would emphasise the tensions embedded in Ferguson's writing, the keynote is to be found in the article which he contributed to the *Dublin University Magazine* in November 1833: 'A Dialogue Between the Head and Heart of an Irish Protestant'. The issues which it raises have set the tone for discussion of his poetry.[2] But the 'Dialogue' is in fact more of a commentary on contemporary affairs than a personal manifesto. It offers a graphic disentangling of the conflicting motives which might be supposed to affect enlightened Irish Protestants (*viz*, *Dublin University Magazine* readers) in late 1833, hot on the heels of Catholic Emancipation and the Reform Act. The question of tithes, which was to remain a vexed one through the mid-1830s, had already exacerbated sectarian animosities; the Party Processions Act of 1833 had forbidden public displays of religious differences; and the Church Temporalities (Ireland) Act in August of the same year, intended to slim down the structure of the hierarchy and administration of the established church in Ireland, was regarded by the Anglican communion as unwarranted government interference in ecclesiastical affairs. 'From 1831 to 1838 the Church of Ireland felt it was in a state of siege, while the government waited to see if the storm would wear itself out.' [3] The 'Dialogue' was written to engage with these issues of the moment, rather than to offer itself as a portrait of the artist.

In later life, having moved south and married into Dublin society, Ferguson gravitated more towards the Church of Ireland. But by formation he was an Ulster Presbyterian, and consequently when writing the 'Dialogue' in 1833 he could remain somewhat apart from problems specific to the established church. Indeed, just a couple of generations previously the northern Presbyterians had made common cause with Irish Catholics as United Irishmen. It remains a moot point as to what degree Ferguson himself can be identified with the 'Irish Protestant' whose position he analyses in the 'Dialogue', or how far he is using his background as an outsider to observe and dramatise the issues confronting his readership. And if he is to be identified with either of the two voices in the 'Dialogue', it is with that of Head, who both initiates and ends the exchange and takes the lead throughout. Head coolly preserves an attitude of detached rationality, in opposition to the emotional susceptibilities of Heart.

Initially, Heart's animus is directed along party lines, against the Whig government which is promoting the measures. He proclaims a sympathy for, and some affinity with, the Irish Catholics, who also have cause, albeit a different one, to mistrust the London government. Heart continues:

> I am tormented and enraged by the condition which our loyalty has brought us. – Deserted by the Tories, insulted by the Whigs, thwarted by the Radicals, hated by the Papists, and envied by the Dissenters, plundered in our country-seats, robbed in our town houses, driven abroad by violence, called back by humanity, and, after all, told that we are neither English nor Irish, fish nor flesh, but a peddling colony, a forlorn advance guard that must conform to every mutinous movement of the pretorian rabble – all this, too, while we are the acknowledged possessors of nine tenths of the property of a great country, and wielders of the preponderating influence between two parties; on whose relative position depend the greatest interests in the empire. – I love this land better than any other. I cannot believe it a hostile country. I love the people of it, in spite of themselves, and cannot feel towards them as enemies.

Head is more inclined to consider the position of Ireland in the wider context of radical politics as pursued by 'British democrats' such as Hume and Cobbett in an opportunist allegiance with Roman Catholics. Turning aside from the heated rush to action – any action – which Heart advocates, Head wins him over to a programme of persuasion and propaganda:

> We must fight our battle now with a handful of types and a composing-stick, pages like this our field, and the reading public our arbiter of war.

And Ferguson the author is following just such a course in this article. Head attempts to pick a middle course between the twin dangers posed by a radical international alliance of republican ideologies and the exclusively confessional nativism which was later to take the specific form of Irish nationalism.

But the remarkable feature of the 'Dialogue' is not the degree to which Ferguson himself might be aligned with one or other of the speakers, but the fact that he is able to marshal and elucidate so effectively two different strands of Irish Protestant thought, and to set them off one against the other. Running through a range of attitudes from bigotry to sympathy, Ferguson represents them in an adversarial structure which allows for a balance of extremisms while at the same time all but abstracting himself from favouring one side or the other. There is a broad but non-committal inclusiveness of vision.

This inclusiveness was to be fundamental to his poetry and prose writing, which time and again seeks to explore areas unacknowledged by the culture in which he lived. There is a number of other pieces in which he adopts a polemical stance, and which derive much of their force from his writing as an outsider making an attempt to acquire and use a tradition from which he might be excluded. It is a device used to comic effect in 'Father Tom and the Pope', a piece of religious burlesque which is tied to contemporary events as much as is the 'Dialogue'. In the 1849 poem,'Dublin', which was to be Ferguson's last real excursion into polemics, it is the sense of exclusion which prevails; the poem is spoken mainly by an Irishman about to leave his native country for America, despondent at a nation in which he had hoped to find fulfilment but which offers him nothing.

Ferguson's extension into another tradition of thought is to be seen again and more strikingly in his four-part review of Hardiman's *Irish Minstrelsy*. Here the vigour of the polemicist is combined with quick perception of a hitherto unappreciated body of literature. In arguing against the politics which underpins Hardiman's presentation of the Irish poems, Ferguson created a diversion which allowed him to move in and take

possession of the texts themselves for writing in English; the
vigorous antagonism of his criticism partly occludes that mix of
generosity and opportunism which was capable of responding to
and valuing the poems even though, as parts of his review
indicate, they seemed wilfully strange to him in their rhythms
and thought.
   Confrontation with a body of literature at once unfamiliar yet
native was to be a constant in Ferguson's writing life. The
steadfastness with which he adhered to the purpose he eventually defined for himself, in spite of critical neglect and scorn
during his own lifetime, is not the least remarkable aspect of his
achievement. To us, over a century later, it seems natural and
even banal that a writer in Ireland should respond to and speak
through material drawn from Gaelic literature. But that it does
seem so is due in great part to Ferguson's example; he set out to
establish a poetic idiom in which such images, themes and
narratives might be appropriated by writing in English, and he
partly succeeded.
   In making the first sustained attempt at giving that material
formal qualities proper to the English tradition, while at the same
time preserving something of the differences which
distinguished writing in Irish, he succeeded in that he managed
to provide a nucleus of translated Gaelic verse narratives and
lyrics. The limitation to his success was that these of themselves
did not initiate a new type of poetry, nor win over a significant
new readership.
   Ferguson's importance lies rather in the fact that, for successive
generations of Irish writers, from Gavan Duffy and *The Nation*
anthologisers on through Yeats and AE to Clarke and Kinsella,
his work provided a necessary precedent. Irish poets have long
felt a need of that sort of endorsement deriving from some line of
continuity of their own, reaching back on a different course from
that of the dominant English mainstream. The name of Samuel
Ferguson has been one of the straws clutched at in any effort to
sketch a continuing tradition of Irish poetry extending back
through the nineteenth century. That his work, with the
exceptions of the nationally neutral 'Forging of the Anchor' and
the comic 'Father Tom and the Pope', was signally neglected or
even rejected by critics in England only served to confirm a
necessary sense of difference in the eyes of his successors.
   In the charting of an Irish tradition, Ferguson's name has
become inextricably linked with those of his shorter-lived

contemporaries, Davis and Mangan, as if the trinity invoked by Yeats in 'To Ireland, In The Coming Times' had defined all the possibilities for Irish writing in the nineteenth century. But Ferguson's career might have taken an altogether different shape had he chosen to follow up his early successes in *Blackwood's Edinburgh Magazine*. His entry into the pages of the leading periodical of the day, made with such *éclat* in 1832, could have established him as one of the group of Irish writers who were then prominent in the magazine press of London and Edinburgh: William Maginn, Francis Mahony ('Father Prout'), Thomas Crofton Croker, Gerald Griffin, the Banims, William Johnstone, Thomas Colley Grattan and others.

On the strength of his admission to *Blackwood's* Ferguson was furnished with introductions to members of the literary world in London, and he made use of them when keeping his terms there as a law student at the inns in the early 1830s. The group of expatriate Irish writers in London fluctuated in its membership, and was not cohesive enough in aims or background to warrant its being regarded as anything like a 'movement', but it contributed a distinctive element to British literary life during the 1820s and 1830s through the pages of the *Literary Gazette*, the *London Magazine*, and *Fraser's*, as well as *Blackwood's*. It was from these writers, rather than from Thomas Moore, that Ferguson took his early lead; and it is among them that one can discern, if not the beginnings of, then the preliminaries to, an Irish literature in the nineteenth century. The strong presence of these writers is a clear indication that, at the time when Ferguson made the first steps in his career as a writer, the centre of activity lay across the water. It was the establishment of the *Dublin University Magazine* in 1833 which enabled him to ground his work more specifically in Ireland; he in turn was foremost in giving to what was at the outset a mainly political periodical a distinctively literary cast.

Ferguson wrote not about himself but about Ireland, an Ireland that a poet might imagine. Ireland, as an abstract ideal, had long been a theme of poetry in Irish during the seventeenth and eighteenth centuries; the preferred method of presenting this abstraction was to give it a name, so that Ireland appears variously as *Banba*, or the *Sean Bhean Bhocht*, or Cathleen Ny Houlihan; but Ferguson explicitly rejected one such personification in 1834, when quarrelling with Hardiman's reading of *Róisín Dubh* as a veiled naming of the country.[4] Ferguson's interest was directed more towards the parts and places of the physical landscape. The allegorical names were generated by the imagination in poetic texts and songs; he fastened more on to those places which had, or ought to have had, a history. He had announced the need for such a theme, also in 1834, in the sonnet 'Athens':

> Yet I, methinks, so love my barbarous isle,
> That more I could not, though each nameless Dun
> Had been an Areopagus of old.

It was the first publication to which he deliberately attached his name; he shed anonymity while drawing attention to the namelessness of his own landscape. Ferguson's endeavour over the next fifty years, in his prose as well as in his poetry, was to try and compensate for that namelessness by writing in a history which would attach to the localities. It provided the impulse for his work on the Hardiman poems and on the *Hibernian Nights' Entertainments*; it was restated in 'Mesgedra'; it found a further outlet in his archaeological work on ogham, where he collected and deciphered vestiges of the past inscribed as names on the very stones of the fields and hillsides.

In discussing Ferguson's work it is useful to give attention to what may seem to be pedestrian details of date of composition and sources drawn upon. A knowledge of these yields a much clearer understanding of the shape and purpose of Ferguson's career as a writer. His writing life extended over half a century, longer than that of any of his contemporaries, with the exception of Aubrey de Vere. During that time the nature of his poetry, and the cultural conditions of the Ireland in which he wrote it, underwent great changes. He cannot be fully understood without some awareness of those developments; for instance, 'A Dialogue between the Head and Heart of an Irish Protestant' of 1833 offers a valuable and intriguing insight into the issues facing Ireland under William IV; as a key to reading Ferguson's narrative poetry of the 1860s and later it should be used with caution. By the later date the duality to which that article gives expression was being seen not in terms of the individual but of the society in which he lived.

It is of course natural and useful to think of a writer's work as a unified whole; we can speak quite properly of 'Dickens' or 'Shakespeare' or 'Yeats' when using their writings as a benchmark against which to set a particular concept or body of ideas. And one can equally well speak of 'Ferguson', when wanting, for instance, to rank him with Davis and Mangan, as Yeats did. But although Ferguson's name is readily known to anyone with more than a passing interest in Irish writing of the last century, his name is better known than the substance of his work; he is perceived as a presence rather than as an actual historical component of the tradition. Furthermore, he wrote at a time when Anglo-Irish literature, in so far as it was Irish, was attenuated, and, in so far as it was English, was seen as peripheral to a flourishing matrix which overshadowed it. Ferguson's significance for us today is so bound up with the subsequent formation of modern Irish literature that can be difficult to see his work on its own terms.

Some sense of the order of his writings is all the more necessary in that for the most part his poems, when they are known at all, are known from anthologies or selections which, while they do make the texts of (some) poems available, cannot of their nature indicate their relative positions within Ferguson's work as a whole; even the most comprehensive gathering of his poetry, A. P. Graves's edition of the *Poems of Sir Samuel Ferguson*, pays scant heed to their order of appearance. The chronological line taken in this study is designed to go some way to compensate for this, in the absence of any full edition of Ferguson's writing.

Wherever possible I quote from or refer to the various sources which Ferguson used as material for his poetry. One benefit of this is that it allows us to see the particular transformations which Ferguson makes in 'converting' (his term) the originals to the uses of his age. Apart from the fact that poetry in translation is more enjoyable when the reader has some knowledge of the original, in the particular case of Ferguson the use of a source text is so frequent as to be almost a constant in his major work; his was a poetics of scholarship rather than of the imagination, and any treatment of his poetry which did not give space to the texts on which he drew would be partial at best. Determinedly giving a new cast to the writing of Ireland, Ferguson required the authenticating presence of a written source for the material of his poetry, whether it be Hardiman's anthology, the publications of the Irish Archaeological Society, O'Curry's *Manuscript Materials for Ancient Irish History* or Juvenal's Third Satire. He is at once the most innovative and the most unoriginal of Irish poets.

2

Early Periodical Writings

Reviewing Lady Ferguson's biography of her husband, *Sir Samuel Ferguson in the Ireland of his Day* (1896), Yeats was unable to conceal his dismay at what was revealed there.[1] The poet whom he as a young tyro had admired, and had commemorated nobly in his first published articles as the one who had led Ireland to the threshold of a confident new age in literature, was scarcely distinguishable among the archbishops, judges and other worthies of ascendancy Dublin drawing-room society. Anyone seeking to know more of the background to Ferguson's poetry cannot avoid a great indebtedness to his wife's book, but it is a memorial compounded of respectfulness and respectability. The Ireland of Ferguson's day as it emerges from the biography is very much the high Victorian Ireland of the later nineteenth century, when its subject had attained eminence in several spheres of cultural and social activity. This was the period best known to Lady Ferguson herself, for the couple first met in 1847 when he was already in his late thirties and with a considerable part of his writing career already behind him.

A more continuous, and more immediate, account of Ferguson the writer is to be had from his letters to successive editors of *Blackwood's Edinburgh Magazine*. This correspondence, which extended from 1832, when he was twenty-one, until his death in 1886, is now preserved among the 'Blackwood Papers' in the National Library of Scotland; it was evidently not available to Lady Ferguson, even though the biography of her husband was published by Blackwood. There are ninety-seven letters in all, most of them concerned with actual or possible contributions to the magazine but touching also on matters of personal and general interest. They give a particularly detailed picture of the earliest and most active period of his long association with *Blackwood's*, between 1832 and 1838, when he was still in his mid-twenties and in his formative years as a writer.

Before making the breakthrough to *Blackwood's*, Ferguson's earliest pieces had appeared in the *Ulster Magazine*, a monthly published in his native Belfast and edited by Charles Teeling. Containing a mixture of commentary, fiction and verse, it lasted only from 1830 to 1832. Between March 1830 and April 1831, during his twentieth year, Ferguson contributed at least six poems to it, beginning with 'Sir Kenneth Kerr', a ballad in Scottish style which mixes narrative and song. As Ferguson's first published work, it gives early evidence of a penchant for romantic medievalism, complete with turrets, plumes and casements, and throws in a 'ween' and an 'athwart' for good measure:

> The midnight rain fell fierce and fast,
> And lightnings gleam'd along;
> When mingling wildly with the blast
> That thro' the Douglas turrets past
> Was heard the voice of song.
> In the castle-yard there stood a Knight,
> His drenched plume dripping hung –
> I ween he was a fearful sight
> As his harness glanced in the fitful light
> That athwart the gloom was flung.
> And at her casement stood above
> The bright-eyed Ladye of his love
> To whom his lay he sung.

The subsequent description of the flight by the knight and his lady southward across the border into England shows Ferguson's ability to move a story along in vigorous undemanding verse.

His other poems in the *Ulster Magazine* make up a mixed bag. There are 'To the Anti-**** Society', a humorous song defending drink against the strictures of the temperance movement, an ironical anti-Reform squib called 'The Expostulation of Honourable Lord Augustus Touchmenot with Earl Grey', and versions of two lyrics by Horace. The most significant items are the two pieces labelled as 'Ulster Ballads', 'The Rescue of the Mare' (January 1831) and 'Una Phelimy' (March 1831). These are Ferguson's first excursions into specifically Irish material, and his only contributions to the *Ulster Magazine* which he considered worth reprinting.

Blackwood's Edinburgh Magazine

The poems in the *Ulster Magazine* were just a preliminary to his first appearance in *Blackwood's Edinburgh Magazine* in February

1832, when his poem 'The Forging of the Anchor' was part of the 'Noctes Ambrosianae' instalment for that month and his career as a writer got properly under way. Several decades later Ferguson was to claim that the poem, which became one of the best-known pieces of verse in the nineteenth century, 'underwent a rejection before its appearance in 'Blackwood".[2] It seems likely that Teeling was the editor who had let 'The Forging of the Anchor' get away from him.

'The Forging of the Anchor' is some eighty lines of thumping rhyme which hymn the making of an anchor and its service to mariners on the high seas. It is distinguished for its unreflective energy, and for its passage of underwater description as the anchor sinks to the seabed.

O deep-Sea-Diver, who might then behold such sights as thou?
The hoary monster's palaces! methinks what joy 'twere now
To go plumb plunging down amid the assembly of the whales,
And feel the churn'd sea round me boil beneath their scourging tails!
Then deep in tangle-woods to fight the fierce sea-unicorn,
And send him foil'd and bellowing back, for all his ivory horn:
To leave the subtle sword-fish of bony blade forlorn;
And for the ghastly-grinning shark, to laugh his jaws to scorn.

'The Forging of the Anchor' did not make its appearance as an isolated piece in *Blackwood's* but was included in the 'Noctes Ambrosianae'; this was a sort of ongoing freewheeling conversation conducted in the pages of the magazine from month to month. It was one of the leading features in periodical journalism of the 1820s and early 1830s, and it provided a prominent platform for the poem and for its author whose name was mentioned approvingly in the text surrounding it. Ferguson found himself in notable company, for another poet given approving mention in the same 'Noctes' was Alfred Tennyson, who had just published his first solo collection, *Poems, Chiefly Lyrical*. For the rest of his lifetime Ferguson was to remain conscious of Tennyson's long career as it unfolded over the next half-century, an impressive example of what might be achieved in poems whether lyrical or narrative.

In the aftermath of his poem's publication Ferguson wrote eagerly to William Blackwood, offering to follow up his success by supplying others in a similar maritime vein, and disclosing also that he was engaged on a 'metrical romance in six cantos containing about five thousand lines'.[3] His letter further indicates that two other poems included in the same 'Noctes'

were written by him; these, which he had submitted anonymously, were 'Roger Goodfellow', a translation of Pierre de
Beranger's song '*Roger Bontemps*', and a version of the seventh
epode of Horace, '*Quo, quo, scelesti ruitis?*'. Both are given an
explicitly contemporary reference as published in the 'Noctes'.
The winter of 1831–32 was a season of political uncertainty as the
Reform Bill stumbled along its way to becoming law, and 'Roger
Goodfellow' is presented as a rallying-song to the downcast Tory
readers of *Blackwood's* who felt menaced by the aims of Grey's
government. Contemporary political reference is more pointed in
the 'Horatian Version', which is headed 'On Meeting the Birmingham Mob, Dec. 1831'. In adapting Horace's poem on civil
unrest, Ferguson engages with the high-running feelings which
had followed the Bristol riots, and which had led the Political
Union in Birmingham to organise itself as an independent local
militia,

> Whither away, ye dirty devils?
> Why have ye drawn your fire-shovels,
> Shoulder'd your pikes, and left your hovels?
> Not enough yet of your Bristol revels?

Ferguson had two other contributions in *Blackwood's* during
1832: 'The Wet Wooing; A Narrative of '98' and a poem 'Light
and Darkness'. 'The Wet Wooing', a long prose fiction set in
Ferguson's native Ulster during the autumn of 1798, tells the
story of a young soldier who meets and falls in love with the
daughter of a rebel Irish commander; the courtship leads him
steadily into the fugitive society of the rebels as they wait to
escape to France. It represents, however clumsily, an attempt to
bring two traditions into conjunction. The obvious model is
Scott's *Waverley*: the young soldier in the service of the crown
embarks on a discovery of the alternative tradition and becomes
sentimentally involved with it. In this it anticipates very clearly
the concerns and structures of what would be Ferguson's main
effort in fiction, the stories gathered as *Hibernian Nights'
Entertainments*: these are set in earlier times, but they also
dramatise possibilities of crossover, exploring the opposite sides
of conflicts in Irish history without necessarily mediating
between them or synthesising them.

To judge from Ferguson's letters, his principal narrative work
at this time was the metrical romance in cantos which is
mentioned several times during the year. In the end of June he

wrote of it as being nearly complete,[4] and soon afterwards he submitted it to *Blackwood's*. It did not meet with approval, however, and in August he wrote: 'I purpose altering my long Poem in the arrangement of the Cantos and will probably be obliged to keep it for a few months before I can satisfy myself in the change and submit it again to you'.[5] This is the last we hear of his early attempt at long narrative poetry, at least as far as *Blackwood's* is concerned.

Other pieces were written and submitted by Ferguson during this, his first year as a *Blackwood's* author. Some of them were not to be published until 1833, while others failed to find their way into the magazine at all. Among these was a tale called 'The Clouded Honeymoon', which was apparently a follow-up to the success of 'The Wet Wooing'.[6]

The most important event in Ferguson's relationship with the magazine during this first year was a visit he made to Edinburgh in April 1832, *en route* from Belfast to London to keep his terms as a law student at Lincoln's Inn. He spent ten days in the Scottish capital, and Lady Ferguson prints an enthusiastic letter to his brother describing his contacts with the Blackwood family and with other writers for the magazine. Even allowing for a natural tendency to try and impress the recipient, it is evident that Ferguson had been welcomed as a promising addition to the panel of *Blackwood's* authors.[7] He was given introductions to a number of people in London: Thomas Cadell, the publisher, William Johnstone, who wrote in *Blackwood's* on Irish affairs, and George Cruikshank, the illustrator.

At this time, fifteen years after its commencement, *Blackwood's Edinburgh Magazine* enjoyed a comfortable superiority over its rivals and imitators. Its affairs were prospering, with a monthly circulation of 8,000 having been reached the previous year.[8] It was a vigorous unofficial mouthpiece of Tory political opinion, it published some of the liveliest periodical fiction, and its reviews of current literature could be crucial to a reputation. The founder and publisher, William Blackwood (1776–1834), had in the early years enlisted the distinguished editorial assistance of John Wilson ('Christopher North'), J. G. Lockhart, James Hogg and William Maginn, but by the 1830s he and his sons had taken over a greater degree of editorial control themselves. An indication of the magazine's increasing success was its move to imposing new offices at 45 George Street in 1830, and in the same year the Blackwood family moved up to Ainslie Place in Edinburgh's New

Town; it was at this address that the young Irish recruit was received on several occasions in April 1832.

The various introductions from Blackwood served Ferguson well in London, where he remained until his return to Belfast in early July. With the Reform Bill reaching its crisis, it was an exciting summer to be in London, even for one who considered himself 'a bad authority on politics'.[9] Bad authority or not, his next contribution to *Blackwood's* was made up of political squibs – verses gathered under the heading 'An Irish Garland' and so positioned in the magazine as to form a tail-piece to an article on Ireland and Protestant Unionist interests. In these four songs, apprehensions about the state of the country are set in a wider context of international unrest rather than limited to Ireland. The Irish 'levellers' who gather for the lifting of the revolutionary Tricolour trace their lineage back through the Bristol riots to the July Revolution in Paris in 1830:

> When last to the banquet we gather'd around her,
>   The Seine for three days with our feasting was dyed;
> Blest Paris we left more enslaved than we found her,
>   And Bristol in flames to our revels replied.

The indulgent romanticising of rebellion in 'The Wet Wooing' is here quite absent. Displaying more vigour than elegance, the verses are as unsubtle as one could wish for in a political song. The conservative defenders, whose fathers held out against the Tricolour in 1798, are the gentlemen who preserve the hereditary values; opposed to them are the unschooled upstarts led by O'Connell, jackasses braying of freedom.

'An Irish Garland' inaugurated a very active year in Ferguson's association with *Blackwood's*, and seven of the thirteen numbers for 1833 carried his work. In February there was 'The Forrest-Race Romance', another short story set in the latter half of the eighteenth century, but this time on the south coast of England and with a lot of marine action. Ferguson was a keen amateur sailor in his youth, and this experience provided him with useful imagery on several occasions, from 'The Forging of the Anchor' through to the sea-passages in *Congal*. In 'The Forrest-Race Romance' there is a fine scene in which the narrator finds himself alone on an unignited fire-ship under full sail in the Channel before ending up in the quiet waters of Forrest-Race where the ship catches fire.

The following month's number contained a poem, 'The Fairy

Well', and the circumstances surrounding its publication shed some light on the background to another of Ferguson's poems, probably the most admired and influential of all his lyrics. 'The Fairy Well' had been submitted to *Blackwood's* together with 'The Fairy Thorn', but only the one poem was published, much to Ferguson's chagrin: ' "The Fairy Well" is doubly unfortunate – it should *follow*, not precede the "The Thorn" and the printers have managed to deform it by the greatest blunders'.[10] 'The Fairy Thorn' eventually made its appearance in the *Dublin University Magazine* the following year, and in theme, imagery and rhythms established itself as a prototype for later Anglo-Irish poetry, being reprinted on many occasions. Its intended companion-piece has meanwhile languished in relative obscurity, leaving 'The Fairy Thorn' rather less than Ferguson originally intended it to be.

'The Fairy Well' tells of Una Baun, a young girl weighed down by great sorrow, apparently because of her desertion by Jurlagh (*recte* Turlagh) Daune, who is mentioned in the last stanza of the poem. She wishes she could escape into fairy-land, away from the burden of memory, like Anna Grace – the girl whose abduction by fairies is described in the other poem. Accompanied by her sister, Ellen, she goes to seek the ease of forgetfulness by bathing herself with the waters of the well of Lagnanay and pacing three times round its rim. Thereupon she fades away and is seen no more. The distant languor which characterises 'The Fairy Thorn' is less evident here, and it relies for its effects on narrated incident combined with the returns of a refrain built in to each stanza. However, it is so closely related in theme to the better-known poem as to be almost integral to it, yet the two have never been published together as originally intended.[11]

Ferguson's next contribution to *Blackwood's* was four 'Songs After the French of Beranger', a return to a source which had provided the material for one of his first appearances. Almost forgotten nowadays, Pierre de Beranger (1780–1857) enjoyed immense popularity as a writer of songs in early nineteenth-century France, and the extent of his fame in Britain was sufficient to warrant his inclusion in *Fraser's* 'Gallery of Illustrious Literary Characters' in March 1835. Ferguson was among the earliest of his translators; later ones included Francis Mahony ('Father Prout') and Thackeray.

Other pieces from Ferguson during 1833 were 'The Death-Song of Regner Lodbrog', and two short stories, 'Nora Boyle' and 'The Return of Claneboy'. The first is a version of a long poem, supposedly a song chanted by the eighth-century Norse king and poet as he went to execution in a snake-pit, and recorded in a Latin text by Olaus Wormius. Ferguson's translation is accompanied by footnotes and a long commentary on the recorded details of Regner's life. The scholarly apparatus was the fruit of Ferguson's spells in the British Museum, which he frequented while back in London during the winter of 1833, and it is a first indication of his abilities as antiquarian and scholar which were to underpin all his significant poetry and fiction from this time on. A Latin text of the 'Song' had already been published among the prefatory material to an edition of Macpherson's *Poems of Ossian* in 1819, as an example of what the early poetry of Northern Europe may have been like,[12] and Ferguson in his commentary is at some pains to show the connections between the background to the poem and early Irish history.

The story 'Nora Boyle' is a short and melodramatic tale about an attempt to dispose of an infant heir so as to benefit the evil Sir Richard Morton; he has beguiled the servant-girl Nora into aiding him, but, after a night-time encounter in which she comes to realise the wickedness of Sir Richard, the child is saved, the villain drowned, and Nora dies repentant and forgiven.

When sending in 'Nora Boyle', Ferguson had written to Blackwood: 'It is not one of the projected series I spoke of but a short tale independent of history'.[13] This series of historical tales eventually took the form of the *Hibernian Nights' Entertainments*; most of those tales were to appear in the *Dublin University Magazine*, but two of the earliest, 'The Return of Claneboy' and 'Shane O'Neill's Last Amour', were published in *Blackwood's*. These tales, which are discussed along with other stories in the next chapter, reflect Ferguson's growing interest in Irish history, fed by the material he found in the British Museum and in the Lambeth Palace library. A letter written in March 1834, after his return to Belfast, tells Blackwood that he has now 'accumulated a great quantity of matter on Irish history & antiquities', and offers further pieces of the same kind as 'Shane O'Neill', 'which took very well here'.[14] The letter indicates Ferguson's growing awareness of specifically Irish subjects and readership, and he was soon to find the *Dublin University Magazine* a more convenient and effective outlet. But it was in *Blackwood's* that he had begun to discover himself as a writer, and his links with it were never abandoned and remained a factor in his literary career to the end.

Dublin University Magazine

The *Dublin University Magazine* had started publication in January 1833, at a time when Ferguson was in London. On his return to Ireland in June of that year he naturally began to cultivate the *University* as somewhere to place his writing. His first piece in its pages was an unremarkable poem, 'Don Gomez and the Cid', in August 1833. Over the following four years the magazine carried one or two pieces from him nearly every month, and with some interruptions he was to continue a contributor until 1853, furnishing well over eighty items. Notwithstanding his often close associations with the *Dublin University Magazine* in its early days, Ferguson was not one of the founder members, and he did not come to live in Dublin until 1834 when he was registered as a student at Trinity College.

Several of his early articles in the *University* were ones that had failed to make the pages of *Blackwood's*. Apart from the series of 'Hibernian Nights' Entertainments' which, as we have seen, was originally intended for *Blackwood's*, there were also 'The History of Pierce Bodkin' and 'The Fairy Thorn'; it is also likely that 'The Stray Canto', a verse tale set in England at the time of the crusades, has in fact strayed from 'the metrical romance in 6 cantos' which Ferguson had submitted unsuccessfully to *Blackwood's* in 1832. Of the 'Three Ballads' published in the *University* in January 1836, both 'Una Phelimy' and an earlier version of 'Willy Gilliland' had already been printed in the *Ulster Magazine*; in the interim Ferguson had incorporated both of these, as well as the the third of the trio, 'Young Dobbs', into a tale offered to *Blackwood's* in May 1832;[15] this tale was not published, so the three ballads were recycled for the *University* nearly four years later. This would indicate that, initially, Ferguson ranked the Irish magazine as a second string to his bow.

Even so, much of his most enduring work appeared in its pages. 'The Fairy Thorn' tells how Anna Grace was drawn away to by the fairies associated with the thorn tree. There is no real sense of any past transgression or yearning on her part which might have resulted in this, unless it be the mere fact of her daring to be one of the four who approach and dance around the tree. In Ulster folklore, the fairy thorn is a whitethorn, or hawthorn, which is found growing singly; there are many stories which outline the awful consequences of human interference with them.[16] The thorn in the poem is not solitary, but grows alongside another tree with a supernatural aura in folklore, the rowan or mountain-ash. Ferguson is not interested in particularising the events, and concentrates more on conveying the uncanny atmosphere of the landscape as the four girls succumb to 'A Power of faint enchantment'. Anna Grace is twice lured away in the course of the poem: first she is persuaded by the three sisters, to leave her house and venture 'up above the crags with them', and then she is singled out to be taken by the fairies.

The basic line of this prosodically inventive poem is a twelve-syllable iambic one, with a shorter last line in each quatrain which usually contains eight syllables but sometimes nine or ten. The variations are achieved by additional unstressed syllables in the course of a line, or by playing the rising iambic rhythm against a falling sense rhythm, as in

> They're glanc |ing through | the glimm|er of | the qui|et eve,
> Away | in milk|y wav|(ings) of neck | and ank|le bare
> The heav|y-slid|ing stream | (in) its sleep|y song | they leave,
> And the crags | in the ghost|ly air,

where the iambic pattern is all but abandoned in the final line.

The most notable of Ferguson's writings in the *University* was his four-part review of James Hardiman's two-volume *Irish Minstrelsy* (1831), which appeared between April and November 1834. This too had originally been intended for *Blackwood's*; indeed, the evidence indicates that these essays and the accompanying translations of Irish poems, which stand at the very fountain-head of modern Anglo-Irish criticism and poetry, owe their existence to a suggestion made by William Blackwood. Such being the case, some of the often-remarked peculiarities of Ferguson's review immediately become less puzzling.

Just before he left London in 1833 Ferguson wrote to Blackwood:

> The Museum is closed till the 3rd of June so that I cannot make out the collection you mention. I am but a grammar scholar in Irish as yet, but I hope soon to be able to translate and would be delighted to follow up your suggestion.[17]

Blackwood had suggested to Ferguson that he work on a collection of translations from the Irish; the phrase 'make out' as used here may mean 'decipher' or 'discern', but more probably

'compile'. The idea was prompted by Ferguson's having already
furnished *Blackwood's* with verse-translations from a number of
sources, especially 'The Death-Song of Regner Lodbrog'. There
were also his Irish prose romances which showed a growing
familiarity with the Irish background. That William Blackwood
should have been the begetter of Ferguson's work on Irish poetry
is not so unlikely as might at first appear. One of the
characteristics of his magazine was its eclecticism regarding
literatures other than English, and a decade previously it had
already published six of J. J. Callanan's versions from the Irish.[18]
Three months after Blackwood's floated the idea, Ferguson,
by now on friendly terms with some of the leading Irish scholars
of the day, was writing to George Petrie: 'Pray make my respects
to O'Donovan, and tell him I have begun Irish, and have
translated all I want of Hardiman'.[19] This work on Hardiman is
evidently what Blackwood had had in mind, and in Ferguson's
next letter to him the project has taken on the character of a
review.

> As you anticipated I find ample materials for a service to the Irish
> Minstrelsy. I hand you the two first Nos and if you like can have as
> much more. I tried it first with as grave a treatment as I could give it,
> but I found no other style than that I have adopted would answer. . . .
> If you like the Review I would take it as a great favor if you would send
> on the proofs to correct.[20]

Ten days later he was still concerned about the tone of what he
had written: 'You will find in No 1 of the Minstrelsy that I have
said somethings perhaps too broadly; I trust to your better
knowledge of what is correct to mark such on the proof that I may
if necessary alter them'.[21] The papers were not to appear in
Blackwood's, however, and by January he was writing 'I send you
something which I hope you like better than the Minstrelsy'.[22] It
is clear that the review as it began appearing in the *Dublin
University Magazine* from that April on was familiar to Blackwood,
for in March Ferguson remarked to him parenthetically 'I have
been doing a good deal lately for the University Magazine where I
begin the Minstrelsy next month'.[23]
As printed in the *Dublin University Magazine* all four papers
exhibit that broad liveliness of style about which Ferguson was so
apprehensive, and none of them more than the first, which
Malcolm Brown has called 'the most interesting, enlightening,
and perverse critical essay in the canon of Irish literature'.[24]

However, the exact relationship between the two (of a projected four) essays submitted to *Blackwood's* and the four which subsequently appeared in the *University* is not altogether clear. For instance, are the 'translations' first prompted by Blackwood the same as those mentioned in the letter to Petrie? And in the review there are two sets of translations: the literal prose renderings embedded in the text of the papers, and the verse translations in the appendix. The former are provided by Ferguson primarily to facilitate discussion of the substance; the latter are intended to remedy the unfeeling inadequacy of those by Hardiman's team of translators. Were these poems, so important in the course of Irish lyrical versification, the end-point envisaged from the outset when William Blackwood made his suggestion, or were they a later addition which grew out of the criticism of Hardiman's collection? It is in the course of the second instalment of his review, published more than twelve months after the initiation of the project, that Ferguson first gives an undertaking to supply those at the end.

Although two instalments at least of a review of Hardiman's *Irish Minstrelsy* were offered to *Blackwood's* and turned down, it was not simply a matter of transferring those manuscripts from one periodical to another and then patching on some further articles. The second, third and fourth papers contain much internal evidence of having been written, or at least revised, with Irish publication specifically in mind. For example, the second paper makes a comparison between the songs of Scotland ('theirs') and the songs of Ireland ('ours'); the third opens with a panegyric to 'our' capital city of Dublin; and the second and fourth both begin with extended references to the time of year in which they were written, references which accord strictly with the months of their appearance in the *Dublin University Magazine* and not at all with what might have been done the previous year for *Blackwood's*. It seems clear from the opening paragraphs of the fourth instalment, with its mention of Clashganny and the mills on the river Barrow in autumn, that it was written, certainly in part, during Ferguson's excursion into south Leinster during September and October of 1834. Both the tone and substance of these sections of the review are quite consonant with their having been written by an Irishman for the Irish readership of an Irish magazine.

Such is not the case with the first of the papers. It stands apart from the others in that it contains more actual translation and quotation of the Irish material than any of the succeeding instalments, and in that a gap of four months intervened before the review was continued and completed. (This interval may have had something to do with a change of editor at the *Dublin University Magazine* as Isaac Butt took over from Charles Stanford.) Brown has, as we have seen, singled out this first essay as being, among other things, 'perverse'; Robert O'Driscoll, while upholding Ferguson's analysis of Irish poetry as 'one of the most significant and original pieces of literary criticism in nineteenth-century Ireland', feels compelled to concede apologetically that in the opening pages Ferguson wrote 'as one of the ascendancy, and in his initial declarations of sympathy for the repressed Catholic Irish there is a touch of arrogant condescension'.[25]

The difficulties which are engendered by the tone of the first paper are greatly diminished if, instead of taking it as an ascendancy Irishman's address to his peers, we read it as an essay by a Tory Protestant observer standing a little apart from Ireland – by a *Blackwood's* contributor in other words. When looked at thus, the rhetorical questions posed in the long opening paragraph become much more intelligible.

Oh, ye fair hills of holy Ireland, who dares sustain the strangled calumny that you are not the land of our love? . . . Who is he who ventures to stand between us and your Catholic sons' goodwill? What though for three centuries they and we have made your valleys resound with clang of axe and broadsword, ringing on chainmail and plate armour, or with the thunder of artillery tearing their way in bloody lanes? . . . What though in times long past they startled your midnight echoes with our groans under the knife that spares neither bedridden age nor cradled infancy? . . . What though in sacred vengeance of that brave villainy we fattened two generations of your kites with heads of traitors?

The personal pronouns in this might be disentangled as follows: 'you' and 'yours' refer to the personified territory of Ireland, whose 'fair hills' are invoked; 'we' and 'our' encompass at once the authorial voice of a *Blackwood's* writer and the natives of the larger island of Britain whose love for Ireland is witnessed by their willingness to fight for possession of it, and who make up most of the readership of *Blackwood's*; 'they' and 'theirs' indicate the indigenous original inhabitants of Ireland. The opening salvo is thus removed from a strictly internal dialogue between Catholic native and Protestant settler. The 'heads of traitors' are the heads of those executed by the crown on charges of treason, and when a little further on Ferguson speaks of 'the nuptial knot' that is 'tied and consecrated between us', the reference is specifically to the Act of Union between Britain and Ireland, not to some fancied reconciliation of Catholic native and Protestant ascendancy. The attitude throughout this essay is that of a superior, even ironically detached, outsider endeavouring to bring two quarrelling factions to a better understanding of each other:

> We will not suffer two of the finest races of men in the world, the Catholic and the Protestant, or the Milesian and Anglo-Saxon, to be duped into mutual hatred by the tale-bearing go-betweens who may struggle in impudent malice against our honest efforts.

It can only be conjecture, but it seems highly probable that we are indebted to William Blackwood for the original idea of a discussion of the poems in Hardiman's *Irish Minstrelsy*, and also that the first of these papers is made up of material earlier presented to the Scottish magazine, and that this accounts in part for its idiosyncrasy of tone. Such verbal belligerence was not, of course, so extreme by the standards of the periodical journalism of the day. In some respects he is continuing 'A Dialogue Between the Head and Heart of an Irish Protestant', which belongs to just the same part of 1833 as the initial idea for the review for of Hardiman. As in the 'Dialogue', a debate is set up – this time between the Catholic editor and the Protestant reviewer, with the latter coming to see himself in the role of mediator between extremism and ignorance. In the review he is urging the claims of the Heart, as represented by the songs of the country and the response they awaken; he asks that they be examined and recognised by the Protestant intelligence of the Head. Where the debate represented in the 'Dialogue' had been internal to the article, here there is an engagement with an outside point-of-view, and the adversarial disputatiousness would have appealed to the aspirant barrister in Ferguson.

The review of Hardiman pursues a dual track; it is at once a discussion of the most effective means of making poetry in Irish available to readers of English, and a polemic on the nationhood of Ireland leading up to its present membership of the 'imperial confederacy'. Perhaps the most remarkable aspect of the whole enterprise is that a writer in the signally Tory, Protestant and Unionist *Dublin University Magazine* should be given so much

space to argue that the 'Irish Minstrelsy', the often dissident
songs of Gaelic Ireland, were part of a heritage common to all
Irishmen. Irrespective of the grounds or presuppositions of his
argument, the claims made by Ferguson betoken something of a
new radicalism in the overlap of literature and politics; the inertia
that had set in to Irish culture after the Act of Union was being
replaced by assertion and questioning.

Some of his exhortations are addressed to the Protestants in
particular, as these constituted the principal readership of the
periodical: 'But let it first be our task to make the people of
Ireland better acquainted with one another. We address in these
pages the Protestant wealth and intelligence of the country'.
More generally, Ferguson suggests that Hardiman's recovery of
these literary remains is an enterprise of value to a larger public –
a public that corresponds closely to the bulk of *Blackwood's*
subscribers: 'Let us contribute our aid to this auspicious
undertaking, and introduce the Saxon and the Scottish Protestant
to an acquaintance with the poetical genius of a people hitherto
unknown to them'.

Ferguson's quarrel with Hardiman lay in what he saw as
Hardiman's attempt to appropriate Irish songs as exclusively
expressive of Irish Catholicism, and so make them instruments of
opposition to the Protestant ascendancy. Placing his faith in the
national character of the Irish people, he looks forward to a time
when sectarian and factional disagreements will be eroded by
enlightenment and education.

> It is to the excess of natural piety, developing itself in over loyal
> attachment to principles subversive of reason and independence, that
> we would trace the tardiness, nay, sometimes the retrogression of
> civilization and prosperity in Ireland. Natural piety we would define
> as the religion of humanity, the faith of the affections, the
> susceptibility of involuntary attachment to arbitrary relations in
> society, that constitution of character most favourable to legitimate
> religious impressions, were it not that its superabundance of devotion
> too often runs to waste on sublunary or superstitious dissipating
> objects.

Hardiman's collection of songs and poems provides a basis for
this melioristic possibility, but it needs a Ferguson to interpret it
aright.

Ferguson found in the two volumes of Hardiman the Irish texts
of some 125 songs, poems and fragments. These were
accompanied by extensive prefatory material and editorial notes,

and most had been provided with English verse translations by a group of writers whom Hardiman had approached for the task. The contents are divided into four sections: songs by the eighteenth-century harper Carolan, sentimental songs (which are mostly anonymous love songs), patriotic and national songs from the Jacobite wars, and more formal odes and elegies drawn from a much greater period of time. The four parts of the review correspond loosely to Hardiman's sections, but with many digressions and excursions as Ferguson uses the poems as a means of access into a wide range of Irish history.

The first paper, after its rumbunctious start, concentrates on Carolan and the the difficulty of finding variety in a group of what are essentially praise-poems or songs written for patrons. But the first piece to which Ferguson gives his attention is 'County Mayo', taken from the second section, the 'Sentimental Songs'. Ignoring the parallel verse translation in Hardiman, he gives a full English line-by-line text of the song and asks

> Is this not better than a version? Here are the words, and unmutilated thoughts, and turn, and expression of the original; only observe, that the idiomatic differences of the two languages give to the translation an uncouth and difficult hesitation, which in the original did not affect the Irishman.

This is the opening of Ferguson's discussion of the problem of rendering Irish poetry adequately in English, a discussion which will punctuate the course of his review. In the remainder of this first paper there are fourteen linear translations of songs by Carolan, in whole or in part, after which Ferguson comments: 'Our readers have, in the translated parts of these pages, read such writing as they have never read before; and many, we would hope, have obtained some glimpses of the character, such as they never before knew or cared for'.

Resuming the review after four months, this is the point which Ferguson picks up as he moves on to discuss the 'sentimental songs', songs 'such as the speakers of the English language at large have never heard before, and which they could not see and hear now but for the pious labours of a man who, however politically malignant and religiously fanatical, has yet done such good service to his country in their collection and preservation, that for her sake we half forgive him our own quarrel, and consent to forego a great part of its vindication'. The recognition of Hardiman's work is less than unstinting, and in the areas which Ferguson does not forgive or forego he leaves himself ample scope to pursue his quarrel.

These sentimental songs are the material which Ferguson finds the most attractive, and they are the ground on which he engages with Hardiman politically. 'Sentiment is the soul of song', writes Ferguson, 'and sentiment is one imprescriptible property of the common blood of all Irishmen'. He hopes to demonstrate the particular qualities of this sentiment 'by adhering to the strict severity of literal translation', and begins by giving it a character of 'savage sincerity', which is 'the one great characteristic of all the amatory poetry of the country'. The racial taxonomy underpinning Ferguson's reading of the poems distinguishes between (Catholic) Irish, (Presbyterian) Scottish, and (Anglican?) Saxon, with the first two closely allied in temperament; desire and pathos are the dominant traits of these songs, and help to mark out the Irish sensibility, which produced them, and the Ulster Scottish, which is now responding to them, as essentially different from that of Saxon stolidity.

Another fourteen songs are translated, or partly translated, in the course of this instalment, among them '*Róisín Dubh*'. Ferguson was never to offer a versified translation of this, but he makes it the occasion of a notable skirmish with Hardiman. The song is a plaintive expression of love for 'Dark Roisin', or 'Dark Rosaleen' as Mangan was later to render it. Hardiman reads it as an allegorical political ballad: 'By "Roisin Dubh", supposed to be a beloved female, is meant Ireland. The toils and suffering of a patriot soldier, are throughout described as the cares and feelings of an anxious lover addressing the object of his affection'.[26] Ferguson, in his anxiety to neutralise the song, ripostes that it seems to him 'to be the song of a priest in love, of a priest in love, too, who had broken his vow, of a priest in love who was expecting a dispensation for his paramour, of a priest in love who was willing to turn ploughman for his love's sake', and he goes on to exclaim against the celibacy of the Catholic clergy. The priest in the poem seems to be a pleasant figment of Ferguson's enthusiasm; otherwise, the truth of the matter seems to lie between the two readings. Where Hardiman suggests that the original political meaning became submerged in the traditional love song, a recent editor states that it was a love-lyric at the outset and took on a political significance subsequently.[27]

The third paper concentrates on the second volume of Hardiman, taking the odes and bardic poems as an occasion for a dis-

cussion of the history of Ireland's nationhood. The literal translations become fewer in the second half of the review, and in the
fourth paper there are none at all until the appendix. This final
paper concentrates on assailing Hardiman's competence as 'antiquary, herald, historian, patriot, scholar, critic, and pacificator'.
It is a headstrong performance by Ferguson, swinging from
bravura assurance to niggling pedantry as he questions the
editor's motives and accuracy. It all made – still makes – for a
good read, but later on Ferguson had cause to feel a little
embarrassed by his youthful vigour. In August 1843 he was
writing to James Hardiman to acknowledge receiving a copy of
the older scholar's edition of the *Statutes of Kilkenny*:

> I have often felt since I first had the pleasure of knowing you
> personally, that your treatment of me as a friend, after the petulant –
> tho' really not ill-designed – attack on your first publication in which I
> had been engaged shortly before, ought to give me a lesson of
> forbearance & good feeling in after life; and the consideration you
> show me, now, in presenting me with your last piece, renders it
> impossible for me to refrain from expressing that sentiment. I believe I
> would not have had occasion to make this acknowledgement, if you
> had not perceived from my writings and conversation that, however
> we might differ on means, we agreed in an ardent desire for the same
> ends, the elevation of Irish literature, & the aggrandisement in all
> good gifts of the Irish people. It is vain to repent disagreements; but it
> is a satisfaction & pleasure to feel that there is one great, fixed, and
> blessed object in which all who are engaged become not only better
> citizens but kinder and gentler men.[28]

The chastened tone of this letter suggests that Ferguson had
come to recognise that, for someone who had seized on the Irish
songs as a reservoir of common Irish feeling, he had been unduly
divisive in his notice of them. But he had been writing as a young
man without many connections or obligations in the Dublin
community as yet, and the 1830s under William IV were years
which generally tolerated a more freely robust journalism than
did any of the Victorian decades which followed.

Something of Ferguson's method of translation can be gleaned
from the examples and comments in the review, and the poems
included in the 'Appendix' after the last paper. The first stage is
to arrive at a literal line-by-line translation, preserving as far as
possible the imagery and idioms of the Irish; this then becomes
the basis for a rhymed version. Here, for instance, is the second
stanza of 'Nora of the Amber Hair' – *'Nora an chúil ómraich'*:[29]

Oh Valentine of my heart within,
Make not for me a lie;
Since you promised to marry me
Without a farthing in the world:
I would walk the dew with you,
And I would me [*recte* not] bruise the grass with you,
Oh Nora of the amber hair,
'Tis prettily I would kiss your mouth!

This is a close version of the Irish, and final rhymed poem changes the meaning only minimally:

Oh valentine and sweetheart!
Be true to what you swore,
When you promised me you'd marry me
Without a farthing store:
Oh we'd walk the dew together,
And light our steps should be;
And Nora amber-coolin;
I'd kiss you daintily!

'Oh Valentine' is given for 'A bhaill íntinne' in the Irish, one of a number of instances where Ferguson is guided as much by the sound as by the sense; this is also the case in 'amber-coolin' for 'chúil ómraich'.

From some of his comments in the second instalment it would seem that the work of translation was, in part at least, a co-operative one; he speaks of having 'assistants' in the task. In 1833 he described himself to William Blackwood as 'but a grammar scholar in Irish',[30] and there is no reason to believe that he ever advanced much further in his command of the modern language. He had been one of a small group studying Irish in Belfast at about this time; other members of the class were his schoolfellows George Fox and Thomas O'Hagan. Fox was subsequently identified by Ferguson as the principal author of 'The County Mayo', a translation quoted in the first instalment of his review. Evidently poetic translation formed part of the activity of the group, and some of Ferguson's prose versions may well have emanated from this. Furthermore, he was in contact with the Irish scholars George Petrie and John O'Donovan at this time, and may have looked to one or both of them for guidance. An instructor closer to hand was Thomas Feenaghty, author of an Irish grammar, who in 1833 was appointed a teacher of Irish at the Royal Belfast Academical Institution.[31] By all acounts he had only a few students in the Institution itself, and would have had the time available to tutor a group of enthusiasts such as that to which Ferguson belonged.

Ferguson praises Thomas Moore, not as a 'translator' or for any Irish quality in his poems, but rather for showing that the Irish temperament is capable of producing fine lyric poetry and so, incidentally, preparing the way for the reception of the pieces which Ferguson is about to introduce to his readers. Of Hardiman's own team of translators, Ferguson withholds comment as long as possible and then disposes of them in a footnote. Their versions are 'so strangely unlike the originals both in sentiment and style, as to destroy alike the originality and the interest of the Irish minstrelsy for those who can appreciate it only through such a medium'. Having noted that they had generously contributed their efforts without payment, he continues:

> All the versifiers seem to have been actuated by a morbid desire, neither healthy nor honest, to elevate the tone of the original to a pitch of refined poetic art altogether foreign from the whole genius and *rationale* of its composition. We are sorry to be obliged to add, that the majority of these attempts are spurious, puerile, unclassical – lamentably bad.

The only one to be let off lightly was W. H. Drummond. Drummond (1778–1865) was, like Ferguson, an Antrim man, and their poetical careers touched at several points. In 1812 Drummond had published a long poem called *The Giant's Causeway* which includes a passage describing the floor of the ocean in terms which, even making allowance for conventionality, were very like those to be used subsequently in Ferguson's 'The Forging of the Anchor'. In later life he produced *Ancient Irish Minstrelsy* (1852), narrative fragments in verse based on old Irish poems which explore the material Ferguson drew upon for his 'Lays of the Western Gael' and *Congal*.

At the very end of his review, introducing his own translations, Ferguson discusses some of the practical problems encountered. Of these the chief was the compression of the Irish texts

> so that the translator is driven either to lengthen the measure, and thus make his version incompatible with the tune of the original, if a song, and indeed with its spirit and character in any case, or else to double each stanza, and by a dilation as prejudicial to the genius of its

subject as the over compression, of too strict adherence, to lose the raciness of translation in the effete expansion of a paraphrase.

Apart from length, there is also the problem of finding a suitable register of language. Neither the the classic poetic diction of the eighteenth century nor the idiomatic spoken English of Ireland is wholly appropriate to the particular tone allowed in Irish. There are nineteen versified translations in the Appendix. They are numbered I to XX, but without any XVIII; perhaps a poem was omitted at a late stage, but more likely it is a simple printer's error. Most but not all of them are of poems to be found in Hardiman's *Irish Minstrelsy*. For the most part Ferguson's treatment of the poems is unremarkable enough. They read now as competent renderings of the Irish material into straightforwardly rhymed stanzas. Their intrinsic virtues are mostly negative; they avoid introducing any undue refinement of language or inappropriate poetic conventions. The verses are allowed to stand as simple statements, although the degree of their restraint is perhaps less apparent now. It can best be appreciated by taking a stanza from '*Stuairín na m-Bachall m-Breágh Réidh*',[32] which is given here with an interlinear crib:

Trí nídh' do chídhim tres an n-grádh
(Three things I see through love:)
An peacadh, an bas a's an pian;
(Sin, death, and sorrow;)
Agus m'íntinn dá' ínsin gach lá dhamh,
(And my mind tells me daily)
M'aigne gur crádh sí le ciach; –
(She tormented my thoughts with despair.)
A mhaighdean, do mhíll tú a'm lár mé,
(Young girl, you have wounded me to the heart)
Agus m'impídhe ó'm láimh chúghat-sa n-iar,
(And my entreaty from my hand back to you[?])
Mé leigheas ó na saighiodaibh-si a'm lár,
([Is] to cure me from the arrow in my heart)
S go bh-fághaidh tú na grása ó Dhia.
(And that you may get grace from God).

Hardiman's translator for this poem was John D'Alton. If one puts aside for a moment the obloquy heaped on his work by Ferguson (and which subsequent commentators have generally accepted without question as merited), D'Alton's offering is a song altogether worthy of a nineteenth-century music room:

> The various emotions that sway me,
>   A lover alone can impart;
> The heavy forebodings that weigh me,
>   The anguish that tortures my heart.
> Relieve me, my love! I implore thee,
>   From pangs thou alone couldst excite;
> And oh! may the heavens shed o'er thee
>   An Eden of smiles and delight.

It is a very finished piece. There are only vestigial traces of the original Irish emotion, but that is largely a consequence of the *degree* of translation which D'Alton evidently felt to be required. As a minor poem inspired by an Irish song, it does very well; as an indication of the intrinsic qualities of that song it is next to useless. At best, D'Alton and the other Hardiman translators build on Thomas Moore's accomplishment which, as Ferguson himself pointed out admiringly, had been to indicate the possibility of an Irish lyric poetry.

But all poetic translations have to negotiate between the twin extremes of offering a new poem or maintaining a close semantic contact with the source text, and Ferguson was arguing the need for the latter. His own version of the above stanza forgoes the polish and balance of D'Alton's and, for the first four lines at least, comes close to achieving a poetry of statement:

> I through love have learned three things,
> Sorrow, sin, and death it brings;
> Yet day by day, my heart within,
> Dares shame and sorrow, death and sin.
> Maiden, you have aimed the dart
> Rankling in my ruined heart;
> Maiden, may the God above
> Grant you grace to grant me love!

The particular quality of Ferguson's translation is the extent to which he is willing to rely on a line-for-line reproduction of the ideas and images of the original, rather than seek for 'equivalents' in English poetic techniques; it is a gesture of considerable confidence, and it served the purpose of startling his readers with the newness of an unfamiliar material. It could lead to some striking individual lines:

> From all the girls in the world I'll go,
> But from you, sweetheart, oh, never, oh no,
> 'Till I lie in the coffin stretched cold and low!

('Pastheen Finn')

Great God, why am I thus denied
My Uileacan Dubh O!

('Uileacan Dubh O!')

Or to a stanza such as the following, which expands slightly on
the Irish:

Oh love, do you remember
When we lay all night alone,
Beneath the ash, in the winter storm,
When the oak wood round did groan:
No shelter then from the blast had we,
The bitter blast or sleet,
But your gown to wrap about our heads,
And my coat round our feet.

('Coolun – II')

The most prosodically distinctive of the translations in the
appendix is 'Cashel of Munster', especially the first two stanzas:

Phósfainn thú gan bha gan púint 's gan mórán spréidh,
A's phógfainn thú maidin drúchta le bánadh an lae;
Mo ghalar dúbhach gan mé a's tú, a dhian-grádh mo cléibh!
A g-Caisiol Múmhan, 's gan de leabaidh fúinn ann, acht clár bog deal.

A chaoin-bhan! an cuímhin leat-sa sliabh na m-ban fionn?
Nó an cuímhneadh leat n'uair do bhídhinn-si 's mé fiadhach 'fá'n ngleann?
'Nois ó chaith an aois mé a's gur liath mo cheann,
Ni cubhaidh dhuit mé dhíbhirt, a's tá'n bliadhain-so gann.[33]

Ferguson renders this as

I'd wed you without herds, without money, or rich array,
And I'd wed you on a dewy morning at day-dawn grey;
My bitter woe it is, love, that we are not far away
In Cashel town, though the bare deal board were our marriage bed
    this day!
Oh, fair maid, remember the green hill side,
Remember how I hunted about the valleys wide;
Time now has worn me; my locks are turned to grey,
The year is scarce and I am poor, but send me not, love, away!

The echo of internal- and cross-rhyme in this reaches an unusual
intricacy, and opens up to the delayed rhythms which were also
found in 'The Fairy Thorn'. The repetition of a word or phrasal
pattern in the first and second lines is a device which is continued
throughout the translation, and is closely derived from the
original poem. However, the first two lines of the Irish turn on
the similarity of Phósfainn thú and phógfainn thú ('I'd wed you'

and 'I'd kiss you' respectively); Ferguson restricts the sense and substitutes repetition for rhyme in order to preserve the structural feature. Furthermore, throughout the opening stanza the four '-ay' endings not only rhyme with each other but also with the original Irish, which uses a closely similar sound, while 'dawn' in 'day-dawn grey' rhymes with *bánadh an lae'*, matching it in sound, position and sense. The advanced rhyme of 'day' in the second line anticipates the proper rhyme-word 'grey', which (with its pair 'away') in turn anticipates the last two lines of the next stanza. The first rhyming complex, 'rich array', finds its sounds redistributed in 'marriage', which is placed where the end-rhyme of the fourth line would have been had it contained the same number of syllables as the preceding three. This regularity of line-length is not picked up again until the last three lines of the fifth and final stanza. The flexibility makes for the remarkable capacity of the eighth line above, which can contain three separate and fully expressed statements and still find room for a term of endearment as well without losing the prosodic shape.

Another element for which Ferguson finds room is the Irish weather, which in these translations begins to appear in Anglo-Irish verse for the first time and to provide a distinctive set of images. The occasional billows and tempests have no particular local force, but the native wet grass figures in the polite but frequent references to the 'dew', and after its conventional first line this stanza from 'Timoleague' has a ready familiarity:

> Ivy from your eaves is growing,
> Nettles round your green hearth-stone,
> Foxes howl where in your corners
> Dropping waters make their moan.

This is a vernacular imagery which has been carried over directly from the language of the old vernacular poetry, and its introduction into the current of Anglo-Irish must be seen as one of the side-effects of Ferguson's initiative.

The last instalment of the review of Hardiman was followed the next month by the first of the *Hibernian Nights' Entertainments* which ran over the next year and a half; these and other pieces of fiction from the late 1830s are discussed in the next chapter. For the ten years or so after 1834 Ferguson produced next to no poetry. The most significant contributions to the *Dublin University Magazine* during those years were three articles in late

1836 called 'The Attractions of Ireland', which were followed in January 1837 by a sequel 'The Capabilities of Ireland'. The publication of these essays was to have far-reaching effect on Ferguson's poetic career subsequently, for they were instrumental in attracting the favourable attention of Charles Gavan Duffy; Duffy was pleased to spot such nationalist fervour in the notably Protestant *University*, anticipating by some years aspects of the editorial line which would be pursued by *The Nation*. He was later to write of these essays as having 'exercised a wide and powerful influence in nationalizing the sentiments and pursuits of the literary and professional classes in this country',[34] and privately recommended them to an appreciative Thomas Carlyle as useful preparation for the latter's visit to Ireland in 1849. It was partly due to Gavan Duffy's recognition that Ferguson's poetic reputation was re-established in 1845, when he gave prominence to a significant number of Ferguson's lyrics in the anthology *The Ballad Poetry of Ireland*.

Ferguson's active association with the *Dublin University Magazine* was to last until the 1850s. His contributions included a number of poems and translations, but were mostly book reviews. His relationship with *Blackwood's* was much more intermittent, but lasted to the end of his life; he was always considered a *Blackwood's* author by the magazine, and was sent a copy of it every month; the last thing by him to appear in its pages during his life-time was 'A Word with John Bright' in 1882, a political squib in verse like his very first anonymous pieces there fifty years before. His work for *Blackwood's* and the *University* during the 1830s set Ferguson on course as writer. In their pages he found a platform for himself as reviewer, polemicist, translator, poet, and as story-teller.

3

Hibernian Nights' Entertainments and Other Fiction

The translations from Hardiman have made Ferguson one of the recognised initiators of a specifically Anglo-Irish tradition in poetry; the month after that review was completed he commenced in the *Dublin University Magazine* a series which gives him some claim to being a pathfinder for a particular kind of Anglo-Irish fiction also. The *Hibernian Nights' Entertainments*, which ran over the next year a half, was innovative on two counts: it was the first serial fiction to be published in the *Dublin University Magazine*, so paving the way for later serials in its pages by Carleton, Lever, Le Fanu and others; it was also one of the earliest examples of Irish historical fiction, setting out with the definite intent of bringing alive the Irish past rather than using it simply as a scenic backdrop to a romantic tale.

There are in all seven stories which might go under the heading of 'Hibernian Nights' Entertainments', although the seven have never been grouped all together under the serial title, either in the original periodical publication or in the posthumous collection edited by Lady Ferguson. They were written between late 1833 and the middle of 1836; five appeared in the *Dublin University Magazine* over the eighteen months between December 1834 and May 1836, ranging in length from a single instalment such as 'The Captive of Killeshin' to the novel-length 'The Rebellion of Silken Thomas' which ran to six parts and 55,000 words. These five stories from the *Dublin University Magazine* were subsequently published as a single-volume edition in New York in 1857; it was Ferguson's first book, and was apparently brought out independently of him and without his authority.

In 1887, shortly after Ferguson's death and more than fifty years after their first appearance, the *Hibernian Nights' Entertainments* were gathered into three volumes by his wife. Given the collaborative nature of their relationship and her role as his literary executor and biographer, this edition can be taken as

34

representing the form in which Ferguson himself would have wished them to be re-issued, and it shows some differences from the original serial publication in both arrangement and selection. It includes six stories: 'The Death of the Children of Usnach', 'The Return of Claneboy', and 'The Captive of Killeshin' in Volume One, 'Corby Mac Gillmore' and 'An Adventure of Shane O'Neill's' in Volume Two, and 'The Rebellion of Silken Thomas' which takes up all of Volume Three. The final story of the *Dublin University Magazine* series, 'Rosabel of Ross', is silently omitted, and two earlier stories which had been separately printed in *Blackwood's* are included: 'The Return of Claneboy' and 'Shane O'Neill's Last Amour' (the latter primly retitled by Lady Ferguson). As set out in the 1887 edition, the stories follow an approximate chronological order with regard to the subject matter: first comes a story from the legendary past, then three from the Hiberno-Norman period in the fourteenth and early fifteenth centuries, and finally two from the sixteenth. The span thus ends just before the 'actual conquest' of Ireland in the 1580s, as Ferguson dates it in 'A Dialogue between the Head and Heart of an Irish Protestant'. The order in which the stories had appeared in the *Dublin University Magazine* was rather different, and the two stories from *Blackwood's* had appeared earlier, in December 1833 and February 1834 respectively, where they lacked the framing device which ostensibly generates the series.

The *Hibernian Nights' Entertainments* are supposed to be a collection of tales told to the three Irish princes, Red Hugh O'Donnell, Henry and Art O'Neill, kept prisoners in Dublin Castle during December 1592. The dramatised narrator is the bard Turlogh Buy O'Hagan, who has infiltrated into their cell in the guise of an attendant and whiles away the three weeks before their planned escape by storytelling.

'The Death of the Children of Usnach'

The first story he tells, 'The Death of the Children of Usnach', is set in Ulster the legendary past. It is a straight retelling of one of the great romantic tales of Ireland without the introduction of any new fictional characters or incident around the received events of the story, or any attempt to modernise the narrative techniques such as one finds in each of the other *Hibernian Nights' Entertainments*. It is in fact a rendering of an Irish manuscript version of the tale which had been printed some twenty-five years before. 'Rendering' is perhaps too kind a description; in effect Ferguson has more or less silently plagiarised the work of an earlier editor, Theophilus O'Flanagan, who had produced a version of the tale for the *Transactions of the Gaelic Society* in Dublin in 1808. Lady Ferguson years later was to to describe her husband's work both as a 'literal translation' and as 'a free rendering of the Irish original'; the former is more accurate, as Ferguson's version is not free, and neither is it based on the Irish original, but on O'Flanagan's translation of it.

O'Flanagan gives two texts, one of them from a manuscript made in the eighteenth century by Hugh O'Daly. The story is printed with an English translation on the facing pages. The occasional passages in metrical quatrains are given a literal prose translation by O'Flanagan, while in footnotes there are versified translations by a Mr William Leahy, ' a young gentleman from whom Ireland has yet to expect much celebrity'. A principal concern of O'Flanagan's had been to claim the story for Ireland in the face of Scottish appropriation of it following on Macpherson's 'Darthula' in *Ossian*. His 1808 edition, while it has been found defective by subsequent scholarship, is notable as a pioneering attempt to get some of the early Irish material into print. Ferguson's follow-up is no less notable for bringing it into the popular domain.

As put into the mouth of Turlogh O'Hagan, Ferguson's text is no more than a minimal easing of O'Flanagan's parallel translation. Whereas the other *Entertainments*, for all their melodramatic staginess and set-piece descriptions, retain the vigour of a tale in the telling, 'The Death of the Children of Usnach' has in its style much of the self-conscious awkwardness that comes from an attempted fidelity to an original. Ferguson's text is everywhere close to O'Flanagan's; for instance, where O'Flanagan has

> and he moved off from the place in great wrath; and Ardan, and Deirdri, and the two sons of Fergus followed him, and they left Fergus sad and sorrowful after them (p. 53),

Ferguson writes

> and he departed from Fergus in great wrath; and Ardan, and Ainli, and Deirdre, and the two sons of Fergus followed him, and they left Fergus sad and gloomy behind them.

Ferguson's text supplies the name of Ainli, which appears in the original Irish but which O'Flanagan omits.

Elsewhere, O'Flanagan translates

> And then it was that Conor said, 'Where is my own son Fiacara the fair?' 'I am here my sovereign,' says Fiacara. 'By my troth,' said Conor, 'it was on the same night that thou thyself and Iollan the fair were born.' (p. 95)

This appears in the *Hibernian Nights' Entertainments* as

> Then it was that Conor cried, 'Where is my own son Fiara Finn?' 'I am here, my king,' cried Fiara. 'As I live,' said Conor, 'it was on the same night that thou and Illan Finn were born'.

And in the passage immediately preceding the description of the climactic fight, where Naisi sits playing chess with his brother Ainli, Ferguson interpolates an explanatory clause: 'for the sons of Usnach would not let their calm hearts be troubled by that alarm'. This is not in the Irish text, but it is the substance of a footnote by O'Flanagan, added to account for the unwarlike conduct of the brothers in the face of the impending crisis.

One of the few departures which Ferguson makes from his source is in shortening and tidying up the death of Deirdre, especially in omitting the detail of her drinking the blood of her slain companions, a feature which O'Flanagan had felt obliged to excuse and explain.

In the Irish tale there are several metrical passages, the matter of which is closely related to the narrative. Ferguson silently omits a number of these, but in place of two of them he offers his own poetical versions, both from the mouth of Deirdre. The first is sung at the moment when Deirdre, Naisi and Naisi's brothers sail from Scotland, returning from their refuge and trusting themselves to the safe-conduct of Fergus; Ferguson uses it as part of the transition from one locale to another. The second is her song of lament at the end of the story as the three brothers are buried, just before her own death.

In later selections of Ferguson's poetry, and in his own collection *Lays of the Western Gael*, these two poems are placed alongside his translations from Hardiman. Certainly they belong to the same period of activity in Ferguson's life; 'The Death of the Children of Usnach' appeared the very next month after the end of the Hardiman review and its appendix. Indeed, the whole story as told by Ferguson may well be a product of the same study of Irish in which those 'versions from the Irish' were conceived; O'Flanagan's edition, with its dual language text, would have provided a convenient and interesting learning aid. For the verse passages in it Ferguson had available to him a literal and a metrical translation as well as the Irish text.

Ferguson's treatment of the two verse passages for which he does offer versions is however very different to that in the Hardiman songs; here his approach is much freer and departs significantly from the base text. In 'Deirdre's Farewell to Alba', to use the title given later when it was published separately, he rearranges the ordering of the stanzas, omits recalcitrant matter, and expands on the length of the line. Each stanza of the 'Farewell' salutes a locality in Scotland which had sheltered Deirdre and her companions. As in the original, Ferguson lists the attractions of each place, but in doing so picks out particularly associations deriving from her love for Naisi which found its expression there.

There is no direct Irish equivalent for Ferguson's first stanza, but his second and third correspond to the fifth and eighth respectively in the Irish. Here is O'Flanagan's literal English version:

> Vale of Masan, O! vale of Masan;
> High its hart's-tongue, fair its stalks;
> We enjoyed a rocking sleep
> O'er the grassy harbour of Masan.
> . . . .
> Vale of two Roes! O vale of two Roes!
> My love each man to whom it is inheritance;
> Sweet is the cuckoo's note on bending bough,
> On the cliff over the vale of the two Roes.

William Leahy's versification of these lines is more compact in form than Ferguson's, if not in language, and he keeps as close to the original as his chosen diction will allow:

> Adieu to Masan's verdant vale!
> Where herbage sweet perfumed the gale;
> My cares were often lulled to rest
> Enroll'd in Masan's grassy vest.
> . . . .
> No more I'll rove in Daro's vale –
> I love each claimer of that dale:
> How sweet the cuckoo's melting strain
> From bending bough, o'er Daro's plain.

Such is a specimen of the raw material on which Ferguson

worked, and the second and third stanzas of the six in his poem (the original had nine) read

Glen Vashan! Glen Vashan! where roebucks run free,
Where my love used to feast on the red deer with me,
Where rock'd on thy waters while stormy winds blew,
My love used to slumber, Glen Vashan adieu!

Glendaro! Glendaro! where birchen boughs weep
Honey dew at high noon o'er the nightingale's sleep,
Where my love used to lead me to hear the cuckoo
'Mong the high hazel bushes, Glendaro, adieu!

Ferguson manages to preserve many images of the original as translated by O'Flanagan, but gives them greater particularity. The 'inheritors' of Glendaro are dropped, and the matter of the third line of that stanza, 'Sweet is the cuckoo's note on bending bough', is expanded to include a nightingale as well. Ferguson's innovation may be ornithologically unlikely in Scotland, but it contributes to a quatrain of fine sensuality. The roebucks and the red deer of the other stanza are also Ferguson's introduction, perhaps suggested subliminally by O'Flanagan's 'hart's tongue' (cneamh, or wild garlic).

Ferguson's poem is strongly formulaic, with an emphatic anapestic metre and a refrain linking the final two lines of the first and last stanzas. Each intermediate stanza begins with the repeated name of a glen, and ends with it being named again in conjunction with 'adieu' or 'farewell'. In between, there is a listing of its attractions, and also a mention of 'my love', associating the place of Deirdre's refuge with the companionship of Naisi.

The 'Farewell' shows Ferguson responding to and reproducing material which focuses on the appeal of topography and nature. The metrical passages in the tale which contain more dramatic exchanges are elided or incorporated into the prose telling by him. He does, however, allow for Deirdre's great outburst of grief over the death of Naisi and his brothers, 'Deirdre's Lament for the Sons of Usnach'. Here again, the warriors are presented in imagery which immediately associates them with the landscape and animal life – not animals native to Ireland, but ones symbolic of their prowess. This natural imagery figuratively subsumes the three men into the earth as the grave takes and covers the bodies of the protagonists, while at the same time something of the erotic passion of love is suggested:

The lions of the hill are gone,
And I am left alone – alone –
Dig the grave both wide and deep,
For I am sick and fain would sleep!

The falcons of the wood are flown,
And I am left alone – alone –
Dig the grave both deep and wide,
And let us slumber side by side.

The dragons of the rock are sleeping,
Sleep that wakes not for our weeping:
Dig the grave, and make it ready;
Lay me on my true-love's body.

The lions, falcons and dragons are taken from the original, but in
general this second poem is even more remote from the original
Irish than the 'Farewell'. Its characteristic measure is nearer that
of a Percy ballad than a Hardiman song. Nevertheless, the two
poems, because they are rather freer than the Hardiman pieces,
are trial-pieces in the finding of a voice for Anglo-Irish verse.

'The Captive of Killeshin'

Like the other stories in the *Hibernian Nights' Entertainments*, 'The
Captive of Killeshin' combines the use of historical material with
Ferguson's own experience of the Irish landscape. Four of the
stories are set in and around his native north-east Ulster; the
other three – 'The Captive of Killeshin', 'The Rebellion of Silken
Thomas', and 'Rosabel of Ross' – take place in Dublin and south
Leinster. In September and October of 1834, shortly before the
Hibernian Nights' Entertainments began appearing in the *Dublin
University Magazine*, Ferguson set off from Dublin on a tour
through the counties of Kildare, Carlow and Kilkenny.[2] By
mid-September he was at the home of his cousins, the Haughtons
in Carlow. The Haughtons were a prominent family in the area,
owning several mills there, and Alfred Haughton had been a
schoolfellow of Ferguson at the Belfast Academical Institution.[3]
    By early October Ferguson had progressed further south to
Clashganny on the river Barrow near Borris, where the
Haughtons also had milling interests; from there he wrote to
George Petrie, and it is clear from the letter that a principal object
of his tour was to visit and note the various antiquities on his
route.[4] The landscapes and sites encountered fed his growing

interest in field archaeology – he had become a member of the Royal Irish Academy earlier in the year – while at the same time they provided background locations for his fictions. The siege of Maynooth Castle in County Kildare forms a protracted climax to 'The Rebellion of Silken Thomas'; Killeshin, near Carlow town, Leighlin Castle, Ullard and the surrounding hills are the setting for 'The Captive of Killeshin', and 'Rosabel of Ross' has the walling of the town of Ross as its focal event.

While staying in Carlow he was invited to contribute to the album of Sarah Jane Haughton; the piece he chose to write in was the sonnet 'Athens', which had appeared in the *Dublin University Magazine* earlier in the year.[5] The first eight lines of this sonnet hail the newly recovered freedom of Greece; it had been composed, like a number of Ferguson's writings, in close response to contemporary happenings. After the Greek war of liberation in the 1820s, England, France and Russia combined in support of autonomy for Greece: Otto of Bavaria was installed as king, and Athens was named the capital in 1833. After dwelling on the cultural riches of the Greek past which have now achieved freedom, Ferguson turns to Ireland in the sestet. He does not transfer any of the political implications of a movement towards national independence; he contents himself instead with contrasting the unstoried landscape of Ireland with the classical heritage of Greece:

> Temple and tower, and tale heroic told
> In her own tongue, can give the natal soil
> Claims unimagined on her conscious son:
> Yet I, methinks, so love my barbarous isle,
> That more I could not, though each nameless Dun
> Had been an Areopagus of old.[6]

Now he was gathering background and material to remedy this 'nameless' state. The *Hibernian Nights' Entertainments* would people some of the localities of Ireland with romantic and stirring characters associated with the hitherto inscrutable landscape – inscrutable, that is, in the English vernacular. For instance, *Dun Dealga*, 'the fort of Dealga', is no 'nameless dun', although anglicised as Dundalk it becomes a sign with a diminished referent. When Ferguson writes 'in her own tongue' he presumably has in mind his own tongue, English; there was a rich body of place lore, or *dindsenchas*, in Irish writing.

Ferguson's eagerness to compensate for this perceived lack by 'writing in' an Irish history would lead to an exchange such as the following in 'The Captive of Killeshin'. The Irish chief O'Nolan has just learned that his son Ever has been killed by a neighbouring faction of the MacGillpatricks; as he is about to ride out to wreak vengeance, another chieftain arrives to claim his service against the English instead.

'What say you, Sir Donell Kinshella?' cried O'Nolan, 'see you not that I am bound on my own feud against another? – Donell, Donell; my son, my Ever, my only stay and promise is scarce yet cold from the murderous hands of MacGillpatrick! – King of the elements! how can Kavanagh crave service of a father in such an extremity? . . . . I conjure you, as you love the memory of your mother's father, stay me not; urge me not; for by the blessed bells of Ullard, I will ride against no man save Rickard Roe, the bastard of Ossory, and his abettors, who this day slew my son in Shrule forest . . . . '

'Then ride against the English, noble Brian, 'said Kinshella, his countenance clearing . . . . 'ride on with a safe conscience against the general enemy; for Rickard MacGillpatrick is even now fighting against his natural allies, under the banners of Edmund of March, in Kildare. It was on his way to the traitor's rendezvous at Castledermot, that the red dog of Durrow came through the pass of Shrule: my own scouts saw his party crossing the fords above Coole-banagher.'

The proper reaction to a passage such as this seems to be to reach for the road-map of Ireland. The place-names are driven into the text like so many stakes, as if to fasten it on to a storied landscape.

The topographical truthfulness which is characteristic of both the Ulster and the Leinster groups of stories is an early instance of Ferguson's project of 'writing in' an Irish history. The major thrust of his life's activities, as poet, antiquarian, and archivist, was to gather, decipher and record the traces of the Irish past. His work on ogham stones and state papers was part of this endeavour, but it found its most enduring expression in his 'storying' of the Irish landscape. The tales told by Turlogh O'Hagan are offered as example or inspiration to the three noble princes in Dublin Castle; but for Ferguson's readers in nineteenth-century Ireland they extended the temporal dimensions of the island. The communal history of Irish Protestant settlers dated from the completion of the conquest at the end of the sixteenth century; the *Hibernian Nights' Entertainments* granted access to a more remote time.

This imaginative exploration of the past may be seen as a sort of retrospective colonisation, but in Ferguson's treatment there is little that is settled. The most remarkable feature of his stories is the mobility of allegiance which they portray, with an interchange between conqueror and conquered taking place at a time when the roles of that relationship were not yet fully defined on either side. All the pieces in *Hibernian Nights' Entertainments* are, in one way or another, fictions of crossover, in which the loyalties of a character are, through misunderstanding or persuasion, transferred at least in part to the opposing side. Such a move from one side to the other could be presented as one of openness rather than of betrayal when set in the distant age of transition before the conquest was completed. The possibilities of such a transfer entailed a very personal and pointed urgency when debated with contemporary reference, as in the 'A Dialogue between the Head and Heart of an Irish Protestant'; cast back several centuries, dramatised as romantic adventure, and put into the mouth of a bard speaking to an audience of Gaelic princes in an enforced sojourn among their enemies, those possibilities became less painful and more speculative. After all, they were not history, not even stories, but entertainments.

So, in 'Corby Mac Gillmore', the timid monk Virgil from the abbey at Carrickfergus finds himself among the unbaptised Irish of Mac Gillmore's clan in the glens of Antrim; Talbot, the protagonist of 'The Rebellion of Silken Thomas', is torn between loyalty to the crown forces of Henry VIII and his friendship for the doomed rebel; and in 'The Captive of Killeshin' the English knight Fitz Thomas is won over to sympathy with the Irish during his convalescence and captivity among them. The obvious example for describing such crossovers was provided by Scott's *Waverley*, and Ferguson had already explored the theme humorously in 'The Wet Wooing'.

For 'The Captive of Killeshin' there was, however, an actual historical precedent: Froissart tells the story of Henry Castide who was taken prisoner when his horse bolted in battle and one of the Irish leaped on the horse's back behind him and captured him. Castide remained among the Irish, learned to speak the language, and married his captor's daughter. When after seven years his father-in-law was taken by the English, his mount was recognised as Castide's; an exchange was agreed, and Henry returned to England. Ferguson's story is based on this, but he recasts it by having Turlogh claim that the version he tells was handed down by a monk of Killeshin monastery: 'Froissart tells a somewhat different story, I confess, . . . but, as he was never in the Sacred Island, and speaks marvellously ill of the Irish, I think the Killeshin monk's must be the truer'.

In the fictional account the captive is named Sir Robert Fitz Thomas; he is an Englishman almost by accident (his mother was an O'Maley from Connaught) and is in despair at the prospect of an imminent forced marriage at the behest of his uncle the Earl of March. Fitz Thomas is won over by his love for Una O'Nolan, daughter of the Irish chief, and his enthusiasm for the Irish cause is much more wholehearted than anything indicated by Froissart. But his first encounter with Una reveals something of the conflicting loyalties.

'Would to heaven', he exclaimed, 'that these dissensions which keep us from knowing one another were at an end! Ah, lady, if instead of waging a vain war against England, you would abide by the surrender of the realm made by your ancestors and confirmed by the church, what a happy people might the Irish be! We should have no more of intestine feuds, of barbarous manners, of princes murdered by their usurping successors, or of any of these disgraces to a nation which the people of England now allege against this country, as an excuse for whatever rapacity or oppression they may choose to practise upon its ill-fated inhabitants.'

It would be difficult to find another paragraph which sets out so clearly and naively English colonial attitudes regarding Ireland: all would be well if only the Irish would behave themselves. Una speaks out with passion against these prejudices inculcated into Fitz Thomas through his upbringing.

I would I were an ollamh or a bard, to make thee blush for thine own country's disfigurements, before thou didst arraign these blemishes in mine: – but this I cannot do – I can only bear witness with my tears to the holy indignation my heart is burning with, when I hear these specious sophistries of sordid, rapacious men, blindly repeated by one who himself groans under the oppression of a Saxon tyranny, so hateful, that death itself would, he confesses, be a happy alternative!

This exchange which initiates their relationship is again cast in the form of a dialogue. Seen in the terms of that which Ferguson had written for the *Dublin University Magazine* sixteen months before, Una clearly speaks for the 'Heart', and hers clearly emerges as the dominant claim in this story, if not in history. But the speakers in this dialogue, being characters rather than fixed viewpoints, undergo change and arrive at an understanding and the story ends with Fitz Thomas becoming *tanist* to O'Nolan and betrothed to his daughter.

'The Rebellion of Silken Thomas'

A similar trajectory, fleshed out to greater length, is followed by
the protagonist of the next story, 'The Rebellion of Silken
Thomas', which ran over six instalments between February and
August 1835, with a break in May. It is the most achieved of all
Ferguson's historical stories in prose, and the most extensive. In
it he successfully portrays a fictional character against the
background of a critical moment in Ireland's history. The two
levels of event, personal and national, intersect for a sustained
account of the siege, defence, and eventual betrayal of Maynooth
Castle.

The fall of this stronghold in March 1535 signalled the collapse
of the Geraldine rebellion led by Thomas, Lord Offaly ('Silken
Thomas'). Written on the three hundredth anniversary of the
campaign, Ferguson's story centred on an occasion which was
dramatic of itself and which also had a far-reaching effect on the
course of affairs in Ireland, in that it marked the end of the power
of the Geraldines. This Norman family had, as Earls of Kildare,
become the dominant force in Ireland; from their lands astride the
Pale they operated as virtual rulers of much of the island and had
become almost independent of the monarch in London. In 1534
the Earl, father of Silken Thomas, was called to London where he
faced an allegation that he was misusing for his own ends military
equipment supplied to him by the crown. When Thomas learned
of his father's arrest, and heard a false report that he had been
executed, he embarked on a rebellion in which he was joined by a
number of allies in Ireland.

The episode is one of the best-known in Irish history, marking
as it does the virtual end of medieval power structures in Ireland.
Ferguson would have found accounts of it in Stanihurst's
contributions to Holinshed's *Chronicles*, and in Thomas Leland's
History of Ireland from the Invasion of Henry II which had been
published in Dublin in 1814. These give the progress of the
rebellion, including Thomas's dramatic throwing down of the
sword of state in the council chamber, the shipwreck and killing
of Archbishop Alan of Dublin, and the treachery of Parese who
handed over Maynooth Castle to the besiegers. Each of these
events is incorporated into Ferguson's story in a way that makes
them integral to it. For instance, he has it that the archbishop is
treacherously murdered while in the custody of the protagonist
Sir John Talbot. Talbot has been brought up as a protégé of the
Earl of Kildare, and so is tied by the strong claims of fosterage to

Thomas. But there is another tie on his affections: he is betrothed to Ellen Dudley, the daughter of a Dublin trader, and his prospective father-in-law, in common with the citizens of Dublin generally, is loyal to the crown.

The conflict within Talbot is acute. On the one hand he is bound by a proper feeling of loyalty to the crown, and by his love for Ellen and her family; against that there are his feelings for the Earl and his foster-brother Thomas. When Talbot does eventually throw in his lot with the rebels, he finds that because of his background he is mistrusted by them and assigned an inglorious petty command north of the city. When the Archbishop is murdered in his keeping he is accused of the deed, and the climax of the second episode is the scene of his excommunication by bell, book, and candle in St Patrick's Cathedral. Ferguson contrives to have the disguised Talbot present in the congregation while it is pronounced, with his newly-wed bride Ellen beside him.

Cut off from his church, from the party with which he had sided, and from his erstwhile friends in Dublin, Talbot sets off with Ellen on a journey through the troubled country in attempt to clear his name. They go northward to Monasterboice and Drogheda, then south again into mid-Leinster. Eventually the couple are taken prisoner by a wandering band of Irish, to be held in Maynooth Castle throughout its siege and fall.

In this story also Ferguson has managed to dramatise the problem of uncertain allegiance. His description of the campaign by Silken Thomas has the character more of a civil war than of a rebellion against the crown. The opposing sides are not marked territorially, and in Talbot's own case he finds that the fighting splits friendship and family. Although in the end Talbot arrives at a resolution of his own position, the wider crisis is not settled so easily by Ferguson. The last paragraphs describe Thomas and the Irish lords setting sail for London, where they think to avail of the terms of a pardon. But Talbot's last comment foresees their eventual end on the executioner's block:

> 'Such has been the end of our Irish Rebellions from the first; and such now, if tyranny and treachery remain as close friends as they have been of late, will be the end of the Rebellion of Silken Thomas'.

In these stories, with the exception of 'The Death of the Children of Usnach' which moves to a different beat, Ferguson typically finds a personal reconciliation for his protagonist while the larger national questions which are opened remain unresolved.

Other *Hibernian Nights' Entertainments*

The last two stories in the *Dublin University Magazine* series are of lesser quality than the others. In both 'Corby Mac Gillmore' and 'Rosabel of Ross' the presence of historical individuals and events is at best tangential to the action of the story, and even though Ferguson had difficulty in bringing such areas of experience to a satisfactory narrative conclusion they still provided him with the most effective contexts for his characters. 'Corby Mac Gillmore' is set in early fifteenth-century Antrim; the Franciscan monk Virgil from the monastery at Carrickfergus becomes the enforced companion of the unbaptised Mac Gillmore and his clan. The main lines of demarcation in this story are not between English and Irish, or between conqueror and conquered, but between Christian and pagan; this anticipates a division which will become important in Ferguson's later narrative poems.

'Rosabel of Ross' was the last of the series to appear in the *Dublin University Magazine*. At 55,000 words it is the second longest of them, but it shows some signs that Ferguson was getting weary of his project. The principal historical event is the walling of the town of Ross, or New Ross, in Wexford, which took place in the 1260s. The titular Rosabel, or Rose, whose generosity provided for the building of the walls, plays little part in the story, which is concerned with the incursions into the town by Irish clansmen from the surrounding district and the machinations of her deceitful steward.

Ferguson would have found in Stanihurst a detailed account of the construction of the defences around New Ross and of other incidents. He quotes a version of a Norman-French satirical poem, apparently composed by Friar Michael of Kildare in the thirteenth century; this had been published in *Archaeologia* in 1829.[7]

The distinguishing feature of 'Rosabel of Ross' is its use of set-pieces, in particular the description of the assembly of the townspeople as they turn out *en fête* to begin the building of the town walls. The static nature of this indicates a certain loss of narrative impulse while Ferguson indulges in a page or two of enthusiastic medievalism:

Never before was seen in an Irish town before such a waving of plumes and mantles, such a flashing or laughing of bright eyes, such a glancing and twinkling of pretty little feet, such a wreathing of radiant smiles, and bending and bestowing of gracious salutations.

The most engaging character in 'Rosabel of Ross' is *Donnell-an-Teanga*, a stock type of the fast-talking inveigling Irishman. At the beginning of the third episode Donnell, acting as interpreter and explaining the story so far, gives some insight into the meshes in which Ferguson has entangled himself in this story, as sundry narrative plots multiply like the conspiracy plots of the characters:

'There are so many plots I scarce know which to begin with. There is a plot against the Bantierna More, and a plot against the Bantierna Oge, and a plot against *Gibby-na-lung*, and a plot against *Emon-na-t'saggart*; and the villains who have plotted it all have plots besides the one against the other . . . . '.

Donnell shares some of the author's exasperation, but is rewarded by being one of the few characters left alive at the end of the story. In a cursory ending a shipload of the protagonists is drowned after their craft is lured on to the rocks outside Waterford harbour; others die, of old age or on the scaffold, or else retire to a nunnery. The final comment by the narrator Turlogh, as he ends the story hastily, cuts off any questions on loose ends:

'So ends Rosabel of Ross, my friends', said Turlogh to Henry, who was preparing to ask a number of perplexing questions, 'but as we have already trenched on the hours of repose, I think it better for us to go to sleep than to play the critic.'

And in that uncritical sleep the series came to an end. The stories had run their course, and Ferguson did not publish any more prose fiction in the *Dublin University Magazine*.

The series had commenced in the *Dublin University Magazine* in December 1834, a seasonally appropriate time. In his preliminary talk with the captives, Turlogh remarks that there are twenty-one days and nights to wait until the escape attempt can be made on Christmas night, and as each instalment is headed 'First Night', 'Second Night', 'Third Night' and so on, it looks as if it was originally intended to run over twenty-one parts. In the preamble to 'Corby Mac Gillmore' Turlogh lists the titles of some of his tales: 'Shall I tell your nobleness that ancient legend of the walls of Ross, or the story of Dame Kettle, or Coghlan na Cashlean,

Corby Mac Gillmore, – ?'. Only the first and last of these were subsequently told before the abrupt ending, and the opportunity of finishing with an account of the escape of the princes to the Wicklow hills in the depth of winter is lost; it was left to Standish O'Grady to exploit its fictional possibilities in his *Flight of the Eagle*. The two stories which had been published earlier in *Blackwood's* were 'The Return of Claneboy' and 'Shane O'Neill's Last Amour'. The former is the longer and more achieved of the two. Its historical moment is the killing of Earl William de Burgh near Carrickfergus in 1333, and its publication in 1833 fell on the five hundredth anniversary of the event it narrates, just as 'The Rebellion of Silken Thomas' a couple of years later marked the three hundredth anniversary of that event. Although the killing of de Burgh was part of a struggle among the great Anglo-Norman families in north-east Ulster, Ferguson makes it part of their reaction to the pressures of a frontier existence, caught between the power of the crown in London and the resistance of the clan structures in Ireland. The story is told from the perspective of Phelim, youngest son of Aodh O'Neill of Claneboy. Part of an expedition from the clan's territories west of the Bann to Carrickfergus, stronghold of the Anglo-Norman power, he encounters and falls in love with Honora. She, in company with her mother, Lady Gyle, is also on the way to visit de Burgh to plead for the release of her brothers who are imprisoned in Carrickfergus on suspicion of disaffection to the crown.

The crossover characters in the story are these two women, especially the younger who ends up married to Phelim. The initially unlikely marriage of the two is brought about by Loughlin Phelimy, the wily negotiator who schemes to suborn the Anglo-Norman lords and to win them over to Irish ways and sympathies. He outlines the position to his ardent young companion, O'Neill:

> Shrewd clerks, Brehons, and Erenachs like myself . . . have wrought their government more mischief in one day than centuries of unequal war could have accomplished. Have we not already in times past stirred up both the De Lacys to rebellion; won over the MacMurrough and O'More to our alliance of late in Leinster, Fitz-Thomas in Desmond, and, in Ormonde and Kilkenny, the stout Lord Tipperary?

The story explores the wavering allegiances of the Anglo-Norman overlords in the decades immediately before the enactment of the Statutes of Kilkenny in 1366, which sought to prevent precisely this assimilation of the governing families into the culture of the governed. The struggle between the two powers, as represented by the competing claims of the Irish Brehon law code and the imported feudal law, was described by Ferguson a few years later in an article which he wrote for Charles Knight's *Penny Cyclopedia*.

> It was not surprising therefore that the lapse of a Norman noble into mere Irishism, by which he acknowledged the brehon code alone, was anxiously encouraged by his dependents; and such were the inducements of the system itself for turbulent and ambitious spirits, that few of the adventurous nobles who first established themselves in Ireland resisted the temptation. (p. 386)

This is the sort of situation which the ambitious Erenach tries to exploit in 'The Return of Claneboy'.

The actual recapture of the lands east of the Bann which is announced by the title of the story is only told cursorily in two final paragraphs, which are little more than afterthoughts to the working out of the personal story of Honora and Phelim. There is a similar defect in 'Shane O'Neill's Last Amour' which tells how the Scot Randall MacDonnell enters the camp of Shane O'Neill in 1567, where his cousin Lady Catherine has been supplanted as O'Neill's wife by another woman, the wife of Calvagh O'Donnell. Shane O'Neill is present only on the periphery of the action, and the incidents of the story shed little light on the broader political and strategic issues of the sixteenth century.

Later stories

Between 1834 and 1837 nothing from Ferguson's pen appeared in *Blackwood's*. An obvious reason for this was the availability of the *Dublin University Magazine* as a more readily accessible outlet for his work. In February 1834 he had registered as a student at Trinity College, Dublin, and soon afterwards he moved to that city which was to be his home for the rest of his life. Through 1835 and 1836 the continuing *Hibernian Nights' Entertainments* absorbed most of his energies; this was, as we have seen, one of the projects diverted from *Blackwood's* to the *University*. The death in the summer of 1834 of William Blackwood, the editor who had fostered Ferguson's early work, may have brought about a change in relationship when *Blackwood's* was taken over by

William's son Alexander. He continued the process of consolidating it as a more staid and weightier magazine. Ferguson returned to its pages, however, in October 1837, with a remarkable story called 'The Involuntary Experimentalist'. This story is of some significance in the history of nineteenth-century short fiction generally, in that it stands as the last of a number of sensation tales which were characteristic of *Blackwood's* during its first two decades of publication. '*Blackwood's* fiction' became a shorthand term for a type of story which concentrated on the state of consciousness of a suffering individual in a death-bed, death-cell. or similarly *in extremis*. One of the earliest of these stories had been William Maginn's 'The Man in the Bell' in November 1821; through most of the eighteen-thirties the genre was continued by the successful and long-running 'Passages from the Diary of a Late Physician' by Samuel Warren. When that series eventually reached its end in the middle of 1837, Ferguson's story provided an opportune tailpiece, having as it does a medical protagonist also.

Ferguson had already made a tentative approach to the sensation tale in 'The Forrest-Race Romance' with its blazing fire-ship, but the romantic element of that story dilutes its more sensational aspects. There is no such dilution in 'The Involuntary Experimentalist'. A young doctor is returning to the centre of Dublin late one night after a sick-call in Harold's Cross when he comes upon a burning distillery. He joins in the firefighting efforts, but becomes trapped in one of the distillery's huge copper vats as the building collapses around him. In the vat he is isolated from direct contact with the flames but not, of course, from the rapidly increasing heat. His predicament is awful but, good medical man that he is, he takes the opportunity to note down some first-hand observations on the reaction of the human body when subjected to great heat.

The story's central event is grounded on fact, as the opening sentence makes clear: 'The destruction by fire of the distillery of Mr B — in Dublin, some time since, will be in the recollection of many of your Irish readers'. The distillery was that of Mr J. Bushby in Fumbally Lane, in the Liberties area of Dublin.

Ferguson's story had a resonance which extended far beyond Dublin, however. As the last of the *Blackwood's* sensation stories it triggered Edgar Allan Poe's delicious piece of fun, 'How to Write a *Blackwood's* Article' and the accompanying tale "The Scythe of Time". Poe portrays Mr Blackwood offering advice to an earnest young aspirant contributor and listing the stories which have succeeded in the magazine. The list includes ' "The Involuntary Experimentalist", all about a gentleman who got baked in an oven and came out alive and well, although certainly done to a turn'.[9] But while he parodied this type of writing Poe also learned from it. 'The Involuntary Experimentalist' is recognisably one of the models for his own *Tales of Mystery and Imagination*, so that Ferguson must be seen as having made a minor contribution to a literary tradition far removed from the Celtic renaissance.

The issue of *Blackwood's* for May 1838 carried no less than three pieces by Ferguson: 'A Vision of Noses', which poked fun at the phrenology fad, a sonnet on a painting of Niagara Falls by a Mr Wall, and the exuberant 'Father Tom and the Pope; or, A Night at the Vatican'. This last has been acclaimed as one of the high spots of nineteenth-century comic writing, although it was conceived as part of a sectarian skirmish. Like the 'Dialogue' and 'Athens' and a number of Ferguson's pieces, it is closely tied to contemporary events.

The piece has survived on the strength of its humour, but it had an urgent reference to what was going on in Dublin at the time. The 'Father Tom' of the title is a caricature of Father Thomas Maguire (1792–1849), parish priest of Ballinamore in Leitrim and 'modern Hercules of dogmatical controversy'.[10] In 1827 he had established his reputation in a six-day public debate on the subjects of infallibility, purgatory and transubstantiation; the chairmen for that debate were Admiral Robert Dudley Oliver and Daniel O'Connell, and a transcript of the proceedings was issued afterwards.[11] Maguire's opponent then had been a Protestant clergyman, the Reverend Richard Pope, whose name is punned upon in passing in the title of Ferguson's article. However, Pope is of no more than peripheral relevance to the events of 1838.

In the spring of that year Maguire was again active in Dublin, giving a series of sermons in the Church of Adam and Eve on Merchant's Quay; these attracted large congregations, including some Protestants. 'Father Tom and the Pope' was written as a debunking exercise to counteract the effect of Maguire's rhetoric. After the piece had been posted to *Blackwood's* there was a further development; Maguire was challenged by the Reverend Richard Tresham Gregg to a public debate. Gregg was minister at Swift's Alley, aggravatingly close to Merchant's Quay along which Maguire's audience thronged. Ferguson was apprehensive about the outcome of this debate, given the reputation of Maguire as a popular controversialist and the possibility of the upholder of the Protestant cause being confused with a much more able namesake, the Reverend John Gregg – at that time Bishop of Cork, Cloyne and Ross, and later one of the most eminent of nineteenth-century Irish churchmen.[12] Ferguson's article was given added urgency by the imminent debate, and it was published most opportunely in the May issue; the nine-day debate began on the twenty-ninth of that month.

'Father Tom and the Pope' takes the form of a series of letters from one Michael Heffernan , a Leitrim schoolmaster on a visit to Dublin; he is introduced mainly to allow the story to be told in the dialect of Maguire's own parish and from a viewpoint of blind partisanship. He tells how Maguire, on meeting the Pope for 'a night at the Vatican', first beats him in a drinking bout and then outwits him in theology, Latin, metaphysics and algebra. Maguire also shows signs of making off with the Pope's attractive young housekeeper. This last was a piquant thrust by Ferguson, for ten years before Maguire had been in court accused of abducting a young girl; the oratory of Daniel O'Connell secured his acquittal of what appears to have been a trumped-up charge.[13]

But Ferguson's principal object was to try and demonstrate the speciousness of Maguire's reasoning. This he does through a mixture of sectarian side-swiping and wholesomely vulgar fun, in a spirit which is typical of the eighteen-thirties, a much more robust decade than those which succeeded. Maguire's 'dexterity' is apparent in the contest in bog-Latin, which has the Pope and Maguire trying to sustain a conversation without recourse to any English words. Maguire wins by pretending that the amount of drink he has taken has put him in pressing need of a vessel in which to relieve himself and making as if to use one of the Pope's prized ornaments; the latter's alarm is so great that he breaks into the vernacular to protest. The night's entertaiment ends with the Pope being carried off to bed considerably the worse for wear, while an unruffled Maguire lets himself out of the Vatican taking with him his dog and what little is left of the poteen he had brought with him.

Whether or not it affected the outcome of the debate, 'Father Tom and the Pope' enjoyed a long afterlife. Yeats admired the piece before he knew Ferguson to be the author, and in an anthology of Irish writing ascribed it to William Maginn. This misattribution and others were sufficiently widespread at the end of the century for Lady Ferguson to ask Blackwood in 1894 for a statement that her husband was indeed the author.[14] The confusion had been not altogether unforeseen by Ferguson, although it had not been Maginn whom he had had in mind as putative author when requesting that 'Father Tom and the Pope' be published anonymously.

> I am very desirous not to be known as the author. It will be laid at Carleton's door or Maxwell's and they can both bear the misimputation; but, for myself, I am just about to be called to the bar here, and I confess I wouldn't like to lose the patronage of every Papist attorney as I infallibly would if they suspect me of breathing a syllable against their dogma.[15]

During the second half of the century the piece was frequently printed as a pamphlet up and down the east coast of the United States, variously attributed to Maginn or John Fisher Murray, another Irish magazine writer. There it fed into the continued religious sniping between Roman Catholics and Protestants.

Apart from the unauthorised reprintings of the *Hibernian Nights' Entertainments* and 'Father Tom and the Pope' across the Atlantic, a number of Ferguson's prose pieces from *Blackwood's* were included in the *Tales from Blackwood's* series published between 1858 and 1861. An important publishing initiative for short fiction, these twelve volumes gathered together stories from the magazine since its inception. Among the seventy and more pieces selected there were four by Ferguson: 'Father Tom and the Pope', 'The Wet Wooing', 'The Forrest-Race Romance' and 'The Involuntary Experimentalist'. In this cheap and popular format the stories reached a new audience some twenty or twenty-five years after they had been written.

Ferguson's prose stories have rather faded from view. They get scarcely a mention in any of the standard histories of Irish fiction,[16] probably because of the long time which elapsed between their first publication and their posthumous appearance in book form. But during his own lifetime, thanks to unauthorised republication in the United States and to the inclusion of some in the *Tales from Blackwood's*, they reached a wider readership than did most of his poetry.

4

The 1840s: A New Beginning

In the course of the 1830s Ferguson had achieved prominence as a contributor to the periodical press. After finishing his law studies and being called to the bar in 1838 his writing diminished, and for a number of years he wrote and published little. His major involvement with poetry was in assisting Edward Bunting, who was preparing the third series of his *Ancient Music of Ireland* for the press. This he was able to do while in Belfast as part of his work on the north-eastern circuit. No doubt it came as a welcome diversion from the struggles of a young barrister. As he wrote to *Blackwood* early in 1841,

> It is term time & I am busy with my briefs which begin to make a merest show in the bottom of my bag, though alas they are still sadly disproportionate to the capacity of that roomy receptacle.[1]

The north-eastern circuit, taking him as it did on a regular sweep twice a year up through Dundalk, Lisburn, Carrickfergus and other towns meant that he never lost contact with his native east Ulster, even though his home was henceforth to be in Dublin. That knowledge of and contact with place, first given expression in the sonnet 'Athens', is always a fundamental aspect of Ferguson's poetry; in this, as in so much else, he sounded a note that was to be heard again in subsequent Irish writing.

It was Charles Gavan Duffy's *Ballad Poetry of Ireland* (1845) that kept Ferguson's poetry before the public and provided encouragement at a time when it seems to have been needed. This anthology was published in August 1845 and went through three editions in the course of a month; it sold more rapidly than any other book published in Ireland since the Union, and reached a fortieth edition by 1874. The book was dedicated to a mutual friend of Ferguson and Gavan Duffy, Thomas O'Hagan, who had been one of the youthful 'private class' studying Irish in Belfast a dozen years before. Gavan Duffy's anthology gave ten of Ferguson's poems, more than by any of the other poets. Although it included 'The Forging of the Anchor' and 'When

this Old Cap was New' – the latter added at Ferguson's suggestion – most of the poems were taken from his contributions to
the *Dublin University Magazine* in the 1830s.

More of Ferguson's poems were included in a sequel to Gavan
Duffy's anthology, D. F. MacCarthy's *Book of Irish Ballads* which
came out the following year. Ferguson had nine more poems in
this, a representation exceeded only by that of MacCarthy
himself, who exercised his editor's prerogative to the full. Again,
nearly all Ferguson's poems in this were taken from the *Dublin
University Magazine*; the one exception was 'The Fairy Well of
Lagnanay'. There was even room for his most recent work, the
long narrative poem 'The Welshmen of Tirawley'.

Also in 1846 came two other anthologies, Henry R. Montgomery's *Specimens of the Early Native Poetry of Ireland* and Thornton
MacMahon's *Casket of Irish Pearls*. Montgomery arranged the
translations along a historical account of Ireland, and included
pieces by Charlotte Brooke, William Drummond, Mangan,
Thomas Furlong and others; again, Ferguson was the most
heavily represented of all, with fifteen of his translations
selected. *The Casket of Irish Pearls* offered examples of prose and
verse from the eighteenth and nineteenth centuries; there were
three of the Hardiman review poems 'translated from the Irish'
by Ferguson, who was among the youngest to be included.

The first three anthologies were reviewed as a group in the lead
article of the *Dublin University Magazine* for August 1847. In the
course of this review, which quotes both 'The Fairy Thorn' and
'The Coolun' entire, there is high praise for Ferguson, and it is
possible to detect in some of the comments an attempt to place on
record his primary role in initiating a type of poetry which now
seems to be developing independently of him.

> To a series of papers [on Hardiman's *Irish Minstrelsy*], in our own
> pages, from the pen of Mr Ferguson, who has been one of the most
> distinguished labourers in the field of Irish literature, the success of a
> movement which is now rapidly gaining popularity is mainly to be
> attributed . . . We think it only due to this gentleman that the world be
> made aware that it was by the efforts of his accomplished pen that
> public attention was, in the first instance, directed to those lights of
> Irish song . . . It is only fair that his claims to the honour of being the
> leader of this movement should be publicly and satisfactorily
> adjusted.[2]

By this time, however, Ferguson had moved on to a very different
type of poetry, of which 'The Welshmen of Tirawley' provided

the first inkling. But these anthologies of the 1840s, followed in the next decade by Edward Hayes' *The Ballads of Ireland* (1855), played a part in keeping Ferguson's name before the public. It was to be another twenty years before his first collection of poems was published.

For Ferguson, the most significant of the anthologies was undoubtedly the first. Its editor Gavan Duffy was to be a long-term champion of Ferguson. He had recognised in Ferguson's *Dublin University Magazine* contributions an attitude to Ireland which chimed with and in some respects anticipated the new assertiveness of *The Nation*, of which he had been co-founder in 1842, and to the end of his long life Gavan Duffy was to speak warmly of Ferguson's work in his various reminiscences of mid-nineteenth-century Ireland. Duffy's anthology gave considerable space to his original poems as well as to the poems and versions from Irish. The poet was properly appreciative, and wrote to Gavan Duffy on the book's appearance to say how gratified he was at the 'handsome things' said of him, for which 'my own party have left me to wait a sufficiently long time. They are now doubly pleasing coming from your side of the house'.[3] One can discern in these comments some resentment at having been neglected.

Although Gavan Duffy's introduction named Mangan as indisputably entitled to the first place among 'the recent native poets whose ballads enrich our collection', Mangan had at that stage written only four translations from the Irish, which is the extent of his representation. Next for mention is Ferguson. Gavan Duffy's assessment of him is probably the earliest printed critique of Ferguson's poetry:

> Mr Ferguson's ballads differ from Mangan's as Scott's poetry differs from Coleridge's. They are not reflective and metaphysical, but romantic or historical. They are not suggestive or didactic, but fired with a living and local interest. They appeal to the imagination and passions, not to the intellect. Their inspiration is external; they are coloured with scenery and costume, and ventilated with the free air of the country.

His prominence in the anthologies ensured that he was constantly before the public as a poet, even though the material came from the previous decade. After the versions from the Irish attached to the Hardiman review in 1834, Ferguson seems to have written practically no new poetry for many years. He published only 'The Pretty Girl of Lough Dan' and the eight-line 'The Sketcher Foiled' in 1836, followed by a sonnet on a painting of Niagara in 1838; the three ballads printed in the *Dublin University Magazine* in January 1836 had all been written some years previously. Although his translations from the Irish were to open up a seam of lyric poetry which would continue to be mined well into the next century, for Ferguson himself this work seems to have been a dead end rather than an avenue to new modes of expression. Lyric translations were not to figure significantly in his subsequent work over the fifty and more years that remained to him.

'The Welshmen of Tirawley'

It was in 1845 that Ferguson rediscovered his poetic voice, with a very different kind of poetry. Ever since O'Donovan's edition of *The Banquet of Dun na n-Gedh and The Battle of Magh Rath* had been published in 1842, he had been toying with the possibility of using the newly available texts published by the Irish Archaeological Society. The *Banquet* mingled history and myth in a prose narrative centred on a battle fought near Ferguson's own place, Moira, at the south-east corner of Lough Neagh. Versifying this, however, was to prove a long term project, and his first completed exercise in the new manner was a long ballad, 'The Welshmen of Tirawley', published in the *Dublin University Magazine* in September 1845. This drew on an episode recounted in the Irish Archaeological Society's publication for 1844, *The Genealogies, Tribes, and Customs of Hy-Fiachrach*, also edited by O'Donovan.

In its notice of the book, *The Nation* had addressed a 'a word to our bards and romancers', urging them 'to read zealously the text and notes, indexes, appendixes, and every tittle of the publications of the Archaeological Society, as containing information always true, and an inspiration original, native and lasting'.[4] Whether or not he needed this hint, within twelve months Ferguson had produced 'The Welshmen of Tirawley'.

For this poem he used a complicated eight-line stanza, in which the lines seem to get successively shorter until the expansion of the last line, which always ends with 'Tirawley' and is usually the refrain 'Sing the vengeance of the Welshmen of Tirawley' or a variation thereof. The story which the poem has to tell is an extended one of clan warfare over the generations, and the recurrent element of the refrain in the thirty-five stanzas effectively counterpoints the narrative sprawl of the poem. The summary of the story which provided Ferguson's starting point is given as follows in O'Donovan's translation:

At one time when the Barretts had supremacy over Tir Amhhalgaidh (as we have said), they sent their steward, who was called Sgornach bhuid bhearrtha, to exact rents from the Lynotts. The Lynotts killed this steward, and cast his body into a well called Tobar na Sgornaighe, near Garranard, to the west of the castle of Carns in Tir Amhalgaidh. When the Barretts had received intelligence of this, they assembled their armed forces and attacked the Lynotts, and subdued them. And the Barretts gave the Lynotts their choice of *two modes of punishment*, namely, to have their men either blinded or emasculated; and the Lynotts, by advice of some of the elders among them, took the choice of being blinded, because blind men could propagate their species, whereas emasculated men could not. The Barretts then thrust needles into the eyes of the Lynotts, and accordingly as each man of them was blinded, they compelled him to cross over the stepping-stones of Clochan na n-dall, near Carns, to se if more or less of sight remained with them, and if any of them crossed the Clochan without stumbling he was taken back and re-blinded! Some time after this the Lynotts meditated how they could revenge their animosities on the Barretts, and the contrivance which occurred to their minds, – one derived from their ancestors, – was to procure a dalta, (i.e. an *adopted son* [O'D]), from some powerful man of the Clann William Burke, who, previously to this period, had inhabited the south of the mountain (Nephin); and to this end Lynott fed a spirited horse which the Lynotts took with them to receive the adopted son, in order that the Burke who should break that steed should be their adopted son. And thus they obtained Teaboid Maol Burke as an adopted son, who was afterwards killed by the Barretts. So that it was in eric for him that the Barretts gave up to the Burkes eighteen quarters of land; and the share which Lynott, the adopted father of Teaboid, asked of this eric, was the distribution of the mulct, and the distribution he made of it was, that it should be divided throughout all Tir Amhalgaidh, in order that the Burkes might be stationed in every part of it as plagues to the Barretts, and to draw the country from them. And thus the Burkes came over the Barretts of Tir Amhalgaidh, and took nearly the whole of their lands from them; but at length the Saxon heretics of Oliver Cromwell took it from them all, in the year of our Lord 1652; so that now there is neither Barrett nor Burke, not to mention the Clann Fiachrach, in possession of any lands there. (pp. 337–9)

Such is the story on which Ferguson based his poem. His treatment of it expands the incident and gives it a clearer dramatic focus, inventing named characters at the centre of the historical action as he had done in his earlier historical prose fictions. The poem begins with the choice between blinding and castration. Once blinded, all the Lynotts are forced across the stepping-stones, and only one man succeeds in picking his way sure-footedly to the other bank.

Of all the blinded Lynotts, one alone
Walk'd erect from stepping-stone to stone;
So back again they brought you,
And the second time they wrought you
With their needles; but never got you
    Once to groan,
    Emon Lynott,
For the vengeance of the Welshmen of Tirawley.

Emon Lynott's plan to exact revenge is the substance of the poem. He begets a son and rears him as an accomplished horseman, hunter and warrior. With him as an example, he then asks to take the Earl MacWilliam Burke's son in fosterage. Lynott teaches him all the manly arts, but at the same time raises him as a self-indulgent libertine. As foreseen, the young Burke wreaks havoc on the neighbouring Barrett's, especially among their daughters, and he is set upon and slain by a group of their outraged young men. The Earl then demands justice for his slain son, and the Barrett's land is confiscated. Lynott as foster father is entitled to a share of that land, but he forgoes it in order to have the right of parcelling out the land given to the Earl. He does so in such a fashion that Barrett's are everywhere surrounded by Burke's, and required to treat them with deference. In this way he ensures that the Barrett's are deprived of their freedom.

'I demand not of you your manhood; but I take –
For the Burks will take it – your Freedom! for the sake
Of which all manhood's given,
And, without which, better even
    Ye should make
    Yourselves barren,
Than see your children slaves throughout Tirawley!

The final extended stanza in trochaic lines of blank verse starts with a close rendering of the end of the O'Donovan passage, although 'the Saxon Oliver Cromwell' is accompanied by 'valiant, Bible-guided,/Free heretics of Clan London'. The latter part is Ferguson's own invention, looking forward to a time of factionless freedom. It is not clear from the writing whether Ferguson considers that time to have already arrived or to be something still awaited. Perhaps the most striking aspect of this, his first attempt at turning some of the Irish historical materials into poetic narrative, was the nature of the episode chosen. When Davis commended the edition of *Hy-Fiachrach* to the bards and romancers of the day as a suitable source-book for a range of Irish subjects, he can hardly have anticipated that it would yield as its first fruit such a vicious and unforgiving tale. But the Ferguson of the 1830s had not been one to shy away from vigorous material, and here he derives the energy for the poem from the strong motives for revenge which drive Lynott.

He did modify the name of the bailiff whose killing prompted the enmity. O'Donovan refrained from translating *'Sgornach bhuid bhearrtha'* (it means something like 'the throat of the shaved prick'), and Ferguson adapted it to 'Scorna Bwee' ('Boy' in a later version) which might signify 'Yellow Throat'. However, he is still careful to indicate the nature of the man who earned the original soubriquet by describing him as 'lewd' and inserting a charge that he 'Rudely drew a young maid to him'. This little invention of Ferguson's serves to round the tale, for eventually Lynott rears the son of MacWilliam Burk to commit a similar outrage against the Barrett girls and, like Scorna Bwee, he is killed for the deed.

'The Welshman of Tirawley' gives a clear indication of the dominant features of Ferguson's poetry in later life: the 'lays of the Western Gael' and *Congal*. It will be poetry with a strong narrative line carried along by incident rather than by development of character. While very much a poetry of the third-person there are noticeable interjections by the authorial voice, as at the end of this poem. But before writing further poems conforming to this pattern, Ferguson was to write three very different but striking pieces during the remainder of the 1840s.

Ferguson and Davis

The death of Thomas Davis on Tuesday September 16th, 1845, was one of those events which set down a marker in the lives of a whole generation, leaving individual memories indelibly printed with details of where they were and what they were doing at the moment they learnt of it. We know what Ferguson was doing on that particular Tuesday; he was lying ill in bed in his room at Henrietta Street, across the Liffey from Baggot Street where Davis died in his mother's house.[5]

Davis, a Protestant with a Welsh family background, had been born in Cork. He was five years younger than Ferguson. Their paths had converged on Dublin in the 1830s, when both were students at Trinity College, and both were called to the Irish bar in 1838, although in different sessions. While Ferguson went on to practise law, Davis turned to journalism, first in the *Citizen* and *Morning Register*, and then in *The Nation* which he co-founded with Gavan Duffy and John Mitchel in 1842.

Ferguson's experience as a writer, and the pride in things Irish which he had voiced in several of his articles, might have made him a potential contributor to *The Nation* in spite of his Tory convictions, but he was never to be among its panel of contributors even though he shared many of the aims. His detachment may have been because of a lack of sympathy for the methods it advocated; quite likely there was also the pragmatic consideration that, as a struggling young barrister in the early stages of his career, he would not have been helped by links with the Young Ireland group. In fact, during the early forties, Ferguson apparently wrote nothing for magazines of any persuasion, apart perhaps from some pieces for Petrie's *Irish Penny Journal* in 1842, which had ceased publication a month or two before *The Nation* commenced.[6]

During 1843 and 1844 Davis and Ferguson shared one area of common ground: opposition to the *Dublin University Magazine*. *The Nation* criticised its unthinking Toryism, while Ferguson's quarrel was more specifically with its editor Charles Lever who had aided and favoured Thackeray's *Irish Sketch-Book* (1842), which Ferguson considered to be outrageously derogatory of Ireland. By August 1844, however, Ferguson was telling Davis that he had 'patched up [his] quarrel with the *University*' and would be contributing an article on Carleton to the forthcoming number.[7] *The Nation* took the hint, and in the following month it was pleased to note some recent improvement in the *Dublin University Magazine*, observing 'It is thorough Tory; but it is kindly, grave and Irish. . . . By far the best article in the current number is the review of Carleton's works'. It is evident from Ferguson's letters to Davis that there was a degree of friendship between the two. Ferguson knew him well enough to show Davis his work in progress and to joke about the sexual imagery of the round tower on Davis's seal. When in April 1845 he found himself unable to complete an urgent proof-reading assignment, it was to Davis that he turned for help.[9] Davis sent to Ferguson a handsomely bound copy of *The Spirit of the Nation* anthology in 1845 which Ferguson acknowledged:

Accept my best thanks for the 'Spirit of the Nation', which I will preserve as a memorial of your friendship and an incitement to my own love of song and country. When I see how we are all working, I hope to see Dublin at least a better Edinburgh.

Edinburgh, which had fostered his early triumphs, was still the reference point in Ferguson's aspirations for Ireland. The letter continued in terms which set the bounds to his own spirit of nationalism:

Self-reliance is all in all, and with the growing self-reliance of the young men, wider prospects may open. In the meantime, I am satisfied with the progress we are making, even though it aim at no greater result than literary and intellectual supremacy.[10]

The two men shared an enthusiasm for cultural nationalism. Where they differed was that cultural nationalism marked the limit of Ferguson's ambitions; for Davis it was to serve as the basis for a much broader political thrust towards repeal of the Union.

'The Welshmen of Tirawley', marking Ferguson's return to poetry, appeared in *Dublin University Magazine* for September 1845. Later that same month Davis died and, on the very same day according to Gavan Duffy[11], the bed-ridden Ferguson gave vent to his feelings in a poem lamenting the loss. It is a remarkable piece for a number of reasons, and was published eighteen months later in an article on Thomas Davis which Ferguson contributed to the *Dublin University Magazine* as part of its long-running series of profiles headed 'Our Portrait Gallery'.[12]

For nearly all of the intervening year of 1846 Ferguson had been out of Ireland, travelling in Europe in order to recover his health, which seems to have collapsed completely in the latter part of 1845. The Davis profile was his return to active journalism. Ferguson makes of Davis a fellow-traveller of enlightened Tories; had he lived, he would eventually have joined the gentlemen and, no doubt, written for the *Dublin University Magazine*. The article ends with the poem composed at the time of Davis's death. It is one of unusual power in

Ferguson's work. His characteristic poetry is narrative and heroic, but his poem for Davis is invested with the language of personal feeling. The poem begins:

> I walked through Ballinderry in the spring-time,
>   When the bud was on the tree;
> And I said, in every fresh-ploughed field beholding
>   The sowers striding free,
> Scattering broad-cast forth the corn in golden plenty,
>   On the quick seed-clasping soil,
> Even such, this day, among the fresh-stirred hearts of Erin,
>   Thomas Davis, is thy toil!
>
> I sat by Ballyshannon in the Summer,
>   And saw the salmon leap;
> And I said, as I beheld the gallant creatures
>   Spring glittering from the deep,
> Through the spray, and through the prone heaps striving onward
>   To the calm, clear streams above,
> So seekest thou thy native founts of freedom, Thomas Davis,
>   In thy brightness of strength and love!
>
> I stood on Derrybawn in the Autumn,
>   And I heard the Eagle call,
> With a clangorous cry of wrath and lamentation,
>   That filled the wide mountain-hall,
> O'er the bare deserted place of his plundered eyrie;
>   And I said, as he screamed and soared,
> So callest thou, thou wrathful-soaring Thomas Davis,
>   For a nation's rights restored!

In some respects it might be regarded as an elegy, but without the meditative calm which normally accompanies such a poem; this may be a consequence of its having been written so close to the event which prompted it, as an almost spontaneous response to the sense of loss. The poem does, however, display one feature often observable in elegy: it is as much about the elegist himself as about the person commemorated. In no other poem of Ferguson's is the first-person pronoun used so prominently and repeatedly.

The place-names mentioned in the three opening stanzas, grounding the poem in specific parts of Ireland, are brought easily into the service of the poem; the difficulties of namelessness, as alluded to over a decade before in 'Athens', are no longer a factor. And the concept of national freedom, so remote from the concerns of the earlier poem that it was subliminally edited out, now springs from 'native founts'.

The three places are all localities associated with Ferguson and not at all with Davis. Ballinderry, a village in County Antrim, is situated in that narrow tract of Ulster between Lough Neagh and Belfast which was Ferguson's boyhood territory in the springtime of his life, and which provides the setting for so much of his work. Ballyshannon is in south Donegal, just over the border from Sligo and Leitrim, and situated by the waterfall of Assroe ('*Eas Ruaidh*') on the River Erne, a notable salmon river; Ferguson had spent some time in the area in the summer of 1842. Derrybawn is an area of woods and rockface at Glendalough in County Wicklow, where Ferguson had been on a walking tour in June 1836 – not, admittedly, in the autumn as mentioned in the poem, where the season is generated by the 'spring-time – summer' sequence set up in the first and second stanzas.

The literalness of the attention given to the poem here is not unwarranted; each place does have connection with Ferguson's life, and in the next stanza, which is near the pivotal centre of the poem's thought and the one which refers directly to Davis's death, he mentions directly his own personal condition at the time. In a letter of sympathy to Gavan Duffy dated the day that Davis died, Ferguson apologised for being unable to call in person because of being confined to bed with illness. (He was sufficiently recovered two days later to attend the funeral.) The circumstance appears in the poem:

> And alas! to think but now, and thou art lying,
> Dear Davis, dead at thy mother's knee;
> And I, no mother near, on my own sick-bed.

The seasonal cycle of the opening section of the poem is completed by the implicit winter of Davis's death, while the present state of Ireland merges symbolically with the aspirations fostered by and embodied in Davis. It is clearly apparent in this stanza, where the idea of motherhood as expressed in the lines quoted above elides into the larger image of mother Ireland bereft of her son:

> But a hundred such as I will never comfort Erin
> For the loss of the noble son.

It is an early instance of an image which will become a commonplace myth in the Irish literary revival.

The next three stanzas revisit the imagery of the first three, showing the devastating change that has come with the loss of Davis.

Young husbandman of Erin's fruitful seed-time,
    In the fresh track of danger's plough!
Who will walk the heavy, toilsome, perilous furrow,
    Girt with Freedom's seed-sheets now?
Who will banish with the wholesome crop of knowledge
    The flaunting weed and the bitter thorn,
Now thou art thyself but a seed for hopeful planting
    Against the resurrection morn?

There are many other quasi-topographical or landscape passages in Ferguson's poetry, but they usually occur in a legendary or historical context. This poem evokes the contemporary countryside.

The time of its writing was the late summer of 1845, on the very eve of the famine which scarred the Irish countryside and the Irish perception of nature and the land ever since. By the time the poem appeared in print the famine in Ireland was approaching its worst. As a result, the change from fertility to the devastation of loss enacted in the poem has a significance which goes beyond the sense of grief at Davis's death. In the midst of natural disaster was published a poem which begins with a retrospective account of *natura naturans* in Ireland – seed being sown in the fertile soil, salmon leaping in clear water, the high solitude of the eagle.

The three successive images of what Davis represented for Ireland are not simple alternatives; they figure different aspects of what Ferguson saw in him. The sower is the cultural animator and propagandist, spreading a new consciousness 'among the fresh-stirred hearts of Erin', while the salmon is the seeker after new modes of freedom for his country, leaping clear of the 'bigotry and hate' which are presumably associated with Daniel O'Connell and his followers. Both of these sides of Davis Ferguson can approve, but not the eagle whose 'clangorous cry of wrath and lamentation' among the deserted mountains is born of anger at a sense of national wrong. When Ferguson repeats these images in the fifth, sixth and seventh stanzas, he refuses to grieve for the loss of the eagle, seeing that side of Davis's character as loaded with potential violence. The poem's lamentation is carefully discriminating, but its recognition of the various tendencies in what Davis had signified is a further instance of Ferguson's ability to assimilate differences.

This poem on Davis (Ferguson left it untitled) is perhaps the only nineteenth-century Irish poem of its kind which enters successfully into the public domain at a level of seriousness.

Other poems about the dead there were in plenty: Richard Dalton Williams's 'Lament for Clarence Mangan', D'Arcy McGee's 'The Dead Antiquary' on John O'Donovan, and a number on Davis, by John Frazer, John Fisher Murray and Mary Eva Kelly among others. None of these combine personal concern and national commitment as does Ferguson's poem. Prompted by occasion, informed by a sense of ceremony, it has the solemnity of an ode. In Ireland the poem is almost without parallel in its own century, but it does have a tangential relationship with the Irish tradition of the *caoineadh*, or keen, the recited funeral lamentation best exemplified in the eighteenth-century *Caoineadh Airt Uí Laoghaire*. Ferguson would have had some contact with this folk poetry in 1839 when working on Bunting's *Ancient Music of Ireland*, and perhaps even earlier when preparing his review of Hardiman. Although a keen is typically spoken by a woman over the corpse, Ferguson, whether by accident or design, incorporates a number of themes which are characteristic of the form. Seán Ó Tuama identifies six such themes: (i) the keener addresses the dead person directly, (ii) beseeches him to come back to life, (iii) praises his manliness, background and generosity, (iv) claims that nature has gone into mourning for him, (v) mentions having had a premonition of his death, and (vi) speaks out against his enemies and opponents.[13] Four of these themes, or variations of them, are to be encountered in Ferguson's poem; (ii) and (v) are absent.

Ferguson's approximation to the *caoineadh* is a further instance of his intuitive feeling for Gaelic poetry, and his ability to marry it with the more formal requirements of poetry in English. Successful as it was, the poem was not reprinted until 1874 when D. F. MacCarthy gave it pride of place at the head of a revised edition of his *Book of Irish Ballads*, a volume which was dedicated to Ferguson. Wrote MacCarthy, 'The first poem in a collection such as this should strike, as it were, the keynote of the volume. This note is now struck, and struck effectively, by the elegy on Thomas Davis, which is not only a most pathetic lamentation on his death, but a powerful figurative picture of his life and work'.[14] Mac-Carthy, with more precision than succinctness, headed the previously untitled poem 'Thomas Davis: His Life; His Death; His Work'.

'Inheritor and Economist' and 'Dublin'

In the summer of 1849 Ferguson published two long poems in the *Dublin University Magazine*. Written in heroic couplets, these treat directly of the contemporary situation in Ireland and are more in the nature of verse essays than poems. Both show the degree of Ferguson's political and social commitment at this time in his life, and represent a high-water mark from which he was subsequently to withdraw.

'Inheritor and Economist' is an allegorical portrayal of the woes of property in Ireland at the mid-century. After the ravages wrought on human and economic life by the famine, the Irish landowner is everywhere assailed by the consequences of an unsympathetic and uninformed government from London. Ferguson's protagonist is Inheritor, who represents primarily inherited wealth and property but also the values of continuity and stability on which a civilised society is built. Opposed to Inheritor is Economist, who outlines the latest theories of political economy concerning land management. Bamboozled by the jargon, deprived of protection by free trade, and above all made vulnerably pliable as a result of the exploitation by English government, Inheritor outlays his capital in a superfluous analytic study of his land, 'botanizing on poor Ireland's grave', as the poem puts it.

There ensues a succession of encounters with minor characters representing aspects of the current state of Ireland: Pauper, Mortgagee, Receiver, Collector, Tenant-in-Tail. In a country weakened by legislative mismanagement, natural disaster strikes with an aggravated force:

> Such was the land's and such the ruler's plight,
> When heaven, at length, in anger sent the blight.
> With silent swiftness, in a mildew blast,
> O'er Erin in one night the mischief passed:
> Where eve had sunk in shining emerald track,
> Morn showed the green potato ridges, black,
> And all the air, as with a sick man's breath,
> Stunk o'er a waste of vegetable death.

The passage describing the effects of the potato blight is probably the most effective part of 'Inheritor and Economist'; it is also the least typical. The burden of the poem is carried by the interplay of the various characters and the ideas they represent, as when the country Rustic attempts to urge the refining values of humanity against the positivist doctrines of Economist.

> 'Civilization, so it seems to me',
> Rustic rejoined, 'implies Society;

And, if my argument, so far, be good,
Society needs Life, and Life needs Food;
And if you take our Food, and Life be gone,
What's left to civilize, or trade upon?'

'Truth, sir, is left,' Economist replies,
'And scientific law, that never dies!
The principle survives; and, just observe –
I'd sooner see you and your nation starve
Than compromise, infringe, impeach, evade,
Or bate one jot the doctrines of Free Trade.'

Rustic's lines here seem to embody Ferguson's own views, but as events are played out in the poem the Irish estate is sacrificed to meet the demands of the British Mortgagee; Inheritor's daughter, Inheritrix, has to drudge at needlework to earn their bread, and his son Tenant-in-Tail is driven to open rebellion.

Tenant-in-Tail from college halls returned,
Saw the land's ruin, and indignant burned:
A mad exploit the hapless boy conceives,
At one good blow to overthrow the thieves,
To raise his bleeding country, and restore
Her Monarch, Lords, and Commons as of yore,
Joins, with rash zeal, a rude rebellious band,
Failing, escapes, and flies his native land.

The impulse towards self-government, such as that seen in the abortive rising of the previous year, is regarded as 'a mad exploit' born of 'rash zeal'. The son's actions are in direct opposition to the establishment 'thieves', and arise from a love for his 'bleeding country' and its lost self-government. Nevertheless he is distinguished from the 'rude rebellious band' whose motives, it appears, might be less worthy than his; in the end he is separated even from 'his native land'.

The state of Ireland, and the disaffection of its population, are a direct consequence of Whig government policies. Justified resentment of these policies does not lead, in Ferguson's view, to a reaction of proud nationalism but to the disintegration of the kingdom. When the final lines of the poem promise Ireland that

the day will come
When heavens shall also give its sign to thee,
Thy Diocletians fallen, thy people free,

he is anticipating not independence, but a change of government.

Soon after its appearance in the *Dublin University Magazine*, 'Inheritor and Economist' was republished as a pamphlet, again anonymously. This poem and its successor, 'Dublin', published two months later, are of a kind with his speech to the Protestant Repeal Association the previous year[15] and his pamphlet *On the Expediency of Taking Stock* (1847). They mark the culmination of Ferguson's active engagement in the agitation for repeal in the late 1840s. But both poems also indicate a withdrawal from that active engagement. 'Inheritor and Economist' ends in fragmentation and exile; 'Dublin' gives the reflections of an Irishman as he is about to emigrate from Dublin to America, where the Californian gold-rush provides a stark contrast to the stagnation of Ireland.

> For sure no hell-on-earth could well be worse
> Than here to hear the alternate altar-curse
> And pistol shot; the weakling infants' moans
> The mother's sobs, the maddened father's groans,
> The evicted cottier's shrieks; the thousand cries
> That swell the ruined nation's obsequies;
> And, 'mid the hubbub of our woes and crimes,
> The daily prate complacent of the *Times*.

Ferguson subtitles his poem 'In Imitation of the Third Satire of Juvenal'; it also imitates Samuel Johnson's version of that satire, 'London', implicitly matching Dublin with the larger capital. But Ferguson's poem adheres more closely to the general lines of Juvenal than does Johnson's. At times the correspondences are quite remarkable. Even so, 'Dublin' is far more than simply a literary exercise in the classical manner; it is one of the most telling of all Ferguson's polemical writings in prose or verse.

It begins, as does Juvenal's poem, with the poet about to bid farewell to a friend who has decided to uproot and quit the unmannerly town and find a world elsewhere. After the initial lines describing the progress of the poet and his companion to the quay-side, the remainder of the poem is spoken by the departing friend as he surveys the decay of the land which he is leaving. In Juvenal, Umbricius inveighs against the predominance of Greeks and Greek manners in Rome; Ferguson substitutes the English hegemony which has afflicted Ireland. It is not just Johnson's 'London' which is targetted:

> Nor here alone the self-abasing game
> Prospers; in London, with e'en less of shame,

As more of profit, 'tis pursued by all
The servile Irish of the capital –
Yes, I confess that crew degenerate
Are they of men I most abominate.

He attacks the expatriate Irish parliamentarians, novelists, pain-
ters (Daniel Maclise and Richard Doyle, but Frederic Burton is
excepted), and the leader-writers in the press who caricature
their own race. But at home also there are the correspondents of
the London press who pander to their market; meanwhile the
institutions of law, and taxation, prey on the hapless country.
Religious discrimination is also apparent:

Besides, for prospering here, just now, I want
One prime ingredient. I'm a Protestant.
And now, by alternation, just but droll,
One makes his way here, as he'd make his soul,
By dint of masses: time was, 'twould affront
A Flood, a Grattan, or a Charlemont,
To hear the bare suggestion: even yet
Our only province not in the *Gazette*
Still sees the minister and elder dressed
Alike; and urchins on the mother's breast,
Through Ulster still, with orthodox affright,
Would squall to see Mess John arrayed in white.
Long may that horror of the surplice try
Their Presbyterian simplicity;
Long knit it undissevered with the hate
Of arbitrary power in Church or State.

Ferguson is returning to his base in Ulster Presbyterianism. The
rancour in these lines comes close to that expressed by Ferguson
himself at times in his letters, but here he is speaking through a
protective *persona*: not only is he imitating Juvenal, these words
are spoken not by the poet but by the departing friend whose
words are reported. A similar dispersal to that noticeable in 'A
Dialogue between the Head and Heart of an Irish Protestant' is
here used to accommodate unwelcome truths.

As a polemical piece, 'Dublin' is in many respects the successor to the 'Dialogue', but whereas in the earlier piece the debate
was internal, now the grounds have shifted to the larger national
stage, with one of the speakers standing on the quayside and
about to get out of the country. In the 'Dialogue' the state of
Ireland was seen as a cause of concern for Protestants living in
that country; now, in a larger vision, religion is one of many
factors feeding into a troubled nation.

After outlining the social and political ills which afflict Ireland, the poem describes the horrors of the famine-stricken countryside of the past few years.

'Tis hard to sleep when one has just stood by
And seen the strong man of sheer hunger die;
'Tis hard to draw an easy, healthful breath,
In fields that sicken with the air of death;
Or where relief invites the living throng
To see the withered phantoms flit along,
Hunger impelling, and exhaustion still
Leaving the weak limbs baffled of the will.

The feeling of 'Dublin' is in urgent contact with contemporary Ireland, even though the form and diction seem to be of a previous century. Given the poem's antecedents, these are explicable. What is worth noticing is that, even in a poem which engages with the events of the day, Ferguson wields his material most effectively when using a pre-existing form. The fact that there is a model for him to imitate warrants his own utterance. This corresponds to his methods in poetry generally, although in the 'Lays of the Western Gael' and his Irish heroic poetry, it was the material which pre-existed and his problem was to find a poetic form for it.

5

Lays of the Western Gael, and Other Poems (I)

Lays of the Western Gael and Other Poems, carrying on its title page the date 1865, actually came off the press in the latter part of 1864. It was published in London by Bell and Daldy, whose list for that season was made up mostly of works of a moral and improving type, such as *Church Doctrine – Bible Truth* and Mrs Alfred Gatty's *Parables from Nature*. The one other volume of new poetry announced was *Pictures, and Other Poems* by Thomas Ashe (1836 – 1889), a poet who was to find his way into the nineteenth-century anthologies. It was left to a London publisher to bring out one of the defining collections of Anglo-Irish poetry.

Bell and Daldy did have some previous connection with Irish poetry; in 1860 they published a reissue of two of William Allingham's early books, *Day and Night Songs;* and *The Music Master*, in one volume. But Allingham's most important book of 1864, *Laurence Bloomfield in Ireland*, was brought out by Macmillan, who in the same year also published *The Ballad Book*, an anthology of traditional English and Scottish ballads which he edited. Bell and Daldy were also to publish Mary Ferguson's *The Story of the Irish Before the Conquest* (1868) and, under its later style of George Bell, the firm also figures on the title page of Ferguson's subsequent books of poetry in conjunction with an Irish publisher.

Ferguson had already had some contact with Bell and Daldy previous to *Lays of the Western Gael*. They were the publishers of the texts of the Dublin *Afternoon Lectures*, a series given annually during the mid-1860s in the Museum of Industry on St Stephen's Green. These were on various subjects and by various speakers, and in 1864 Ferguson contributed to the second series with a talk on 'Our Architecture', returning to a subject on which he had already written reviews for the *Dublin University Magazine*.

William Allingham has left a description of a lecture he delivered in Dublin in 1865:

Friday, May 19. – Dublin. Car with S.F. to Stephen's Green –
'Chemical Preparation Room' (jokes about that). Introduced to
chairman, Dr E. Kennedy, and committee, then march through door
and find myself in lecture-room, as depicted by S.F. Look over
audience and see people I know, but take no special note of any. After
the chairman's introduction, I read my lecture on poetry for an hour,
but often departing from the written text into more colloquial forms.[1]

Allingham, on a visit from London, was the guest of Ferguson
('S.F.') during his brief stay in Dublin. The man who had
formerly been Ferguson's youthful *protégé* by correspondence[2]
was now, at forty-one, established in British literary circles as one
of Tennyson's acolytes, and already had a number of books to his
name. His host, on the other hand, was in his mid-fifties and had
just produced his first collection; Ferguson could not fail to be
struck by the contrast.

That first collection of Ferguson's had been long in the making.
Lays of the Western Gael gathered poems written over thirty-three
years. Some of them were already well-known, and in advert-
isements for the book Ferguson had been described as the
'author of "The Forging of the Anchor"'. Others had been
included in the widely selling anthologies of the 1840s and 1850s
after their initial periodical appearance. And publication in the
pages of a periodical such as *Blackwood's* or the *Dublin University
Magazine* was not as ephemeral an event as publication in a
literary magazine may be nowadays; the bound volumes of the
back numbers had an extended shelf-life in clubrooms and
libraries. As we have seen, an article in the *Dublin University
Magazine* seventeen years before had already hailed Ferguson as
the originator and leader of the movement of poets looking to
write a distinctively Irish ballad poetry and song in English. Now,
in the eponymous poems of this book, Ferguson changed the
emphasis to another form, that of narrative verse.

Lays of the Western Gael is arranged in four sections, of which
only the first, comprising eight poems, is made up of 'lays'.
These are poems of some length; the shortest is forty-eight lines,
the longest several hundred. For subject matter they draw on
events and characters from Irish legend and history, ranging
from the late Iron Age to the sixteenth century. The eight poems,
together with the eight pages of explanatory or digressionary
footnotes at the rear, make up nearly half the book: 'The
Tain-Quest', 'The Abdication of Fergus Mac Roy', 'The Healing

of Conall Carnach', 'The Burial of King Cormac', 'Aideen's Grave', 'The Welshmen of Tirawley', 'Owen Bawn' and 'Grace O'Maly'. The first five of these were written between 1858 and 1864, 'The Welshmen of Tirawley' and 'Owen Bawn' in 1845 and 1833 respectively, with the date of 'Grace O'Maly' uncertain. The second section is headed 'Ballads and Poems', and includes eight shorter poems, unrelated to each other: 'The Fairy Thorn', 'Willy Gilliland', 'The Forging of the Anchor', 'The Forester's Complaint', 'The Pretty Girl of Loch Dan', 'Hungary', 'Adieu to Brittany' and 'Westminster Abbey'. The first five of these 'ballads and poems' date from the 1830s, with one from each of the succeeding decades. Among them are the earliest and the most recent of all the poems in the book: 'Willy Gilliland', which had appeared in the *Ulster Magazine* in 1831 as 'The Rescue of the Mare', and 'Adieu to Brittany' written after Ferguson's tour there in the late summer of 1863.

The third part of the book is made up of four 'Versions and Adaptations', three from classical sources and one from Irish: 'The Origin of the Scythians', 'The Death of Dermid', 'The Invocation' and 'Archytas and the Mariner'. The date of 'The Invocation' cannot be fixed precisely, but the other three all belong to the 1850s.

Finally there are the 'Versions from the Irish', twenty-two short poems prefaced by a lengthy introductory note. They are 'Deirdra's Farewell to Alba', 'Deirdra's Lament for the Sons of Usnach', 'The Downfall of the Gael', 'O'Byrne's Bard to the Clans of Wicklow', 'Lament over the Ruins of the Abbey of Timoleague', 'To the Harper O'Connellan', 'Grace Nugent', 'Mild Mabel Kelly', 'The Cup of O'Hara', 'The Fair-hair'd Girl', 'Pastheen Finn', 'Molly Astore', 'Cashel of Munster', 'The Coolun', 'Youghall Harbour', 'Cean Dubh Deelish', 'Boatman's Hymn', 'The Dear Old Air', 'The Lapful of Nuts', 'Mary's Waking', 'Hopeless Love', and 'The Fair Hills of Ireland'. This section is largely made up of translations from the appendix attached to the 1834 review of Hardiman's *Irish Minstrelsy*, but it begins with the two poems from 'The Death of the Children of Usnach', also written in 1834. Then follow sixteen poems derived from originals in the Hardiman collection. Of these, fourteen had already appeared among the nineteen versified translations in the appendix to the review of Hardiman; they are joined by two others not previously printed, 'Youghall Harbour' and 'Cean Dubh Deelish'. As in

the appendix, 'The Fair Hills of Ireland' is placed as the concluding poem, but the four poems preceding it do not have any Irish
original in Hardiman or elsewhere that I can ascertain.[3]

Such, then, is the substance of this seminal work of Irish
poetry. Clearly, it is a book which encompasses poetry of several
different kinds written over an extended period of time. The very
variety of the book has tended to disperse its impact; the lyric
translations of the final section had been written a generation
earlier and had already enjoyed considerable currency. Among
the 'Poems and Ballads' were two other poems from the same
time which were even better known, 'The Forging of the Anchor'
and 'The Fairy Thorn'; the former, so divergent from the main
line of Ferguson's work, achieved a popularity which typecast
him during his lifetime as a poet of energetic descriptiveness. The
actual 'Lays of the Western Gael' which bear the main burden of
the book were very different in their intent, tentatively exploring
a society and culture which are only dimly understood. English
readers who had followed into the hidden submarine world of
'The Forging of the Anchor', and Irish readers who had delighted
in the glimpse of an occult faery power in 'The Fairy Well', were
generally unwilling to make the imaginative journey back into
the world of pre-Christian Ireland.

'Lays of the Western Gael'

As gathered in the collection, these eight poems inaugurate a
series which Ferguson was to continue in his *Poems* (1880), where
there is a number of further 'lays'. His underlying aim was to
provide a body of poetry which would contribute to a versified
history of Ireland. The term 'lay' was evidently chosen with some
thought. In the same volume other pieces are described as
'ballads', 'versions', 'adaptations', 'poems' and 'songs'. In using
'lay' to describe these poems Ferguson had some warrant from
English and Irish example. Before its meaning became extended
to include almost any type of song, it referred to narrative songs
dealing with historically based adventures; the subject matter
and structure of Ferguson's poems accorded with this description. There was also the superficial affinity with the word '*laid*' in
old Irish, which signified a particular type of metrical composition or, indeed, a poem or song generally. William Drummond
had already suggested an equivalence between the two terms in
his *Ancient Irish Minstrelsy* (1852), where '*Laoidh Magnuis Moir*'

is translated as 'The Lay of Magnus the Great', and the book's contents generally are spoken of as 'Lays', although there is no etymological connection between 'lay' and 'laid' (or the German 'lied').

Drummond had been on the panel of translators which Hardiman had used for the *Irish Minstrelsy*, and the only one to escape censure in Ferguson's comments on their work. The *Ancient Irish Minstrelsy* follows on from Hardiman in some respects, as the title might indicate; one of the poems, 'The Lay of Beann Gulbain', is reprinted from Hardiman. In the dedication Drummond writes that it is his intention to present the poems 'to the reader in an English dress', although he favours a varied versification to avoid the regularity of an English ballad metre or of heroic couplets;[4] throughout the preface Drummond insists on the importance of preserving the sense and spirit of the Irish source, while his actual translations perpetuate a markedly eighteenth-century sensibility.

The appearance of Drummond's book may have provided a spur to prick the sides of Ferguson's intent; Drummond points to the amount of old manuscripts which are receiving the benefits of scholarly editing and publication, and his versifying of fragments of such material anticipates the project Ferguson had in mind at least since 1842 and which so far had resulted in just one success-ful poem, 'The Welshmen of Tirawley', which is set in relatively recent times.

Ferguson, like Drummond, took his material for the lays from contemporary Irish scholarship; his model, however, came from contemporary English writing. The specific object of imitation was Macaulay's *Lays of Ancient Rome*; even Ferguson's title echoes Macaulay's. The *Lays of Ancient Rome*, published in 1842, had shown how ancient and unfamiliar material could be presented in popular poetic form.

Macaulay's source was Livy, and he too had to work on gapped records of a legendary past; the provincial features of Livy's style might even be seen as anticipating in some respects the problems Ferguson would have with establishing the worth of an apparently obscure provincial language, Irish. Macaulay's book contained four lays, narrative poems of moderate length; these were supplemented by two pieces from more recent European history; in thus mixing ancient and modern they cover a time span equivalent to that of Ferguson's. Each of Macaulay's lays is accompanied by an explanatory note giving the background to it, a feature imitated by Ferguson.

It may at first seem unlikely that Ferguson would take as his example the work of a leading Whig historian, but ideologically he was on safe ground. In the society which forms the background to the 'Lays of the Western Gael' there is no sense of a central polity which would provide an arena for plebeian struggles to be enacted, such as is suggested by Macaulay's Rome. Ferguson presented isolated individuals outlined against an institutional vacuum; this neutralised any implications of nationalism in his poems, whereas there is the strongly-felt presence of populist tension in a poem such as 'Virginia'. It made Ferguson's poems safer, but it also lessened their force.

A book as popular as was Macaulay's in the mid-nineteenth century could not have escaped Ferguson's attention, but, even so, he did not lack for reminders that its methods could be applied to Irish history. Davis in *The Nation* had instanced the work of Macaulay in his exhortations to Irish writers. Another prompt came from Ferguson's friend Sir William Wilde. In the preface to his book *The Beauties of the Boyne* (1850) Wilde quoted Macaulay on 'the early "poetic literature" and "ancient lays" of the various nations of the earth', pointing out how Macaulay can demonstrate that the Greek, Persian and European races, and the Africans, have all perpetuated their early history in bardic song, but that there is no mention of the neighbouring island of Ireland. It was a broad hint, and one to which Ferguson would eventually respond a decade later.

As well as Macaulay there was another writer who had provided Ferguson with possible models. William Maginn's *Homeric Ballads* were published in *Fraser's Magazine* during 1838, where they were noticed and praised by Ferguson in the course of a brief review of periodical literature which Ferguson contributed to the *Dublin Evening Mail*.[5] Maginn's ballads versify selected episodes of the Odyssey; the treatment is fragmentary and has recourse to a variety of verse forms. They were published in book form in 1850, eight years after Maginn's death. In his preface the editor J. C. (John Conington) describes the collection as 'a work which, like *The Lays of Ancient Rome*, its natural associate in the public mind, though its junior in point of time, aims at resolving into their constituent elements, whether primary or not, the records of a nation's antiquity'.[6] In 1861 Matthew Arnold compared these 'natural associates' in the course of his lectures

On Translating Homer; while he finds that Maginn's ballad metres travesty rather than imitate Homer, he pronounces the *Homeric Ballads* to be 'vigorous and genuine poems in their own way; they are not one continual falsetto, like the pinchbeck Roman Ballads of Lord Macaulay'.[7] Such then were some of the models available for Ferguson's enterprise. The difficulty of finding a suitable metre for the ancient stories, which is the burden of Arnold's lectures, is reflected in the variety of forms which he tried for his lays and in the course of completing *Congal*. He eventually came to favour the long fourteen-syllable rhymed couplet, or variations thereof, more than any other. This was, of course, the measure used by Chapman in his version of Homer, and so could boast a respectable epic lineage; but it was also that of Ferguson's earliest and most enduring success, 'The Forging of the Anchor'.

'The Tain-Quest'

Nearly thirty years before, in one of his columns for the *Dublin Evening Mail*, Ferguson had jokingly linked a local dispute over cattle which had occurred in Ulster on the preceding July 12th with the old tale of 'Tain Bo Quelgny'.

> The odd-looking words at the head of this article are, we believe, the title of a celebrated Irish Romance, the subject of which is an exploit in this way of Cuchullin.[8]

Thus hesitantly he began the pursuit of the great Irish prose epic and its associated tales.

There are signs that Ferguson put some care into the ordering of his poems, and it is fitting that 'The Tain-Quest' should lead off his first published collection, for 'The Tain-Quest' is by its nature a prefatory poem. However, the book was issued so late in his career that it has the character more of a 'collected poems' than of a first collection. 'The Tain-Quest' tells how the the epic story disappeared from the repertoire of the Irish bards until, in the sixth century, the foremost of them, Sanchan Torpest, was stung into taking steps for its recovery. He sends his son Murgen on a journey in the hope of finding it, and in a vision at the pillar-stone marking the grave of Fergus, credited with being the composer, the *Táin* is narrated by the dead hero.

In the old sources there are two variants of the episode. According to the Book of Leinster, Sanchan found that the *files* of his time could recite only fragments of the great Irish epic, whereupon his son Murgen, accompanied by Eimena, volunteered to journey eastward (probably to Italy) where it was thought a text of the *Táin* might be found. Passing the grave of Fergus, Murgen addressed a poem to the dead warrior-poet; Fergus responded by appearing in a great mist to recite the *Táin* story to Murgen. In another version, Sanchan so trespasses on the hospitality of King Guary that, at the prompting of Guary's brother Morbhen, the king requires the *file* to recover the *Táin*. Having travelled to Scotland in search of it without success, he calls a meeting which brings together the *files* and the saints of Ireland near the site of Fergus's grave; Fergus appears and dictates the story to St Ciaran, who writes it down in the manuscript known today as *Leabhar na hUidhre* ('The Book of the Dun Cow', said to be named after the animal whose hide went into its making).

The latter version occurs in *Imtheacht na Tromdaimhe: the Proceedings of the Great Bardic Institution*, which had been printed for the Ossianic Society in 1860. Ferguson had already adapted 'The Death of Dermid' from one of the society's earlier publications. As a member of the society Ferguson had a copy of the 1860 volume, and he cites it as a source in a note to his wife's *Story of the Irish Before the Conquest*. But another source cited there is O'Curry's *Lectures on the Manuscript Materials of Ancient Irish History*, published in 1861, which gives a summary of both versions of the story of the *Táin's* retrieval.

In developing his own treatment of the story Ferguson combined the most dramatic elements of each. From *Imtheacht na Tromdaimhe* Ferguson took the initial confrontation between Guary and Sanchan; the burdensome exactions of Sanchan, abusing his privileged status as a bard, form the principal concern of that text, and the appearance of Fergus at the end seems no more than an anticlimactic fashion of bringing the tale to an end. The major part of Ferguson's poem follows the Book of Leinster, with Murgen setting off for Rome accompanied by Eimena and then addressing the burial pillar of Fergus which they encounter on the way. O'Curry's *resumé* continues:

> Suddenly, as the story runs, there came a great mist which enveloped him so that he could not be discovered for three days; and during that time Fergus himself appeared to him in a beautiful form, – for he is described as adorned with brown hair, clad in a green cloak, and wearing a collared gold-ribbed shirt, a gold-hilted sword, and sandals

of bronze: and it is said that this apparition related to Murgen the whole tale of the *Táin*, from beginning to end, — the tale which he was sent to seek in a foreign land.[9]

Ferguson makes of this one of his most successful descriptive passages, in which the mystery surrounding the legendary material from the remote past combines with the achievement of sudden insight.

Fergus rose. A mist ascended with him, and a flash was seen
As of brazen sandals blended with a mantle's wafture green;
But so thick the cloud closed o'er him, Eimena, return'd at last,
Found not on the field before him but a mist-heap grey and vast.

Thrice to pierce the hoar recesses faithful Eimena essay'd;
Thrice through foggy wildernesses back to open air he stray'd;
Till a deep voice through the vapours fill'd the twilight far and near,
And the Night her starry tapers kindling, stoop'd from heaven to hear.

Seem'd as though the skiey Shepherd back to earth had cast the fleece
Envying gods of old caught upward from the darkening shrines of Greece;
So the white mists curl'd and glisten'd, so from heaven's expanses bare,
Stars enlarging lean'd and listen'd down the emptied depths of air.

All night long by mists surrounded Murgen lay in vapoury bars;
All night long the deep voice sounded 'neath the keen, enlarging stars:
But when, on the orient verges, stars grew dim and mists retired,
Rising by the stone of Fergus, Murgen stood, a man inspired.

In this passage Ferguson compresses the three days into one night, substituting instead Eimena's three vain attempts to penetrate the mist in which Fergus and Murgen are enveloped. From this and from his amalgamation of the two Irish versions it is immediately apparent that he is aiming at something other than a translation; the result might more accurately be styled a retelling.

Ferguson also adds elements not present in either of the original sources. Most notably, there is the girl whom Murgen leaves behind when he sets off on his journey. At the end of the poem, in another of Ferguson's dramatic inventions, she is given the last bitter word. When the recovered *Táin* has been brought back and performed in Guary's presence, the spirit of Fergus makes a second appearance. As the terrible apparition passes

through the palace hall, Murgen dies, and the anonymous maid
pronounces a curse on the story which has cost her so much;

> So it comes, the lay, recover'd once at such a deadly cost,
> Ere one full recital suffer'd, once again is all but lost:
> For, the maiden's malediction still with many a blemish-stain
> Clings in coarser garbs of fiction round the fragments that remain.

And so, 'The Tain-Quest' is not just the story of the *Táin's*
finding, it is also the story of its loss. In the 'Introductory Note'
Ferguson speaks of the *Táin* as having been a 'heroic poem';
'readers of the *Tain Bo Cuailgne* as it now exists, have to regret the
overlaying of much of its heroic and pathetic material by turgid
extravagances and exaggerations, the additions apparently of
later copyists'. He evidently regards the surviving manuscript
versions, which are of a prose epic with passages of verse in an
older form of language interpolated at various points, as being
the debased remnant of a lost poetic epic. This was the standard
position on the *Táin* and similar tales, and was clearly enunciated
by Standish James O'Grady in 1879: 'A close study of [the *Táin's*]
contents, as of the contents of all the Irish historic tales, proves
that in its present form, whenever that form was superadded, it is
but a representation in prose of a pre-existing metrical original'.[10]
Ferguson's project therefore involved not merely the recovery
and presentation of Irish history and legend in modern narrative
forms, but also an act of restoration in suiting them once more to
the dignity of poetry.

Some two-thirds of 'The Tain-Quest' is given over to direct
speech by the protagonists: Guary, Sanchan Torpest, Murgen.
These speeches generally contain the substance of what Ferguson has invented or elaborated. The longest speech, the kernel of
the poem, is that which Murgen addresses to Fergus persuading
him to come back from the dead to utter the lost poem. The
appeal is based on three points. First, Murgen asks Fergus to take
pity on a young man forced to leave his family and loved one in
search of the *Táin*; secondly, in a recapitulation of the story of
Deirdre and the sons of Usnach (so extensive as almost to
constitute a further version by Ferguson separate from his telling
of it in the *Hibernian Nights' Entertainments*), it is pointed out that
Illan Finn, Fergus's own son, gave an example of filial fidelity
equal to that of Murgen; and the final appeal is for the sake of
poetry itself:

> Fergus, for the Gael's sake, waken! never let the scornful Gauls
> 'Mongst our land's reproaches reckon lack of Song within our halls!

This is the plea which is answered by Fergus; it is also being answered by Ferguson, provider of a set of recovered lays for the western Gaels.

'The Abdication of Fergus Mac Roy'

Associated with the main story of the *Táin Bó Cuailgne* there is a number of pre-tales which tell of events occurring in the run-up to the famous cattle raid which constitutes the substance of the epic. While Ferguson was never to embark on a reworking of the *Táin* itself, he did render a number of the pre-tales as 'Lays of the Western Gael'; this volume contains 'The Abdication of Fergus Mac Roy', 'The Healing of Conall Carnach' and 'The Burial of King Cormac'.

Underlying 'The Abdication of Fergus Mac Roy', both explicitly and implicitly, is the notion of a change of order. The poem tells how Fergus (the same who was the escort of Deirdre and the sons of Usnach, and the composer of the *Táin*) handed over the kingship of Ulster to Conor Mac Nessa. Fergus, falling in love with the widowed Nessa, asks her to marry him. She consents on condition that her teenage son Conor be allowed to sit and observe Fergus dispensing justice to his subjects; the settling of disputes was one of the most important functions of a king. Fergus agrees, and for a time Conor sits by silently. One day a particularly knotty case is presented for adjudication and Fergus, by now thoroughly given over to his love for Nessa, candidly admits that he has neither the wit nor the will to arrive at a solution. He offers the problem to Conor, who unravels it thoroughly, patiently and fairly. Fergus, pointing out that Conor is of blood royal, hands over the crown to the younger man and enters on a life of ease and contentment. Such is the story as Ferguson tells it. Conor subsequently turned out to be one of the ablest kings in Irish history, thus partly absolving Fergus from the reproaches that might have been levelled at him for walking away from his responsibilities.

The story as given in the Book of Leinster was summarised by O'Curry in his *Manuscript Materials for Ancient Irish History*[11], and again this was probably Ferguson's source. It is clear from O'Curry that in the original Fergus's abdication is not nearly so voluntary. It comes about as a result of his subjects seeing Conor out-perform him on the judgment bench, and one is left with the suspicion that Nessa's request may have been an astute ruse to obtain the kingship for her son. Ferguson avoids any implication of this, and so leaves the arrangement that she exacts from Fergus as motiveless as a lover's whim. Ferguson lends a wash of sentiment to the unforgiving outlines of the legend, and he emphasises the love story rather than the dynastic intrigue. Thus the opening stanzas of the poem portray Fergus as a romantic malcontent chafing at the transition from a life of derring-do as commander of the Red Branch Knights to the sedate deliberations of the council chamber where, like Tennyson's Ulysses, he must mete and dole unequal laws unto a savage race. He finds his relief in solitary country walks, composing poetry – an idyllic picture, but not wholly inappropriate to one reputed to be the author of the *Táin*.

Unusually for a poem by Ferguson, the whole of 'The Abdication of Fergus Mac Roy' is spoken by a *persona*. The speaker is the spirit of Fergus, but there is no real connection with the spirit who appears to Murgen in 'The Tain-Quest'. Fergus here speaks from beyond the grave not to lend a dramatic presence to the poem but to offer a retrospective viewpoint on events. As a *revenant* he is able to see his life as a whole, and to evaluate it with more assurance than ever he displayed in his kingly duties. It is a further instance of the comprehensiveness of Ferguson's vision, of a kind with that noticed at the beginning of his career.

Even though Fergus is no longer a bodily presence he is at pains to assert the force of the love experienced for Nessa. His speech does not simply contrast physical and spiritual states; the concern is to set his decision to abdicate in a much broader context, one that is introduced in the opening lines of the poem:

> Once, ere God was crucified,
> I was King o'er Uladh wide.

Christianity is not alluded to again, but the first line ensures that the poem is read as an excursion into the world of pre-Christian Ireland. The past tense here is not simply a tense of reminiscence; it is an indication of the change in the order of things which has since occurred. Fergus's renunciation of his kingship is not only a movement towards personal resolution, it is also part of a larger process of abandonment of old ways and the discovery of contentment. His spirit would not speak so confidently, it is implied, were it not for knowledge of the redemptive effects of Christ's own self-humbling on the cross, at a time soon after the events Fergus describes.

The arrival of Christianity acts as a reference point throughout Ferguson's historical poems, and it is referred to in each of the three 'Lays of the Western Gael' derived from pre-Christian legends. ('The Tain-Quest' is set in Christian times). The coming of Patrick and the subsequent conversion of Ireland is one of the crucial epochs in his scheme of history, as much for the society which ended then as for the enlightenment which began. The figure of Patrick presides over the beginning and end of Ferguson's life, because of the associations with Slemish, the mountain which loomed over his boyhood at Donegore, and because he is the subject of the last work which Ferguson was to publish during his lifetime. But aside from personal associations, the conversion of Ireland in and after the fifth century was probably the most profound cultural change to affect Ireland. The success of Patrick's mission provided Ferguson with a model of a national transition from one order to another. Furthermore, it was a profound change in the state and outlook of Ireland which was brought about not through bloodshed or warfare but through dialogue and example.

There was a particular benefit in referring these poems to the Christianising of Ireland: in the historical continuum it marked a threshold at which Ferguson's imagination entered into a culture and society at once exotic and yet part of the common heritage. In Ferguson's own age, contact with exotic cultures generally came through missionary endeavour or through colonial exploitation and administration. The latter activities, based on commercial and imperial values, were likely to have proved tendentious as models for an Irish experience. The religious model, involving as it did an exchange or transmission of beliefs and values, offered a context for the sort of cultural outreach that Ferguson sought. He too saw himself as trying to make an unfamiliar, and in some respects alien, culture amenable to his age. The missionary impulse of that age, reflected in its fiction by figures as diverse as St John Rivers in *Jane Eyre* and Mrs Jellyby and the Ramification Society in *Bleak House*, had a zeal to encounter new societies and to learn new languages; Ferguson transposed something of this to his workings of Gaelic material. His references to the coming of Christianity are tokens that what he is dealing with will eventually come into a knowledge of the Christian God and, more importantly, into the purlieu of Christian society.

The conjunction of evangelicalism and the exploration of Irish literature need not be surprising. The first set of Gaelic type, which enabled the rudiments of old Irish literature to be printed, had been provided by Queen Elizabeth to facilitate publication of a bible for her Irish-speaking subjects; and Ferguson's own probable teacher of Irish in Belfast in the 1830s, Thomas Fee-naghty, was charged with providing classes at the Belfast Aca-demical Institution for intending clergymen who might be appointed to rural Irish-speaking parishes.

'The Healing of Conall Carnach'

After 'The Tain-Quest', the longest of the 1864 lays is 'The Healing of Conall Carnach'. Conall Carnach was one of the most prominent of the Ulster warriors in the cycle of tales centred on Conor and the Knights of the Red Branch. Ferguson's source seems to have been John O'Mahony's translation of *Foras Feasa Ar Eirinn* (Keating's *History of Ireland*) which had been published in New York in 1857. The poem was written in the autumn of 1861, and was complete by November when it was offered without success to *Blackwood's*. In his accompanying letter Ferguson remarked that he could provide half-a-dozen other pieces of the same kind.[12] The idea of producing a group of related poems mining old Irish heroic material had taken firm root, and it was to be his major poetic project during the 1860s. Ferguson saw these poems as easing the way for his long poem *Congal*, which he had already been planning and writing in one form or another another for two decades and which he had more or less cast into its final form a few months before; however, over another ten years were to pass before its publication.

In Keating's telling of the story, the Connaught warrior Ceat is returning from a winter attack on Ulster when he is pursued and slain by Conall Carnach. Conall himself is severely wounded and Bealchu, a Connaught champion, finds him in this weakened state. Conall invites Bealchu to kill him there and then, so that at least it will be said afterwards that it took the combined efforts of two Connaughtmen to slay him. Bealchu refuses, and instead takes Conall away to be healed so as to have the honour of meeting and killing him in equal combat. The convalescent Conall, however, shows signs of recovering prodigious strength and Bealchu becomes apprehensive; he plots with his sons to kill Conall while he sleeps. Conall gets wind of what is afoot and arranges it that Bealchu sleeps in his bed on the night appointed. (Keating's version does not explain how Bealchu allowed himself to be manoeuvred into this position; in the manner of old Irish tales, it just happens.) When the sons come in, they of course slay their father unwittingly; Conall then kills the three of them and rides off with four severed heads as trophies.

Ferguson expands this brief story into a dramatic ballad 'with some deviations from the original', as his wife puts it in her *Story of the Irish before the Conquest*, where the poem is reprinted entire. She further describes the episode as a 'primitive instance of chivalrous generosity', which is an inappropriate reading of it but does indicate how her husband's lays tend to haul the uncompromising material towards a more readily understood code of conduct. 'The Healing of Conall Carnach' starts with Bealcu arriving just after the combat between Keth (Ceat) and Conall. He takes the injured Conall captive and hands him over to Lee the physician. Lee stipulates that he will heal Conall only on condition that his patient is guaranteed sanctuary while under his care, and that if the recovered Conall defeat Bealcu in single combat he be allowed to depart home freely. Swearing by the pagan god Crom Cruach and by the Sun and the Wind, the Connaughtmen agree to these conditions.

The sons of Bealcu spy on Conall as he recovers his strength and they become fearful for their father. They devise a stratagem in keeping with the letter but not the spirit of the guarantee given to Lee, and resolve to kill Conall with a slingshot fired from outside the bounds of the sanctuary in the physician's garden. Meanwhile, Bealcu too has been observing Conall surreptitiously, and has noticed that his antagonist seems to derive strength from frequent visits to a well in the garden. Bealcu decides to visit the well in secret and to pray to its tutelary god on his own behalf. Next morning, kneeling there, he is slain by the slingshot intended for Conall. When the body is discovered within the forbidden sanctuary, the men of Connaught deem that the offended gods have exacted punishment for a broken vow, and their leader sets Conall free. It is left to Lee the physician to have the last words; he has recognised on the corpse the mark of a slingshot, not a supernatural striking-down by those forces which were invoked in guaranteeing Conall's safety.

'It is a slinger's doing: Sun nor Wind was actor here.
Yet till God vouchsafe more certain knowledge of his sovereign will,
Better deem the mystic curtain hides their wonted demons still.

'Better so, perchance, than living in a clearer light, like me,
But believing where perceiving, bound in what I hear and see;

Force and change in constant sequence, changing atoms, changeless
    laws;
Only in submissive patience waiting access to the Cause.

'And, they say, Centurion Altus, when he to Emania came,
And to Rome's subjection call'd us, urging Caesar's tribute claim,
Told that half the world barbarian thrills already with the faith
Taught them by the godlike Syrian Caesar lately put to death.

'And the Sun, through starry stages, measuring from the Ram and
    Bull,
Tells us of renewing Ages, and that Nature's time is full:
So, perchance, these silly breezes even now may swell the sail,
Brings the leavening word of Jesus westward also to the Gael.'

Here is the familiar turn, in which are displayed at once a quiet
triumphalist Christianity and a reminder that the values proper
to the source material are now obsolete. The action is placed at the
very moment when that obsolescence is first announced: it was
the centurion Altus who, according to legend, informed Conor
Mac Nessa of Christ's death on the cross, whereupon he became
so agitated that he reopened a wound received long before at the
hands of Keth and died. Lee's words have no great force in
casting a pious gloss, but by giving a larger perspective to what
has happened an effect of great poignancy is attained; Conall
rides away, made whole once again, and victorious, but his world
of fixed heroic absolutes is about to be obscured by the new
dispensation of the Christian church and to put on an awareness
of flux and doubt.

The manuscript of the final stanza shows signs of heavy
rewriting, and the ungrammaticality of the verb at the beginning
of the last line is a vestige of one of the earlier versions.
Furthermore, it originally ended 'also to the distant Gael', before
the notion of remoteness was removed and 'westward'
substituted as being more in keeping with the title of the
collection.[13] The general implication is that the Gael is to be
brought under the same umbrella as the inhabitants of the larger
island to the east. The term 'Gael' had usually been used in
English to signify the Scottish Celts, and only recently had its use
been extended to include the Irish; the epithet 'Western' in the
title of Ferguson's book was a reminder that these other Celts
existed too, and had a history to offer. A noticeable sub-text in
some of his poems during this time is an implied reproach to the
Queen for gracing the Scottish Highlands with her frequent

presence while neglecting Ireland. It is discernible in 'The Widow's Cloak' (*Poems*), and in some unpublished stanzas which he wrote to be added to 'Grace O'Maly'. Ferguson's lays frequently find their narrative closure in a movement towards imperial Christianity which, while it might allow for cultural nationalism, would take the union of 'our isles' for granted. As the unpublished ending of 'Grace O'Maly' puts it,

> And long our isles shall sleep secure
> From dream of coming troubles,
> Nor dread lest, mid the clash of arms
> With cries of faction blending,
> We wake to see the Scythian swarms
> Down Hindoo Koosh descending.[14]

Lee's ambiguous attitude to God and the gods, preferring the 'mystic curtain' to the 'clearer light', is an element that Ferguson has introduced to the story. In Keating's account there is no reference at any point to gods or to the supernatural: Conall and Bealcu live in a world unredeemed by larger presences. The machinery of deities with which Ferguson surrounds his characters softens the thrust of their actions and suggests the possibility of progress to a new state of belief, in accordance with a melioristic Victorian world-view. But the central dynamic feature of the poem, Conall's healing, is not generated by any supernatural agency, in spite of Bealcu's suspicions about the well; his improvement is inspired by a sudden recollection of domestic happiness with his wife and children:

> Conall to the green well-margin came at dawn and knelt to drink,
> Thinking how a noble virgin by a like green fountain's brink
> Heard his own pure vows one morning, far away and long ago:
> All his heart to home was turning; and his tears began to flow.
>
> Clean forgetful of his prison, steep Dunseverick's windy tower
> Seem'd to rise in present vision, and his own dear lady's bower.
> Round the sheltering knees they gather, little ones of tender years, –
> Tell us mother of our father – and she answers but with tears.

Such wholesome memories send a gust of recovered energy through the convalescent Conall, and he arises ready for any fray. Ferguson succeeds in placing his central character in an environment of faith and family, a remarkable translation from pre-Christian legendary Ireland.

'The Burial of King Cormac'

For the next poem of the 'lays', 'The Burial of King Cormac', Ferguson had at least two sources. The story of the death of King Cormac is given in Keating's *History of Ireland*, which he had already drawn upon for 'The Healing of Conall Carnach'. However, he had previously come upon the story in 1845 in George Petrie's *Ecclesiatical Architecture in Ireland*; Ferguson was much exercised in the controversy surrounding this book and reviewed it appreciatively in the *Dublin University Magazine*. Petrie quotes and translates a passage from the twelfth-century *Leabhar na hUidhre* telling how Cormac had renounced the adoration of stones or trees in favour of the creator God of the Christians who had power over all the elements. The passage continues:

> He came by his death at the house of Cletech, the bone of a salmon having stuck in his throat. And he (Cormac) told his people not to bury him at Brugh, (because it was a cemetery of idolaters,) for he did not worship the same God as any of those interred at Brugh; but to bury him at Ros na righ, with his face to the east. He afterwards died, and his servants held a council, and came to the resolution of burying him at Brugh. . . . The body of the king was afterwards thrice raised to be carried to Brugh, but the Boyne swelled up thrice, so that they could not come; so that they observed that it 'was violating the judgment of a prince' to break through this testament of the king, and they afterwards dug his grave at Ros na righ, as he himself had ordered.

Petrie says that another manuscript adds that Cormac's death was possibly brought about by the supernatural Tuatha De Danaan as a punishment for turning away from the native gods. The conflict between the two codes of belief is given much greater prominence by Keating, and is represented as a dispute between Cormac and the leader of the pagan priests. According to this version, after Cormac's death his followers endeavour to obey his instructions concerning burial but the Boyne, stirred to fury by the outraged infernal deities, rises to prevent the funeral rites. The body is washed downstream to *Ros na righ* where it is found and buried.

As he had done with 'The Tain-Quest', for which there were also two possible source stories available, Ferguson conflates the two versions. His poem begins with Cormac's rejection of the primitive gods of tree and stone worshipped by the druids, and then continues:

Anon to priests of Crom was brought –
Where, girded in their service dread,
The minister'd on red Moy Slaught –
Word of the words King Cormac said.

They loosed their curse against the king;
They cursed him in his flesh and blood;
And daily in their mystic ring
They turned the maledictive stones.

He marshals a number of factors to heighten the sense of
conflict between Cormac and the paganism which surrounds
him. After the death of Cormac his followers decide to ignore his
dying request to be buried in Rosnaree rather than among his
illustrious ancestors at Brugh:

Then northward forth they bore the bier,
And down from Sletty side they drew,
With horseman and with charioteer,
To cross the fords of Boyne to Brugh.

There came a breath of finer air
That touched the Boyne with ruffling wings,
It stirred him in his sedgy lair
And in his mossy moorland springs.

And as the burial train came down
With dirge and savage dolorous shows,
Across their pathway, broad and brown
The deep full-hearted river rose;

From bank to bank through all his fords,
'Neath black'ning squalls he swell'd and boil'd;
And thrice the wondering gentile lords
Essay'd to cross, and thrice recoil'd.

Keating's account did not fully suit Ferguson's purpose, in that
Cormac's assertion of the omnipotence of the creator God seems
to be contradicted by the power of the pagan spirits who thwart
his intended manner of burial. Ferguson turned to the story
quoted by Petrie; he has the mourners disregarding Cormac's
wishes and the Boyne, now presumably an agent of the Christian
god rather than an elemental force, carries the corpse off their
shoulders to the wished-for resting-place at Rosnaree.

At the end, the temper of the poem changes remarkably from
sub-epic to Christian pastoral.

At morning, on the grassy marge
Of Rosnaree, the corpse was found

And shepherds at their early charge
Entomb'd it in the peaceful ground.

A tranquil spot: a hopeful sound
Comes from the ever youthful stream,
And still on daisied mead and mound
The dawn delays with tenderer beam.

Round Cormac Spring renews her buds:
In march perpetual by his side,
Down come the earth-fresh April floods,
And up the sea-fresh salmon glide;

And life and time rejoicing run
From age to age their wonted way
But still he waits the rising Sun,
For still 'tis only dawning Day.

The pastoral note on which the poem ends is a striking departure from the old Irish source material, but it does provide an effective contrast with the heroic, military and pagan values which predominate in the earlier part of the poem as the bearers try three times to carry Cormac's bier across the river. These are the values from which Cormac has turned away. There is a movement in the poem away from the old Gaelic world towards the post-Patrician society, and in the final stanza the individual experience of Cormac is set within the larger context of the seasonal renewal of the Irish countryside and a steady progress towards a joyful apocalypse.

'The Burial of King Cormac' accords greater prominence to landscape than do the earlier lays, which are all character and foreground. It continues the concerns of 'The Healing of Conall Carnach' even though set in a later stage of Irish history. Ferguson was later to consider the poems dealing with events surrounding the *Táin* and the reign of Conor Mac Nessa as forming a specific group, and these were at the core of the series of poems labelled 'Lays of the Western Gael' as it was to be continued in his 1880 *Poems*. The figure of Cormac is rather detached from that period; as one of the three people in Irish history reputed to have believed in the Christian God before the coming of Patrick, he is well placed to embody the impending change in traditional belief. 'The Burial of King Cormac' articulates more fully what has been implicit in the preceding lays: the passage from one state of society to another. The action of the poem spans an experience of transition.

'Aideen's Grave'

The next poem in the 'Lays of the Western Gael' section of the book also fastens on the landscape; indeed, the subject is a topographical feature rather than a person, as its title when first published separately in 1861 indicates: 'The Cromlech on Howth'. Like 'The Burial of King Cormac', it is associated with scenes of which Ferguson had a close knowledge. Howth was his summer retreat from the city during nearly all of adult life, and it was the home of his friends, the Stokes family, and for a time of the Rev. John Shearman with whom he discussed archaeological matters.

The poem was written during 1858, earlier than any of the lays so far considered. Ferguson first offered it unsuccessfully to *Blackwood's* for publication, before bringing it out in the lithographed 1861 edition ornamented by Margaret Stokes in a manner which is remarkable for the successful use of motifs from old Celtic art.

According to the notes on the poem, the cromlech at Howth was supposed to be the grave of Aideen, wife of Oscar, who died of grief on hearing of her husband's death at the battle of Gavra (A.D. 284). While Ferguson refers vaguely to a 'tradition' connected with the cromlech, Borlase makes no mention of any such association in his book *The Dolmens of Ireland*. We know what Ferguson's source for the story was: the catalogue of an exhibition mounted in Belfast in 1910 to commemorate the centenary of his birth lists 'a translation of an old Ossianic tale made by Eoghan O'Curry for Ferguson, on which he founded his poem "The Cromlech on Howth"'. This document was in private ownership at the time, and I have not seen it; nor have I come across any reference to Aideen (or *Etaín*) in connection with Oscar. It is clear, however, that Ferguson was working in his usual manner, adapting and retelling a story of which he had been provided with an English translation or outline.

The speaker of the poem, apart from one line at the beginning and a verse at the end, is Oscar's father, Ossian. As a poet mourning the death of his son and his daughter-in-law, Ossian is painfully aware of the passage of time. This awareness is set in a specifically poetic context. He first refers back to another poet who had given memorable utterance on the Hill of Howth: the Ulster bard Atharna, who had used it as a platform from which to hurl invective at the men of Leinster in the course of a dispute during the wars of Conor centuries before. More emphatically, Ossian is represented as looking forward to a later age when some future poet, also on Howth, will transfer the burden of his poem into a form more suited to that later time. Whom might he have had in mind, if not Samuel Ferguson?

> The long forgotten lay I sing
> May only ages hence revive,
> (As eagle with a wounded wing
> To soar again might strive,)
>
> Imperfect, in an alien speech,
> When, wandering here, some child of chance
> Through pangs of keen delight shall reach
> The gift of utterance, –
>
> To speak the air, the sky to speak,
> The freshness of the hill to tell,
> Who, roaming bare Ben Edar's peak
> And Aideen's briary dell,
>
> And, gazing on the Cromlech vast,
> And on the mountain and the sea,
> Shall catch communion with the past
> And mix himself with me.

As in 'The Tain-Quest', Ferguson speaks of a damaged tradition, 'imperfect' and 'wounded'. This is partly the conventional rhetorical modesty of the poet, but it also reminds us that Ferguson is engaged on a work of archaeological recovery, and not simply responding to a creative impulse. It can, however, bring an elemental freshness as it feeds into the contemporary age. From Ossian's viewpoint the 'alien speech' is English; such notions of separateness are quickly passed over in the keen delight of utterance, to be replaced by 'communion' and a merging of the two poetic personalities. It is as near as Ferguson gets to stating a credo in any of his poems.

'The Welshmen of Tirawley', 'Owen Bawn' and 'Grace O'Maly'

Like 'Aideen's Grave', 'The Welshmen of Tirawley' and 'Owen Bawn' had been published before. 'The Welshmen of Tirawley' appeared in the *Dublin University Magazine* in 1845; 'Owen Bawn' is taken from 'The Return of Claneboy', the story which Ferguson had contributed to *Blackwood's* in 1833, where it was entitled 'The Parting from Slemish, or The Con's Flight to Tyrone'. Both poems had already been included in the Mac-Carthy and Hayes anthologies. In *Lays of the Western Gael and Other Poems* there are minor changes to the text of each. The penultimate stanza of 'Owen Bawn' is omitted, perhaps because the name of the character is changed from 'Owen Bawn Con' to 'Owen Bawn Quin' and the rhyme-scheme of that stanza was thrown out as a consequence.

'The Welshmen of Tirawley' has the strongest narrative line of all the lays. The final lines of comment can be seen not just as offering an explanation of the judgment; they also fit in with the structure of the later lays, in that they look forward from the time of the events described to a time of greater enlightenment. Here, that enlightenment is ushered in by the figure of

> the Saxon Oliver Cromwell,
> With his valiant Bible-guided
> Free heretics of Clan London

sounding a note of Presbyterian republicanism. He brings in a time of stability and freedom during which (it was to be hoped) differences of creed and race would disappear,

> Which while their children cherish,
> Kindly Irish of the Irish,
> Neither Saxons nor Italians,
> May the mighty God of Freedom
>   Speed them well,
>   Never taking
> Further vengeance on his people of Tirawley.

While 'The Welshmen of Tirawley' is distinguished by its narrative pace, 'Owen Bawn' is undoubtedly the most lyrical of the lays, and the shortest. After five quatrains cataloguing the attributes of Owen Bawn, the remainder of the poem urges a flight away from the oppression (in Antrim) to the woods and rocks of Tyrone. In its vision of the romantic freedom of the countryside it pairs well with 'Grace O'Maly', one of the more enigmatic of Ferguson's poems.

'Grace O'Maly' is a poem of praise for its eponym, obliterating the sixteenth-century pirate-queen Granuaile of popular legend and substituting a restless spirit seeking the open life of the west. One consequence of his treatment is that the political overtones of her name, which had come to be used as a personification of Ireland in Jacobite verse, are safely neutralised. Her fascination

with the proceedings of the Brehon's court and with the 'planx-
ty's gay commotion', and her fondness for the vigour of the
rolling seas, might be taken as reflections of Ferguson's own
penchant for getting out into the countryside on fieldwork and
sightseeing but never as a serious engagement with the claims of
nationhood.

Even this free spirit is not immune to the general shaping of
Ferguson's poetry, and towards the end she is to be found at her
castle window, where she can

> Sit; and while heaven's refulgent show
> Grew airier and more tender,
> And ocean's gleaming floor below
> Reflected loftier splendour,
> Suffused with light of lingering faith
> And ritual light's reflection,
> Discourse of birth, and life, and death,
> And of the resurrection.

The heroine of the poem is at once romanticised and gentrified. In
the end she is presented as a fugitive, escaping from the society
and manners of her own time and place and seeking an alternative code of life among the western Gaels.

> But chiefly sweet from morn to eve,
> From eve to clear-eyed morning,
> The presence of the felt reprieve
> From strangers' note and scorning:
> No prying, proud, intrusive foes
> To pity and offend her: –
> Such was the life the lady chose;
> Such choosing we commend her.

The date of composition of 'Grace O'Maly' is unknown, but the
other seven lays are arranged more or less in reverse order of
writing. The lays associated with Conor and the *Táin* were
written in the early 1860s; then come one each from the 1850s, the
1840s, and the 1830s. As set out in the book they move through
Irish from the earliest times up to the sixteenth century. This
chronological ordering disguises the fact that Ferguson's concern
in successive poems was to move steadily backward into the
remoter ages of his country's past. He too showed signs of a
fugitive spirit absenting himself from the uneasy Ireland of the
1860s.

6

Lays of the Western Gael,
and Other Poems (II)

Although the main emphasis of of Ferguson's collection rested on the 'Lays of the Western Gael', it has been the 'other poems' which have done more to define and fix his reputation. His early work had found expression in lyric celebration, largely free of narrative shaping; where those earlier pieces had been associated with stories, it was as embedded pieces in a containing prose text. One aspect of the new departure in the lays had been the suggestion that their Irish material did have a story to tell.

Ballads and Poems

The second section of the book gathered together eight of Ferguson's occasional pieces, among them some of those earlier poems. 'The Fairy Thorn' is there, of course; that was already a much quoted piece, steeped in melancholy and natural magic. Successful on its own terms, and admired today as perhaps the first shading of the Celtic Twilight poetry, we can all too easily overlook how untypical that poem is of Ferguson's work generally. The singularity is heightened by the fact that its intended companion-piece, 'The Fairy Well', which to Ferguson's distress had been separated from it when published in *Blackwood's* in 1833, is not restored. This poem had been included on its own in MacCarthy's *Book of Irish Ballads* (1846), but now Ferguson passes over it in silence. As a result, while 'The Fairy Thorn' is one of the most frequently anthologised of his poems, and 'The Fairy Well' has occasionally found its way into selections of Ferguson's poetry, the two never appeared together as originally intended.

An inescapable choice for inclusion was 'The Forging of the Anchor', the poem by which Ferguson was known all through the nineteenth century. Its energetic and unsubtle rhythms are much more characteristic of his work than either 'The Fairy Thorn' or his 'Versions from the Irish'. He had first used the long fourteen-syllable iambic couplets for 'The Rescue of the Mare' ('Willy Gilliland'), and was to use them again in *Congal*. Chapman's translation of Homer had demonstrated the possibility of using such a metre for epic poetry, but for Ferguson its first associations were with ballad narrative. The use of internal rhyme is regularised in 'The Tain-Quest' and 'The Healing of Conall Carnach', so that it becomes a structural device rather than an ornament. In these two lays the long line gains an extra accented syllable at the beginning, and the extra tie of the rhyme at mid-line does help to hold the stanzas in one piece – at the cost, it must be said, of an occasional resounding thump.

While 'Willy Gilliland' was included, the poem linked with it in both the *Ulster Magazine* and *Dublin University Magazine* printings, 'Una Phelimy', was not, although it had appeared in the Gavan Duffy and Hayes anthologies. But perhaps the most remarkable absence was that of the poem on the death of Thomas Davis. The omission is emphasised by its being given pride of place in an expanded edition of MacCarthy's *Book of Irish Ballads* just five years after *Lays of the Western Gael*, when it was deliberately positioned as the first poem in the book with Ferguson identified as the author. Introducing it then, MacCarthy wrote:

> The first poem in a collection such as this should strike, as it were, the keynote of the volume. This note is now struck, and struck effectively, by the elegy on Thomas Davis, which is not only a most pathetic lamentation on his death, but a powerful figurative picture of his life and of his work. In the title which I have given it ['Thomas Davis. His Life: His Death: His Work'] (for in the long prose article where hitherto it has been lost, it has none), I have drawn attention to the three aspects of his career which the poem presents with such felicity and power. . . . As a specimen of Anglo-Irish versification, it is, I think, the most successful and vigorous effort of its author, for, though published anonymously, there can be no possible doubt as to who he is.[1]

MacCarthy is right in hailing the piece as a fine poem, and obviously Ferguson agreed to its inclusion; MacCarthy was a friend of his, and the anthology is dedicated to him. As to why it had been excluded from *Lays of the Western Gael and Other Poems* a few years before there is no clear indication. He may have deemed it politically suspect, although events in Ireland had moved on considerably in the seventeen years since its first appearance – had moved more, it might be said, than had Ferguson's career. By the end of the 1860s, when he was installed as Deputy Keeper of the Records for Ireland, he would have felt more secure.

But perhaps the reason for its omission was more general. None of the poems in his 1864 collection touches on anything connected with the recent past in Ireland. Not only was the poem on Thomas Davis omitted, so also were 'Dublin' and 'Inheritor and Economist'. Although the last-named is a long poem, its length was not such as to ensure automatic exclusion from a book containing a number of long pieces. All three poems were written at the time of Ferguson's greatest involvement in public politics, and all three refer to the contemporary situation in Ireland. They would have sat oddly in a collection where the primary emphasis was, as suggested above, to move away from the immediate present.

There are just three poems in *Lays of the Western Gael and Other Poems* which touch on or arise out of contemporary concerns, and they are grouped together at the end of 'Ballads and Poems'. The first is 'Hungary', which is dated 'August 1849' and appeared in the *Dublin University Magazine* the following month. Like the early sonnet 'Athens', it was evidently written as a direct response to the news from Europe. The Hungarian national government was overthrown by the combined forces of the Austrian and Russian emperors after a short campaign which lasted through the summer of 1849. So immediate is the poem's reaction that its line of development twice changes abruptly, as if Ferguson is trying to sort out his rather confused feelings about it all. At first, with the blustering energy that had once hymned 'The Forging of the Anchor', he rejoices in the prospect of a battle between the mighty and dominant Russia and its oppressed neighbour Hungary. Next, recalling the proper attitude of a concerned Christian, he urges the advantages of peaceful co-existence. But then, in the last stanza, comes news of the final defeat of the Hungarian generals Gorgey and Bem by the Austrian Haynau:

> But you fill all my bosom with tumult once more –
> What! Gorgey surrender'd! What! Bem's battles o'er!
> What! Haynau victorious! – Inscrutable God!
> We must wonder, and worship, and bow to thy rod.

Not even the exclamation marks can haul this back from the brink, and the ways of God are not more inscrutable than Ferguson's decision to resurrect it fifteen years after the events which, so to speak, inspired it.

It is tempting to try to read into this poem an oblique comment on relations between Ireland and England, but so confused is its thought that such speculation advances us little.

Two other poems which touch on recent moments in Ferguson's own life are 'Adieu to Brittany' and 'Westminster Abbey'. These are both of a kind in that they show Ferguson contemplating a setting outside Ireland and using it as a springboard into the Irish past. 'Westminster Abbey' carries under its title the a very specific record of the occasion which prompted it: 'On Hearing Week-Day Service There, September, 1858'. The majesty of the Abbey is an embodiment of prayerful devotion and also a witness to the generations which have gone; the dead generations live on in their 'builded prayer'. But as well as travelling into the past, the Presbyterian Ferguson draws on the contrast between the stateliness of worship in England and its simplicity in Ireland, and then attempts to elide that difference under a shared Christianity.

> Fall down, ye bars: enlarge, my soul!
> To heart's content take in the whole;
> And, spurning pride's injurious thrall,
> With loyal love embrace them all!
>
> Yet hold not lightly home; nor yet
> The graves on Dunagore forget;
> Nor grudge the stone-gilt stall to change
> For humble bench of Gorman's Grange.

Pedestrian though it is, the poem graphically illustrates Ferguson's perception of the relative state of the two countries. England is easily identified with its capital, and especially its cathedral, a monument to grandeur accumulated through the ages by the collective effort of its people; Ireland, however, finds its image in the dispersed congregations of Donegore (his native place and eventual burial ground) and Gorman's Grange. The cities of Belfast and Dublin in which Ferguson lived all his life do not figure; the centre of consciousness is moved out of the streets and institutions into the country fields with their mute antiquities.

The most recent of all the poems in *Lays of the Western Gael and Other Poems*, 'Adieu to Brittany', was written after his extended tour though there in the late summer of 1863. This poem too contemplates Ireland from abroad, and the Ireland that is represented is a rural peasant one. Ferguson contrasts the durability of the megalithic remains at Carnac with the crumbling walls of

Roman buildings and the ruins of more recent palaces and minsters around Old Sarum in Wiltshire. Again, there seems to be an implied suggestion that imperial power is somehow less resilient than the more 'natural' qualities of the Celt.

> Like bubbles in ocean, they melt,
> O Wilts, on thy long-rolling plain,
> And at last but the works of the hand of the Celt
> And the sweet hand of Nature remain.

'The Death of Dermid'

The third part of *Lays of the Western Gael* is made up of four 'Versions and Adaptations', three of them from classical sources and one from Irish. 'The Death of Dermid' derives from Fenian legend and might have been expected to have found a place in the eponymous first part of the collection. It was eventually joined with them in the arrangement of his poems which Ferguson later outlined and which were published posthumously as *Lays of the Red Branch*. It differs from the early lays in that it is written in blank verse, and is concerned more with the debate between the dying Dermid and the aggrieved Finn than with vigorous and martial action. Labelled an 'Irish Romance', this description is more accurately applied to the ancient prose tale from which it derives than to the poem Ferguson makes of it. The lays generally embody narratives worked up from hints or anecdotes in printed manuscript sources, or, where there is a sustained narrative original, Ferguson does not scruple to alter the temper or effect of the original. In 'The Death of Dermid' Ferguson remains relatively close to his source passage, although in an introductory note to the poem he denies that it is to regarded as a translation.

Ferguson's source is O'Grady's edition and translation of *Toruigheacht Dhiarmuda agus Ghráinne* published in 1857 as Volume III of the *Transactions of the Ossianic Society*, of which he versifies a brief but climactic episode.[2] Dermid, the lover of Grania, won her away from Finn – his leader, her betrothed. The story of Finn's subsequent pursuit of the pair throughout Ireland is one of the most celebrated in Irish literature and folk-tale. Ferguson's version fastens on the ending of the pursuit, when Finn at last catches up with Dermid who lies dying of a wound received from a wild boar. Dermid beseeches his old comrade to fetch him some water from a life-giving well nearby; twice Finn goes to the well, but each time the bitter remembrance of the wrong done him by Dermid drives him to spill the water from his hands. After further entreaties he goes a third time to the well, but Dermid dies before he can drink. Grania is spoken of but does not figure directly in Ferguson's poem.

It is instructive to compare Ferguson's poem with the literal translation by O'Grady, in order to see how the elements are selected and arranged. 'The Death of Dermid' begins:

Finn on the mountain found the mangled man,
The slain boar by him. 'Dermid,' said the king,
'It likes me well at last to see thee thus.
This only grieves me, that the womankind
Of Erin are not also looking on:
Such sight were wholesome for the wanton eyes
So oft enamour'd of that specious form:
Beauty to foulness, strength to weakness turn'd.'
'Yet in thy power, if only in thy will,
Lies it, oh Finn, even yet to heal me.'

O'Grady, having told how the boar's attack on Diarmuid has left the hunter with his bowels and entrails ripped out of him (a detail subsumed in Ferguson's adjective 'mangled'), commences a new paragraph:

It was not long after this that when Fionn and the Fenians of Erin came up, and the agonies of death and of instant dissolution were then coming on Dermid. 'It likes me well to see thee in that plight, O Diarmuid', quoth Finn, 'and I grieve that (all) the women of Erin are not now gazing upon thee: for thy excellent beauty is turned to ugliness, and thy choice form to deformity.' 'Nevertheless it is in thy power to heal me, O Fionn,' said Diarmuid, 'if it were thy pleasure to do so'.

Although remarkably close in a number of respects, Ferguson reduces the number of persons present to just two. The Fenians who accompany Finn are dispensed with, as is Finn's son Oscar who, in the O'Grady edition, makes a crucial interjection near the end of the episode persuading Finn to bring the water to Dermid. In the poem the directness of the encounter is emphasised and Finn is not surrounded by companions who, while loyal to him, are also sympathetic to Dermid.

Ferguson exploits the confrontation bewteen the two men to some dramatic effect. Apart from fourteen lines of narrative, the encounter is conveyed in direct speech. This mode of direct presentation came to interest Ferguson more and more, and later poems such as 'The Naming of Cuchullin' and 'Deirdre' rely on it completely. In the Irish text Diarmuid advanced various reasons why Fionn should help him, recalling how he had fought to help Fionn on different occasions. Only after all these pleas had been heard did Fionn go three times to the well, twice allowing the water to spill and then 'the third time, because of that speech which Oscar had made to him, and brought the water to Diarmuid, and as he came up the life parted from the body of Diarmuid'. Ferguson interweaves the arguments of Dermid and Finn's journeys for the water. He also gives more prominence to love as a force in man's life. In the O'Grady edition Fionn sees Grania simply as a possession of which he has been deprived, and Diarmuid as someone who has injured him. The common ground of debate between the two men is the heroic code, not the romantic one of love. Whereas in the old Irish story the exchange is limited to the starkly clear obligations obtaining between a warrior and his commander, Ferguson's poem moves through three different stages. First, Dermid claims that he was powerless in the face of Grania's love, and therefore blameless; then he recalls two occasions on which he fought for Finn and saved his life; and finally Dermid reminds Finn of a vision of Christ's crucifixion 'for all men's pardoning'. This last Christian image replaces Oscar's urging in the original.

The progressive nature of the exchange in 'The Death of Dermid' contrasts markedly with the more fixed world of the old Irish text. In the O'Grady edition, the finding of Fergus does not alter or advance the situation or character of those involved. Ferguson on the other hand shows Finn visibly affected by the mention of Christ ('that Just One'), and Dermid is eased to a happy death.

Although the urgency of the situation in 'The Death of Dermid' rests in the prospect of Dermid's imminent end, that critical moment is set in a larger context. Both men appeal to a shared past and to the bonds that were forged between them as members of the Fianna. This at once heightens Finn's sense of outrage at the wrong done him, and provides the grounds of Dermid's appeal for aid from Finn's hands.

Ah, Finn, these hands of thine were not so slack
That night, when, captured by the king of Thule,
Thou layest in bonds within the temple gate
Waiting for morning, till the observant king

Should to his sun-god make thee sacrifice.
Close-pack'd thy fingers then, thong-drawn and squeezed,
The blood-drops oozing under every nail,
When, like a shadow, through the sleeping priests
Came I, and loos'd thee: and the hierophant
At day-dawn coming, on the altar-step,
Instead of victim straighten'd to his knife,
Two warriors found, erect, for battle arm'd.

Such appeals to the past prove ineffective. Finn eventually
resolves to fetch the water when reminded by Dermid of the very
different credal destiny of

'Him, whom once . . .
Thou showedst me, shuddering, when the seer's fit,
Sudden and cold as hail, assail'd thy soul
In vision of the Just One crucified
For all men's pardoning, which, once again,
Thou sawest, with Cormac, struck in Rossnaree'.

Dermid's words align Finn, the last and greatest warrior of the
old heroic order, with the event which will bring an end to that
order. The fact that Ferguson has him succumb to the request
which bases itself on Christ's sacrifice is a demonstration of that
eclipse. The final image of Dermid, his 'face relaxed in death',
brings him out of heroic paganism into the Christian confidence
of a model deathbed, accepting not just his own end but also the
new dispensation which is imminent.

'The Origin of the Scythians', 'The Invocation', and 'Archytas and the Mariner'

Because it links in with the larger poetic project of Ferguson, 'The
Death of Dermid' is of considerable significance in the context of
his work. The other three 'versions and adaptations', all from
classical sources, are of little import. 'The Origin of the Scythians' had first appeared in the middle of a book review for the
Dublin University Magazine in 1852. In the course of discussing the
origins of the early population of Ireland Ferguson mentions a
passage in Herodotus recounting a legend attaching to Hercules.
This gives the originary myth of the Scythae, supposed fore-
fathers of the Scotic Irish. They trace their line back to one of three
children fathered on the monster Echidna by Hercules as he
returned with the captured cattle of Geryon. Ferguson found the

tale told 'with so much feeling and simplicity' that he 'deemed it worthy of being rendered into verse'.[3] Ferguson gives the story in rhymed couplets, telling how, when Hercules departs, he leaves behind him his belt and bow; the son who grows up to wear the belt and bend the bow will be able and equipped to fend for himself. That son is Scyth, who is shown at the end of the poem coming into his adulthood, inheriting the prowess of Hercules and foreshadowing the race he will beget. He,

> . . .striding dreadful on his fields of snow,
> With aim unerring twang'd his father's bow.
> From him derived, the illustrious Scythians name,
> And all the race of Scythian monarchs came.

This final rhyme, implicit with beginnings, anticipates the ending of *Congal*: '. . . while up the hill the hosts of Domnal came'. This is, as we shall see, a characteric turn in Ferguson's poetry.

'The Invocation' versifies the lines by Lucretius at the start of *De Rerum Naturam* asking Venus, the mistress of nature, to help him with his task of writing. The 'Alma Venus' of the original becomes the less specific 'Joy of the world, divine delight of Love' as Ferguson evokes a picture of life in all its forms fulfilling itself. In his vision the fulfilment is neither cyclic, as in the seasonal rhythm, nor a momentary epiphany of becoming; it is a process which endures temporally, at once made by and experienced through time, as though myth and history were reconciled;

> thou, who through waving woods,
> Tall mountains, fishful seas, and leafy bowers
> Of nestling birds, keep'st up the joyous hours,
> Making from age to age, bird, beast, and man
> Perpetuate life and time; – aid thou my plan.

From such a state as this one might well set sail for Byzantium; however, at the time Ferguson's book was published, Yeats, while rather more than a gleam in his father's eye, was not yet born.

An earlier nineteenth-century translator of Lucretius was Ferguson's fellow Antrim man, W. H. Drummond; as before with the versions from Hardiman, he had shown Ferguson the way. It is noticeable that Ferguson can translate from classical sources without Christianising them in any way; when working on old Irish material, however, the addition of a Christian morality seems almost obligatory.

The occasion which prompted the last of these translations, 'Archytas and the Mariner', is spelled out by Ferguson himself. On his visit to the Aran Islands during the summer of 1853 he came upon some bones uncovered by the shifting sands in the graveyard. The incident recalled an ode by Horace (No. 28, Book I) in which a sailor discovers on the shores of the Adriatic the unburied corpse of Archytas, the geometrician and philosopher. As he moralises upon death, the shade of Archytas interrupts him and, pointing out that death is universal, pleads for a handful of sand to be scattered over him so that he might cross the Styx. This poem, published in 1853, was Ferguson's last piece of poetry in the *Dublin University Magazine*.

Versions from the Irish

The final section of Ferguson's book contains the poems for which, then and since, he has been best known in Ireland. These are the short verse translations, mostly from song, the greater number of which had first appeared in the appendix to the papers on Hardiman's *Irish Minstrelsy* in the *Dublin University Magazine* thirty years before. While many of them had been included over Ferguson's name in the various anthologies of the intervening years, their inclusion here served to establish a belated claim to primacy now that Mangan and others had given greater currency to verse translations from the Irish.

Ferguson's 'Introductory Note' to these poems is far more circumspect than his earlier remarks in the review of Hardiman. He begins with an apology, pointing to 'certain faults' inherent in the bardic poems and songs he has translated. Many of them are praise poems for the ear of a patron, and so are hard put to ring the changes on stock themes and compliments. As a result they lack originality. The anonymous songs of the people are commended for their unrivalled expression of sentiment, although he notes that they are deficient in thought and art. Ferguson speaks with less reserve of the remarkable musical qualities of these songs, an aspect of which he had had little to say when reviewing Hardiman, who did not give the airs for the songs he collected. Subsequently, Ferguson's work with Bunting had brought him into contact with the melodies of popular songs, and he quotes his friend Petrie, himself an accomplished violin player, on the musical structures.

One consequence of the musicality is the 'duplications of rhythm' and the internal rhyme which characterises Irish poetry. Ferguson at this stage is uncertain whether to deprecate these features as being quaintly bizarre, or to commend them as valuably unusual. 'It is difficult in English to imitate these duplications and crassitudes, which give so much of its effect to the original, where, owing to the pliancy of the sounds, several syllables are often, as it were, fused together, and internal rhymes and correspondences produced within the body of the line.' By way of illustration he goes on to quote two stanzas of a translation of 'The Boatman's Hymn', beginning:

> Oh Whillan, rough, bold-faced rock, that stoop'st o'er the bay,
> Look forth at the new barque beneath me cleaving her way;
> Saw ye ever, on sea or river, 'mid the mounting of spray,
> Boat made of a tree that urges through the surges like mine today?

This corresponds to the following lines in Hardiman (I give a literal translation):

> *A Dhaoileinn a chrom-charraig gharbh, gan sgáth*
> (O Whillan, you rough hunched rock without [any] shelter)
> *Air an nuadh-bharc-so fum-sa breathnuigh do sháth,*
> (On this new boat beneath me look your fill)
> *An chuimhin leat 's an g-cuan-so go bhfeaca tu bád*
> (Do you [ever] remember seeing a boat in this bay)
> *Gan chontabhairt, tonn-bharra ghearradh, mar táim.*
> (Without danger, cutting the wave tops as I am).

Ferguson's example is not very happily chosen, in that the Irish text offers only a few irregular examples of internal assonance across the line – just *'leat'* and *'bhfeaca'* in the third line of the piece quoted, for instance. Ferguson introduces internal full rhymes in the third and fourth lines of his version, but these smack more of the internal rhyming of 'The Forging of the Anchor', which owes nothing to Irish prosody. More directly derived from the Irish is the use of a single end-rhyme throughout each quatrain.

Ferguson's version in the 'Poems' is a considerable refinement on the lines as he translates them in the introductory note:

> Whillan, ahoy! old heart of stone,
> Stooping so black o'er the beach alone,
> Answer me well – on the bursting brine
> Saw you ever a bark like mine?

This is unremarkable in itself, but it shows very clearly the degree to which Ferguson was willing to pare down the Irish texts of these songs. There is no straining after an effect of fey 'Irishness', nor is there undue poeticisation in the manner of earlier translators; it relies on the virtues of simplicity.

Of the new poems added in the 'Versions from the Irish' section, the four penultimate ones – 'The Dear Old Air', 'The Lapful of Nuts', 'Mary's Waking' and 'Hopeless Love' – seem to be without any Irish original; certainly none is to be found in Hardiman's *Irish Minstrelsy*, nor in Bunting's *Ancient Music of Ireland*. The temper of these poems is rather different to that of the others in the section. One senses on reading them that they were written apart from, or in different conditions, to the other pieces, and they exhibit none of those signs of language under the stress of a foreign idiom which are nearly always apparent in even the most accomplished of translations. Perhaps Ferguson simply wanted to slip in some lyrics of his own unobtrusively. Whatever the origin, one of them, 'The Lapful of Nuts', is as beguiling a lyric as ever he wrote:

> Whene'er I see soft hazel eyes
> And nut-brown curls,
> I think of those bright days I spent
> Among the Limerick girls;
> When up through Cratla woods I went,
> Nutting with thee;
> And we pluck'd the glossy clustering fruit
> From many a bending tree.

There is a languid grace about this and the other three of this group; they lack the urgency and unease which Ferguson himself had discerned in the Irish sentimental songs when writing about them in the *Dublin University Magazine*.[4]

The two other newly added poems among the versions are 'Youghal Harbour' and 'Cean Dubh Deelish'. They both come from Part II of Hardiman's first volume, the 'Sentimental Songs' which were Ferguson's preferred material. 'Youghal Harbour' enacts an encounter between a man and a distraught young girl whom he meets on the road from Youghal to Cappoquin; he wins her over in spite of her mistrust by promising her shelter, care, and eventually a child. Ferguson slightly tones down the blandishments; one which clinched matters in the original was the offer of a drink-shop. Nevertheless his translation succeeds because it takes the pace of its development strictly from the Irish

version. It also introduces some internal rhyming, especially in
the second-last line of each stanza. This may be an imitation of the
assonantal patterning frequent in Irish verse, but not actually
present in the original in this case.

> One Sunday morning, into Youghal walking,
> I met a maiden on the way;
> Her little mouth sweet as fairy music,
> Her soft cheeks blushing like dawn of day!
> I laid a bold hand upon her bosom,
> And ask'd a kiss: but she answer'd, 'No:
> Fair sir, be gentle; do not tear my mantle;
> 'Tis none in Erin my grief can know.'

The other new poem, 'Ceann Dubh Deelish', is one of Ferguson's most admired translations. The Irish text runs in part (and I
give a literal English crib):

> A cheinn duibh dhílis, dhílis, dhílis!
> (O darling darling darling black head)
> Cuir do lámh mhín-geal thorm a náll!
> (Put your slender white arm around me)
> A bhéilín mheala, bh-fuil boladh na tíme air,
> (O honeyed mouth, that has the scent of thyme on it)
> Is duine gan chroídhe nach d-tiubhradh duit grádh
> (It would be a heartless person who would not give you love)
> Tá cailíneadha air an m-baile-so air builleadh 's air buaidhreadh
> (There are girls around here tormented and troubled)
> Ag tarraing a n-gruaige 's dá léigeann le gaoith,
> (Pulling their hair and letting it to the wind)
> Air mo shon-sa, an scafaire is fearr ann san tuaithe
> (For my sake, the finest young buck in the place)
> Acht do thréigfinn an méad sin air run Dhil mo chroídhe.
> (But I'd leave all of those for my darling sweetheart.)

Then come four final lines which are almost a repeat of the first
four.

Ferguson makes of it the following:

> Put your head, darling, darling, darling,
> Your darling black head my heart above;
> Oh, mouth of honey, with the thyme for fragrance,
> Who, with heart in breast could deny you love?
> Oh, many and many a young girl for me is pining,
> Letting her locks of gold to the cold wind free,
> For me, the foremost of our gay young fellows;
> But I'd leave a hundred, pure love, for thee!

Then put your head, darling, darling, darling,
Your darling black head my heart above;
Oh, mouth of honey, with the thyme for fragrance,
Who, with heart in breast could deny you love?

This keeps remarkably close to the rhythm and meaning of the Irish text in the opening and closing quatrains which carry the real emotional burden of the song. His rendering of the middle four lines departs a little from the original by refining it somewhat: 'pining' dilutes the anguish attributed to the rejected girls; 'locks of gold' over-elaborates on the plain 'hair', but the rhyme of 'cold wind' is a nice addition. All four of these central lines rhyme alternately in the Irish text. Ferguson has not attempted to reproduce this pattern, but rhymes every second line throughout; for the intermediate lines he ends on unstressed syllables, giving a uniformity of cadence to the endings of lines which are often uncompromising in their broken rhythms.

Reaction

Irish matter was unpopular among the larger English readership. If Ferguson had not been alerted to this already by the reluctance of *Blackwood's* to print any of his lays, it was spelt out for him in a notice of *Lays of the Western Gael, and Other Poems* in the *Saturday Review*:

> There is perhaps no class of matters, historical or legendary, in which it is so hard to get up an interest as matters purely Celtic. . . . No one cares for any Welsh hero except Arthur, and people care for Arthur only because they do not realize he was Welsh. . . . The Irishman, the 'Western Gael' of Mr Ferguson, is, if possible, more hopeless still.

The reviewer is patently out of sympathy with what Ferguson is attempting to do, and rapidly loses track of the various characters introduced in the lays. He sighs rather for

> the half-sportive way in which Scott, in the notes to his poems, sets forth and explains his various Highland and Lowland legends, making his notes scarcely less interesting – some people think more interesting – than the poem itself. We had not the least notion, till we opened Mr Ferguson's book, who Nessa and Neesa and Deirdra and Maev were, and we should like to have them introduced to us in a somewhat clearer and less solemn manner. What, for instance, is 'the military order of the Red Branch', to which several of Mr Ferguson's worthies belonged? Mr Ferguson brings in the order and its

'companions' with the utmost seriousness, but without a word of explanation, as if it were something which everybody knew all about. And he ends:

> If the traditions of the 'Western Gael' are to be made attractive to Englishmen, it needs a stronger hand than Mr Ferguson's to do it.[5]

The lays are faulted for taking their material seriously; as an object of detached amusement it might do, but the reviewer is disturbed at being expected to accept Irish, or even Scottish or Celtic, stories on anything approaching their own terms. Alternative terms on which these might be 'attractive to Englishmen' were outlined by Matthew Arnold.[6] The *Saturday Review* was quoted by Arnold as foremost among those voicing a denial of there being any Celtic element in the English make-up. His lectures *On the Study of Celtic Literature* were being prepared at the very moment of the appearance of Ferguson's book; in them he fixed the character of the Celt as dominated by 'sensibility, the power of quick and strong perception and emotion'[7] and in being revolt against 'the despotism of fact'.[8] One may quarrel with Arnold's line of argument; people very soon did. Nevertheless his ideas exerted a powerful and enduring influence on ideas about literature from Celtic countries. His identification of 'style', 'melancholy' and 'natural magic' as the areas in which Celtic poetry excels did little to promote Ferguson's hard-edged vision of the simplicities of a heroic Ireland. Ironically, it was Ferguson's early poems in the periodicals in the 1830s which had helped to establish the Arnoldian mode of Irish poetry. Now, striking off in a different direction in the main section of his first book, he was to be hampered by the very success of his earlier initiative. *Lays of the Western Gael* was out of tune with its time.

An Irish critic, Cashel Hoey, was more appreciative of what Ferguson was doing. Writing on 'Recent Irish Poetry' in the *Dublin Review*, he gave pride of place to *Lays of the Western Gael* among a distinguished quartet of collections (the others were *Poems* by Speranza, Allingham's *Laurence Bloomfield in Ireland*, and *Inisfail: A Lyrical Chronicle of Ireland* by Aubrey de Vere), and concentrated his attention uniquely on the first part of the book, the 'lays', calling them 'the most thoroughly original vein of poetry that any Irish bard of late days has wrought out'.[9]

One of the first reviews to appear, that in *The Athenaeum*, welcomed the book. Noting first of all that Ferguson's poetry was mercifully free of any rancour directed against the English, it claimed that Mr Ferguson had 'lifted Irish poetry out of the mire; furnished some gems with a loving fastidiousness, and given them a worthy setting', and then went on to rhapsodise about Irish nature as 'the maddest will-o'-the-wisp', 'an echo in Elfland', qualities which, the reviewer felt, Ferguson had insufficiently emphasised.[10] Encountering such a gush of disappointed expectations brings home forcefully just how much we are indebted to Ferguson's restraint.

But the *Athenaeum* review is remarkable for a feature which, in spite of the complimentary things said of Ferguson, must have dismayed him: the only pieces discussed are the 'poems and ballads' and the 'versions from the Irish'. 'The Forging of the Anchor' is quoted at length, 'The Fairy Thorn' and 'Anna Grace' (that is, 'The Fairy Well', not even included in the book) are commended, and the translations for which he is known are discussed. Of Ferguson's main poetic endeavour, the 'Lays of the Western Gael' themselves, there is not a word. One could not have a clearer indication of the degree of difficulty faced by Ferguson as he attempted to give currency to Irish historical legend.

7

Congal

Seven years after *Lays of the Western Gael and Other Poems*, Ferguson published *Congal* (1872). This poem, long in the making and, it has to be admitted, long in the reading, was his attempt to develop fully an epic treatment of the Irish past. The endeavour of the lays is carried a stage further, in that *Congal* sets out to portray not just character and incident but also something of the society and conditions of the time. This, together with its publication date, might suggest that the poem follows on from the lays, but such is not the case. The idea for *Congal* predates all the lays except 'Owen Bawn' and, as the manuscripts in the Public Record Office and the Linen Hall Library indicate, the poem as we have it was more or less complete by the summer of 1861. Only then did Ferguson commence work on 'The Healing of Conall Carnach'. He wrote to Blackwood that it and the other lays were 'shoeing-horns' for *Congal*, shorter pieces to prepare the way for his major work; their effectiveness in that task can be gauged from the notices quoted at the end of the last chapter, and from Ferguson's own reference in the notes to *Congal* to his earlier book as 'a little volume, now difficult to obtain'.[1] *Congal* did not come off the press to find a receptive readership waiting for it.

Ferguson had started work on *Congal* in 1842 or soon after. Up to that time he had written mainly lyric or short poems, the ones which had established his reputation. Now he faced into the older, more expansive form of epic. He had already engaged with larger narrative forms in *Hibernian Nights' Entertainments*. In *Congal* and the lays he continued the search to find a suitable treatment for the disjected materials recovered from the Irish past.

The poem's events are based on the prelude to and the outcome of the Battle of Moyra fought in 637 A.D. between forces led by Congal, King of Ulster, and Domnal, the King of Ireland. The quarry from which Ferguson mined his material was John O'Donovan's edition of *The Banquet of Dun na n-Gedh and The*

Battle of Magh Rath, published for the Irish Archaeological Society in 1842.

The society had been established the previous year, with the object of printing the ancient historical and literary documents of Ireland. To do this it relied on the subscriptions of its members to bear the costs of publication, and during the 1840s a number of historical sources were made available to a scholarly readership. In aims and methods it was akin to the English Historical Society, which had commenced its series of publications in London in 1838, and to the Camden Society, founded there the same year. The Irish Archaeological Society's founders had striven for a broadly based membership to prevent its becoming identified with a particular party in Irish life. It certainly satisfied *The Nation* on this particular score:

> It has grown from a knot of two dozen enthusiasts to a national society of 400 gentlemen. It embraces Protestant and Catholic hierarchs, Tory, Whig and Repeal nobles, and journalists and professional men. With another hundred names its list will close, and it will be safe from all hazards.[2]

The optimism was not justified. Although the Irish Archaeologocal Society successfully brought a number of works into print, it never attracted the membership numbers originally hoped for; by 1847 there were still only 458, some way below the necessary 500. The depressed state of the Irish economy was blamed for the difficulty in attracting subscribers, and in 1850 it merged with the Celtic Society.

Samuel Ferguson was not a member of the Irish Archaeological Society, but he was nothing loath to make use of its publications. 'The Welshmen of Tirawley' was drawn from the Society's edition of *The Genealogies, Tribes, and Customs of the Hy-Fiachrach*. With *Congal*, as was often the case with Ferguson's writings, his use of printed and manuscript texts went hand in hand with a direct knowledge of the topography of the story's setting. In the same year as O'Donovan's edition of *The Banquet of Dun na n-Gedh and The Battle of Magh Rath* appeared, Ferguson walked over the battlefield in company with a local antiquary, John Rogan.[3] Within twelve months of this he was mentioning to Robert Blackwood of *Blackwood's Edinburgh Magazine* that he had 'cast a famous Irish Bardic Story into a sort of Celtic epic'.[4] Ferguson refers to this first attempt as if complete, but nothing further is heard of it. The following year, 1844, he began a draft of a version which got no further than twenty-two lines; these, together with some accompanying notes on the battlesite, are preserved in a notebook now in the Public Record Office.[5] Within a couple of years of the story's publication Ferguson had made two abortive attempts at rendering it into verse; the first apparently reached a state of near-finality, the second was barely begun. In the Preface to the 1872 edition, Ferguson says of these early versions: 'After some time, I found the inherent repugnancies too obstinate for reconcilement, and, with some regret, abandoned that attempt'.[6]

That there were problems is not surprising. Apart from the occasional difficulties posed by the subject-matter, with its indelicacy of treatment and its indulgence in far-fetched grotesqueries (as he would have been at one with the *Saturday Review*-er in so considering them), the very form of the long poem in general, and of epic in particular, was open to question as an available form for narrative. Tennyson's 'Morte d'Arthur' was another 1842 publication. It is presented as the one surviving book of an attempted modern epic. A prefatory poem, entitled 'The Epic', gives the supposed background: an undergraduate, Everard Hall, had cast the medieval tale of Arthur into a twelve-book epic but, dissatisfied with the result, had burnt the manuscript. The eleventh book only was rescued from the flames. Asked why he destroyed his poem, Hall replies 'that nothing new was ever said, or else/ Something so said 'twas nothing – that a Truth/ Looks freshest in the fashion of the day'. Ferguson might have taken warning from this, for not only was Tennyson a writer whom he had admired since being linked with him in *Blackwood's* at the outset of his career, but the episode described mirrored his own experience. Ten years before, in the early 1830s, he had written a long six-canto version of a medieval tale[7] which he subsequently discarded, leaving only (as I think) the section which appeared as 'The Stray Canto' in the *Dublin University Magazine* in July 1834.

The choice of a subject like the battle of Magh Rath meant that Ferguson could move towards the medievalism which provided a favoured idiom in Victorian poetry and art. But the early and middle Irish sources which Ferguson used were not directly equivalent to the 'matter of Britain' as rewritten by his English contemporaries such as Tennyson, Bulwer-Lytton, R. S. Hawker and, later, William Morris. The glimpses of a historical Arthur were mediated to the nineteenth-century English writers by late medieval story-tellers; their work found its summation in Malory's *Morte d'Arthur*, a medieval fiction of romantic chivalry which was itself a powerful force in the shaping of a national myth and was given literary currency at an early stage by Caxton's printing press. By Malory's time the story of Arthur had been accepted into the history of England for three centuries.

One part of this process of acceptance was the 'de-celticisation' of Arthur, making him a symbol of England and things English as distinct from the Celtic figure which can be glimpsed in the earliest references to him. As a result it was relatively easy to find an appropriate form when writing of Arthur and the Knights of the Round Table; the stories came rich with associations from being intertwined with the historical consciousness of the nation. Ferguson started from bare narratives devoid of the accretions of myth. That these historical tales are themselves without a history is indicated by O'Donovan's reproach directed at Thomas Moore for having 'so boldly hazarded the unqualified assertion, *that there exist in the Irish annals no materials for the civil history of the country!*',[8] an assertion based on simple ignorance of their existence. The stories are presented by O'Donovan as historical tales, not as imaginative narrative literature. Never before printed, the twin tales of *Dun na n-Gedh* and *Magh Rath* were innocent and unfamiliar. As he set about versifying them, Ferguson would have seen it as a valuable opportunity to highlight evidence that Ireland did indeed possess a wealth of history, but he was primarily concerned to develop a reservoir of heroic literature. In doing this he was faced with the double task of contextualising the tales as well as re-shaping them.

The protracted composition of *Congal* ran parallel to Tennyson's publication of *Idylls of the King*, and the popularity of the *Idylls* was a demonstration of what might be achieved in the handling of legendary material. The body of reworked Arthurian literature which they spearheaded offered a possible meeting-ground for the cultural experience of the two islands. Ferguson's task was complicated by an awareness of the weight of the Arthurian takeover. The dead Arthur might, as legend had it, be fated to come again to Britain, but to Celtic Ireland he was irrevocably lost. Perhaps a fount of Irish heroic narrative might compensate for the loss and take its place alongside the Arthurian matter.

Legends of the Fianna and of the Red Branch Knights seemed to offer equivalents to the Arthurian realm. Already, in his 1847 article on Thomas Davis, when searching for some common ground between the founder of *The Nation* and the readers of the *Dublin University Magazine*, Ferguson had described the energising effect of Davis on 'the young mind of the country, starting us from a trance – or from that fabulous spell which our legends tell us keeps Finn's mighty youths asleep under the green hills, waiting the advent of an Irish Arthur'.[9] Throughout *Congal* itself there are several references to the stories of Arthur, as if Ferguson were reaching out to the potent British figure.

One way in which Ferguson attempted to deal with the 'inherent repugnancies' he found in his originals was to transform them from heroic tribalism to romantic individualism. This can be seen in the published text of *Congal*, which concentrates on a character rather than on an event. Consider the keynote set by the poem's opening:

> The Hosting here of Congal Claen. 'Twas loud lark-carolling May
> When Congal, as the lark elate, and radiant as the day,
> Rode forth from steep Rath-Keltar gate: nor marvel that the King
> Should share the solace of the skies, and gladness of the spring,
> For from her high sun-harbouring bower the fortress gate above
> The loveliest lady of the North looked down on him with love.
> 'Adieu, sweetheart; a short adieu; in seven days hence,' he cried,
> 'Expect me at your portals back to claim my promised bride'.

The heroic note lasts through the first half-line; thereafter the idiom alters radically.

An early draft of these lines, and of *Congal* as a whole, was made during the 1850s. In 1852 Ferguson took up the notebook in which he had made the twenty-two line start eight years before and, starting from the other end, began to set down what is recognisably *Congal*. This occupied him through the decade, by the end of which the poem had assumed the broad outlines of its present narrative shape. In this draft text Ferguson has obviously moved away from any idea of a verse paraphrase of the old Irish narrative, and instead is using the incidents and characters associated with it as the raw material for a new telling of the story. Work on this draft seems to have ended in the summer of 1858. A year later he again broached the subject of his long poem in a letter to *Blackwood's*:

> I have nearly completed a long poem which I hope may live after me. For the present I do not contemplate publishing, and possibly the peculiarly Irish character of the poem – its subject is the great battle of

Moyra, AD 637, when the old Bardic power made its last stand against the new institutions of Christianity – would deter you from having anything to do with it . . . . It will be about 4,000 lines of the long metre, and will I hope be an epitome of the most picturesque and heroic incidents of the Early Irish Tradition before the 7th century.[10]

Just two months later he was having further doubts about the poem, especially the earlier parts, and he set about rewriting it for 'possibly the 4th or 5th time'.[11] The rewriting was severe, for by the end of 1861 the poem seems to have shrunk from the '4,000 lines of long metre' to about 2,500, divided into eight sections.[12] The poem as it stood at this stage is represented by the manuscript in the Linen Hall Library, Belfast, which is marked 'Finished June 1861'.[13] This is more or less the printed text, but not separated into books. On a separate page Ferguson listed possible headings for the eight sections of the poem, as for instance

> The Journey
> The Banquet
> The Ominous Portents
> The Council
> The Muster
> The Battle
> The Defeat
> The End.

When published ten years later, the poem was divided into five books.

As was the case with so many of Ferguson's poems derived from Irish sources, his task was not to translate from Irish to English but from prose to poetry; added to that there was the question of finding an appropriate form. In his working text as he found it in O'Donovan there were two narratives: the account of the battle is preceded by the story of the banquet given by Domhnall at Dun na nGedh, the scene of the quarrel that provoked the battle between him and Congal. 'The Banquet at Dun na n-Gedh' stands as a pre-tale to 'The Battle of Magh Rath', in much the same way as the stories of how Cuchullin and Emain Macha got their names are related to the *Táin Bó Cuailgne*. But while Ferguson never succeeded in reattaching 'The Twins of Macha' or 'The Naming of Cuchullin' to the *Táin*, here he worked on the two stories as an integral unit. In O'Donovan's prose translation they make up together about 36,000 words, with the pre-tale accounting for the first quarter or so of them.

Ferguson's poem is remarkably similar in extent, the 3,300 or so lines of its final version amounting to about 35,000 words. But what Ferguson does within that space, and his manner of presenting the events of the story, differ significantly from his source. His manoeuvrings in and around the stories of the banquet and the battle over a period of thirty years reflect the problems confronting him as he tried to present ancient Irish material in a suitable modern form.

The O'Donovan Text

'The Banquet of Dun na n-Gedh, and the Cause of the Battle of Magh Rath', to give the pre-tale its full heading, tells how Domhnall built the palace of Dun na nGedh on the bank of the Boyne upon becoming King of Ireland. Soon afterwards he has a dream, interpreted by Maelcobha as foretelling that one of his foster-sons, the provincial kings Raghallach of Connaught or Congal Claen of Ulster, will rise up against him. Refusing to believe them capable of such treachery, Domhnall prepares a banquet to celebrate the completion of his new palace. As his servants scour the countryside for the choicest foods, they take goose-eggs belonging to the hermit Erc of Slane, where there is a crossing on the Boyne. Erc curses the banquet, and soon afterwards two mysterious spiky-haired giants approach the palace with a quantity of goose-eggs, consume prodigious quantities of food as it is offered to them, and then disappear with further curses on the feast.

The many guests arrive. As part of the hospitality each king is presented with a goose egg on a silver dish, but at Congal Claen's turn the offering is suddenly transformed into a hen's egg on a wooden platter. Congal and his followers, already discontented by the seating arrangements, take this as a grievous insult and, after lengthy recriminations, they leave the palace in anger, resisting the attempts of clerics and poets to bring them back. Congal meets with his uncle, the aged Cellach, who advises battle to avenge the insult, but first of all to seek aid from Alba and Britain. The second half of the pre-tale is given over to telling how Congal travels to meet the kings of those countries and, after a long series of negotiations, tests, and formal exchanges, he secures their aid. The story ends with a summary account of the battle, the course of which is given in detail in the following narrative of 'The Battle of Magh Rath'.

This begins, after an introductory passage outlining some bardic maxims and other extraneous material, by telling of the peace and prosperity enjoyed under Domhnall's reign; this is the conventional sign of a good kingship. The story concentrates on his preparations for the battle as various forces from around Ireland rally to Domhnall's aid. There are lengthy speeches in counsel, and interpolated verse passages. Dubhdiadh, a druid attached to Congal's army, reconnoitres and reports back on the impressive might of the forces under Domhnall. The account of the battle is given mainly in terms of consultations about tactics on either side, with occasional combat between named persons. There is a long fight between Congal and Conall, in which Conall is defeated through the intervention of Conan Rod. The attempt to carry off the head of Conall as a trophy is thwarted by when Cellach, King of Leinster, slays Conan Rod.

After the account of this combat, the story tells how the imbecile son of Ultan, Cuanna, at a scene removed from tne battle, is seeking firewood to heat the bath water for the women. When taunted with being absent from the fighting, he sets off to Magh Rath to act his part. Getting a weapon, he enters the fray and meets Congal, who is his foster-brother. Congal scorns to fight Cuanna and passes him by, but Cuanna pierces him unawares. The wounded Congal continues to fight on the battlefield, but refuses to fight against Cellach of Leinster. His forces are defeated; only six hundred of the Ulstermen survive, and of all the foreign allies only Dubhdiadh the druid escapes by swimming back to Scotland.

On this raw material Ferguson makes several changes. The most significant is the focussing of attention on Congal the rebel rather than on Domhnall the king, who is at the centre of the original account. He also shapes the events with greater coherence, so that the narrative has the sequence and closure of a story rather than the serial parataxis of a simple chronicle. The eight headings in the 1861 manuscript, which are in effect a catalogue of set-pieces in the poem, show the vestiges of that original structure; they were jettisoned, and the poem re-apportioned into five books with rather more narrative complexity.

Book I

Of these five books, the first two approximate to 'The Banquet of Dun na N-Gedh'. The poem begins with Congal leaving his fort at Rath Keltar, bidding goodbye to his betrothed Lafinda, and setting off southward to Dunangay. On the way he is persuaded to visit his uncle Kellach, whose kingdom is in the fastnesses of the Mourne Mountains; Kellach still clings to the old pagan religion although it is now nearly two centuries since the arrival of Patrick and the start of Ireland's conversion to Christianity. The bards, displaced representatives of the old pagan order, have found a refuge in the remote valleys of Kellach's territory. The invitation to go there poses immediate problems for Congal, but under the rules of hospitality he is bound to accept, as was Fergus in 'The Death of the Children of Usnach'. The example of Fergus is cited in persuading Congal; Ferguson, as he does in 'The Tain-Quest', refers back to the material he has already worked on.

The bards are in internal exile with Kellach as a result of the convention of Dromceat at which Aed, father of Domnall, had pronounced their expulsion. This decree was enacted in about 590 A.D., some forty-five years before the time of the poem. The account in Keating's *History of Ireland* speaks of their finding refuge in the immediate aftermath; it is Ferguson's invention to depict them in the south-east corner of Ulster.

Some by the lonely flood-side walked; and other some were seen
Who rapt apart in silent thought paced each his several green;
And stretched in dell and dark ravine, were some that lay supine,
And some in posture prone that lay, and conn'd the written line.

Apart from getting the positions right, Ferguson is at pains to set up a conflict between the old order and the new, an aspect not present in the source text. This detour on Congal's journey shows the poet's refuge as a physical representation of the interim between the old pagan and bardic Ireland and the new Christian land of Patrick.

While in Kellach's kingdom Congal hears three songs chanted by the bards. The first tells of the legendary colonisers of Ireland. Its elements are assembled from O'Mahony's edition of Keating's *History of Ireland*.[14] The awkwardly allegorical names of Partholan's oxen ('Dig', 'Delve', 'Gather-Increase-In') are based on one of O'Mahony's notes; on the other hand, one of the most successful passages in all of Book I, when the romantic peace of the rhythm sits easily with the long lines of the poem's metre, is that describing Partholan's grave:

Forgotten Partholan himself, lies 'neath his royal mound
On green Moynalty, hushed at eve by drowsy ocean's sound,

> And clangorous song of flocks, by night, when through the wintry air
> The wide-wing'd wild geese to their pools by Liffey side repair.
>
> (I, p. 13)

This brings a post-Keatsian language to bear on images assembled direct from O'Mahony's Keating:

> Partholan died, in the old plain of Magh-n-Elta of Edar, and there he was buried. The reason why it is called the Old Plain, i.e. *Sen-Magh*, is because no wood ever grew upon it, and the reason why it is called Magh-n-Elta, i.e. 'the plain of the flocks', (i.e. *elta*) is because that was the place where the fowl of Eri used to come to bask in the sun.[15]

The first bard ends with a loaded conceit which identifies his principal hearer, Congal, with Slanga, illustrious descendant of Partholan,

> At whose return, when time has brought Fate's pre-appointed hour,
> Long, long withheld, return the days of Ulster's pride and power.

Like Arthur, the national hero is destined to return; Congal is being allotted a role.

The second song recited for his benefit tells of a vision of Borcha, the legendary herdsman of Ulster whose name is still preserved in the Irish name for the Mourne Mountains. Borcha's herds have been much diminished as Ulster's power lessened, but with Congal's arrival he foresees the possibility of repossession.

These two self-contained lays are among the later additions to the poem. 'Lays' is the term used to describe them in *Congal*, and in the manner of the *Lays of the Western Gael* they tell a story drawn from events of the past; they are not included in the 1858 draft,[16] and so must have been written at about the same time as the lays proper. The third poem chanted for Congal, by the chief poet Ardan, is included in the 1858 draft in substantially its present form. Ardan's contribution is rather different in that he does not have a story to tell, but depicts the wrongs which have been inflicted on the bards . His message is conveyed in images of change from wealth and order to blight and decay, a movement of thought which reproduces the progress of the 'Lament for Thomas Davis' rather than looking forward to the *Lays of the Western Gael*. The catalogue of riches recited by Ardan includes the gifts which were due to poets under the old dispensation:

> A hundred steeds, a hundred foal, each foal beside its dam,
> A hundred pieces of fine gold, each broad as Scallan's palm,

And thick as thumbnail of a man of churlish birth who now
The seventh successive seedtime holds a fallow-furrowing plough:
Three hundred mantles; thirty slaves, all females, young and fair,
Each carrying her silver cup, each cup a poet's share
Who sings the ode inaugural.

(I, pp. 18–19)

While all this is reminiscent of the riddle 'As I was going to St Ives', it is also indicative of Ferguson's attempt to fill out the stark foreground of his source material by importing a profusion of props, as if dressing the stage of a costume-drama. Ardan continues his lay with the recollection that Scallan is dead and now 'the skies are altered':

For all the life of every growth that springs beneath the sun
Back to the air returns when once its turn of life is done:
To it all sighs ascend; to it, on chariot-wheels of fire,
All imprecations from the lips of injured men aspire;
And when that lofty lodge of life and growth-store of the world
Is choked with groans from burthened hearts and maledictions hurled
In clamorous flight of accents winged with deadlier strength of song
From livid lips of desperate men who bear enormous wrong,
Heaven cannot hold it; but the curse unbursting from on high
In blight and plague, on plant and man, blasts all beneath the sky.

(I, p 19)

Mindful of Ferguson's reaction to Davis's death, it is possible to read this climactic speech of Book I as having some contemporary bearing. The relationship between Domnal and his sub-king Congal is in some respects analogous to that of Britain and Ireland under the Union; the picture of universal change among 'desperate men who bear enormous wrong' evokes the state of feeling in Ireland during and immediately after the famine, at the time when these lines were written; and while Ardan's expressed wish for the ruin of Domnal is more extreme than anything Ferguson ever voiced, the final more moderate search for the restoration of 'Law and Justice, Wealth and Song' corresponds very accurately to what he desired for Ireland. These were precisely what he felt to be threatened by the centralised indifference to and ignorance of the Irish situation and heritage.

As a result of Ferguson's giving a greater voice to Kellach as champion of the bards, Congal's struggle is altered from a dynastic and territorial one to a fight for a cultural consciousness. Structurally, *Congal* continues in the line of internal struggles for the hearts and minds of protagonists.

The compacted word combinations such as 'fallow-furrowing' and 'growth-store' were a feature of Ferguson's poetic style from the beginning. In 'The Forging of the Anchor' he had described the anchor as a 'deep-sea-diver' plunging into the submarine 'tangle-woods' to meet the 'ghastly-grinning' shark. Although he did not use such constructions in his translations of the Hardiman songs, they are frequent in *Congal* and the Lays of the Western Gael. As the early use indicates, it was a habit of Ferguson's style before he commenced his study of Irish material, but when versifying this section of O'Donovan's translation he encountered lines such as the following description of the waterfall at Assaroe:

> The clear-watered, snowy-foamed, ever-roaring, particoloured, bellowing, in-salmon-abounding, beautiful old torrent . . . The lofty-great, clear-landed, contentious, precipitate, loud-roaring, headstrong, rapid, salmon-ful, sea-monster-ful, varying, in-large-fish-abounding, rapid-flooded, furious-streamed, whirling, in-seal-abounding, royal and prosperous cataract.

Ferguson commented in his notes to *Congal*:

> Had I followed by original, I should have written here –
> The deep-clear-watered, foamy-crested, terribly-resounding,
> Lofty-leaping, prone-descending, ocean-calf-abounding,
> Fishy-fruitful, salmon-teeming, many-coloured, sunny-beaming
> Heady-eddied, horrid-thund'ring, ocean-prodigy-engend'ring,
> Billow-raging, battle-waging, merman-haunted, poet-vaunted,
> Royal, patrimonial, old torrent of Eas Roe –
> or something to that effect.[17]

These lines form part of the draft manuscript version of the poem, but are modified in the published version.[18] Translation, he felt, was unable to reproduce the cumulative effect of the original without introducing tautologies and repetitions. But while the cataract of expressions was unsuited to the English, hyphenated compounds in isolation are characteristic of his narrative poetry.

Book II

The second book of *Congal* follows 'The Banquet of Dun na n-Gedh' more closely than does the first, but at the outset it introduces two reminders of encroaching Christianity. One is a reference to the supposed birthplace of St Brigid at Fochard, near Dundalk, which Congal passes on his journey south; the other, which follows soon after, comes when he encounters Erc at the ford at Slane, still outraged after the theft of his goose eggs. While Erc's anger can be discounted as the posturing of a zealot, the sight of Brigid's cell prompts a resentful comment from Congal on the pervasiveness of Christianity, and he is mollified only by a reminder that Brigid's followers were the early instructors of Lafinda. The incident underlines the changing patterns of belief in Congal's world. Even though Ferguson's verse is not equipped to present rapid and dynamic change, he is at pains to show Congal as a man outstripped by events.

The central concern in Book II is brought back more into line with the Irish text, as Congal seeks to regain and retain what he sees as his hereditary kingdom, 'the whole Rudrician realm, as erst its bounds were known,/Ere Fergus Fogha sank before the Collas' robber sword' (II, p. 31), and to preserve his dignity and his sense of *amour-propre* as king. The re-establishment of the old order of the pagan bards, given such prominence in Book I, now becomes incidental to his cause. Nevertheless, in his harking back to lost territories and status, Congal remains enmeshed in the claims of the past; in one form or another they are the foundation of his enterprise.

Once arrived at the banquet, Congal is first slighted in the seating arrangements, and then by the presentation of an inferior egg on a wooden dish. In the original the transformation of the goose egg is portrayed as a miraculous outcome of Erc's curse on the feast. O'Donovan glosses this instance of superstition with an apologetic footnote, and Ferguson offers a selection of rational explanations for the apparently supernatural event:

> by fate or by mischance,
> Or cook's default, or butler's haste, or steward's ignorance,
> Through transposition of his seat not rightly understood.
>
> (II, p. 27)

The supernatural was an area of particular sensitivity. Ferguson accepts practically none of the marvellous incidents in the source text, and instead introduces his own, generally at differen: points.

The marvellous sat very uneasily with the historical status that was claimed for story; nevertheless, the nature of the material and the epic form demanded some equivalent in the modern version. As Ferguson commented in a slightly exasperated note, 'Nothing more indicates a childish condition of the popular mind than its delighting in mere exaggerations of bulk, of strength, of endurance, such as abound in our old literature'.[19] He felt relatively at ease with the bardic power of prophecy; a supposed capacity for divination accorded with what was known of the bard's social role, and there was example for it in classical literature. However, he omitted incidents such as the arrival of the spiky-haired couple who bring Domhnall the tub of ill-fated goose-eggs. These belong to the realm of the marvellous, a characteristic carried to extreme in old Irish heroic legends.[20] Among the incidents Ferguson introduces are the intervention of the herdsman Borcha, the meeting with the Washer at the Ford, and the appearances of the god Mannanan Mac Lir and Brigid, drawn respectively from Fenian legend, Hiberno-Scottish folklore, Celtic mythology, and Hiberno-Christian hagiography. None of these is introduced for its own sake. Ferguson's solution to what he perceived as a problem of irrelevant exaggeration was to give the supernatural characters a function in the narrative. Uniformly they look forward to later stages of the story, warning of events ahead and predicting a fate which will be fulfilled as the story moves towards its close. Although varied in their dramatic presentation, in their function they scarcely go beyond the prophetic utterances of the bards.

Congal's aggrieved speech at the banquet, rehearsing his claims to Domnal's favour, is a set-piece more closely modelled on O'Donovan's translation than are other parts of the poem. It allows us to see in little some of the transformations wrought on the original. After outlining Domnal's exile in Scotland, O'Donovan's text of Congal's speech runs as follows:

'Thou didst afterwards return to Erin, and I returned along with thee, for I was in exile along with thee. We got into port at Traigh Rudhraighe, and here we held a short consultation. And what thou didst say was, that whoever thou shouldst get to betray the king of Erin, thou wouldst be bound to restore his territory to him whenever thou shouldst become king over Erin. I went on the enterprise, O king, for a promise that my patrimony should be wholly restored to me, whenever thou shouldst become monarch of Erin; and I delayed not until I reached Ailech Neid, where the king held his residence at that time. The king came out upon the green, surrounded by a great concourse of the men of Erin, and he was playing chess amidst the hosts. And I came into the assembly, passing without the permission of anyone through the crowds, and made a thrust of my spear, Gearr Congail, which I held in my hand, at the breast of the king, and the stone which was at his back responded to the thrust, and his heart's blood was on the head of the javelin, so that he fell dead. But as the king was tasting of death he flung a chess-man which was in his hand at me, so that he broke the crooked eye in my head. I was squint-eyed before, I have been blind-eyed since. The hosts and people of the king then fled, thinking that thou and the men of Alba were with me, as I had killed Suibhne Menn, the king.

'I then returned to thee, and thou didst, after this, assume the sovereignty of Erin. My father, Scannall of the Broad Shield, died soon after, and I came to thee to be made king (of Ulster), as thou hadst promised me. Thou didst not perform thy promise except to a small extent, for thou didst deprive me of Cinell Conaill and Cinell Eoghain, and also of the nine cantreds of Oirghiall, the land of Maelodhar Macha, who now sits at thy shoulder, and whom thou hast seated in the place of a king, in preference to me, this night, in thine own house, O king,' said he. 'And a goose egg was placed before him on a silver dish, while a hen egg was placed on a wooden dish before me. And I will give battle to thee and the men of Erin in consequence, as thou hast them assembled around thee tonight,' said Congal. And he then went out of the house, and the Ultonians followed him.[21]

Ferguson's rendering of this passage gains several points of description which fill out the original: Ailech is 'broad-stoned', Troy Rury has 'brown-rippled sands', the green (*faichthi*) becomes a 'sunny sward', and the men grouped around Sweeney are identified as 'nobles' and a 'royal guard'. These descriptions are additional to the old Irish text; they are also utterly unremarkable and conventional. Both features suit well with Ferguson's purpose of visualising the remote unread past of Ireland, conferring on it the expectations of a later age.

This stratagem is fundamental to his enterprise in this type of poetry. The very fact that the vision he presents is commonplace serves to lessen the strangeness of his material. Shklovsky and the Russian Formalist critics have emphasised the concept of *ostranenie*, defamiliarising the material of poetry; but for Ferguson the task was not one of making strange, but of making familiar.

Here is the episode in his words:

> where we first made land
> Was at Troy Rury: there we held a council; and 'twas there,
> Standing on those brown-rippled sands, thou didst protest and
>   swear,
> If I by any daring feat that warrior-laws allow
> Of force or stratagem, should slay King Sweeny Menn, and thou
> Thereby attain the sovereignty, thou straightway wouldst restore
> All that my royal forefathers were seized of theretofore.

Relying on which promise to have my kingdom back,
I left thee at Troy Rury; nor turned I on my track
Till I came to broad-stoned Ailech. There, on the sunny sward
Before the fort, sat Sweeny Menn, amid his royal guard,
He and his nobles chess-playing. Right through the middle band
I went, and no man's license asked, Garr-Congail in my hand,
And out through Sweeny's body, where he sat against the wall,
'Twas I that sent Garr-Congail in presence of them all.
And out through Sweeny's body till the stone gave back the blow,
'Twas I that day at Aileach made keen Garr-Congail go.
But they, conceiving from my cry – for, ere their bounds I broke,
I gave the warning warrior-shout that justified the stroke
By warrior-law – that Eochaid Buie and Alba's host had come,
Fled to their fortress, and I sped safe and triumphant home.
Then thou becamest Sovereign; and, Scallan Broad-Shield dead,
I claimed thy promise to be made King in my father's stead;
Not o'er the fragment of my rights regained by him, alone,
But o'er the whole Rudrician realm, as erst its bounds were known,
Ere Fergus Fogha sank before the Collas' robber sword;
That thou had'st promised; and to *that* I claimed to be restored.
But thou kept'st not thy promise; but in this did'st break the same,
That thou yield'st not Tir-Conal nor Tir-Owen to my claim;
And the nine cantreds of Oriall to Malodhar Macha, he
Who now sits at thy shoulder, thou gavest, and not to me.
And him today thou givest my royal place and seat,
And viands on a silver dish thou givest him to eat,
And me, upon a wooden dish, mean food which I disdain:
Wherefore upon this quarrel, oh King,' said Congal Claen,
I here denounce thee battle.'
                    Therewith he left the hall,
And with him, in tumultuous wise, went Ulster one and all.
                                    (II, pp. 30–2)

Ferguson also makes some changes in the presentation of Congal's adventure here. Twice he insists that Congal adhered to the rules of 'warrior-law' in his attack on Sweeny, and shouted a warning. The Irish text is more pragmatic; it makes no mention of any such warning, and has Domhnal inviting one of his followers to 'betray the king of Erin'.

Ferguson's text, here and throughout the poem, suppresses all mention of the origin of the epithets which attach to Congal's name: *Claen* ('squint-eyed') and *Caoch* ('blind'). An eye had been damaged in childhood, and subsequently lost its vision completely in the incident narrated above. Although Congal is several times styled 'Congal Claen' in the course of the poem

('Claen' allows for an easy rhyme), at no time is there any hint of the meaning of the cognomen. Congal is presented as an unblemished hero, as if any disfigurement would disqualify him as it did the ancient high kings of Ireland. On the return journey northward after the dispute at the feast, Congal takes the opportunity to confer with his uncle Kellach. In the Irish text this is the first meeting between the two, and Kellach's role as protector of the displaced bards is not mentioned. The belligerent old man produces a sword and threatens to use it unless Congal make war on Domnal. In O'Donovan he offers to run it through Congal if he prove less than committed in confronting the king. Ferguson changes this to a more romantic threat: Kellach will turn the sword on himself should his nephew hang back. He advises Congal to seek aid in Britain, and recalls the names of Arthur, Gwendolen, and Merlin. As in Book I, Congal is urged on by having the example of other warriors brought to his mind, and of course Ferguson is here aligning his story of Congal with the larger Arthurian legend.

Before Congal sets out across the Irish Sea Ferguson inserts an intimation of Borcha's presence on the mountain; the herdsman stirs as he anticipates the full restitution of his former greatness. There is also time for a meeting between Congal and Lafinda. She is found by a limpid stream, supervising her handmaidens as they full a cloak. Congal explains to her the dark turn in events, with the consequent delay in their marriage.

Arrived in Britain, Congal is well received both in Scotland and at Caer Leon. The first to see him in Britain is the druid, whose name is altered by Ferguson from Dubhdiadh to Drostan. Ferguson also abbreviates the contest in courtesy which pits the four sons of the Scottish king and their wives against each other in offering hospitality to Congal; likewise, the test of Congal's wisdom in deciding a difficult case at Caer Leon (which of three claimants is the true Conan Rodd, son of the British king) is much shortened. Arrangements are speedily concluded for the invasion of Ireland by a combined force including French and Saxon troops.

Book III

The second book of *Congal* ends with the forces gathered in Britain setting sail 'in an evil hour', and the sense of evil attaching to the enterprise is continued in the opening of Book III, which launches into the preparations for the battle. The narrative runs on without interruption and the supplementary material at the beginning of 'The Battle of Magh Rath' is jettisoned. The arrival of Congal's army is attended by 'a cloud of blood', like that hanging over Emain Macha in the story of 'The Death of the Children of Usnach', and a lightning flash sets fire to all the boats once the troops have landed. These presage doom, and the ominousness is continued by Congal's encounter with Manannan Mor Mac Lir. Manannan appears as a giant striding figure wrapped in a cloak who disdains to answer Congal's challenge. Later, the marching armies come to a ford where they find an old woman, 'The Washer of the Ford', who is rinsing the mangled remains of slain warriors. She tells Congal that he is leading his troops to death, and shows him his own severed head. All these incidents are imported by Ferguson. The apparition of Manannan is modelled on Mangan's 'Churl of the Grey Coat', while that of 'The Washer of the Ford' is taken from a sixteenth-century manuscript account of 'The Wars of Turlough'; Ferguson had already quoted it in his review of Hardiman:

> The multitudes at large gazed altogether at the transparent lake, where they saw on the bank of the smooth water a hideous and ghastly hag, . . . having before her a heap of heads and a load of helms, and a pile of lopped hands and dissevered feet, washing and pouring water diligently thereon, till all the water was full of hair, and blood, and brains from her abominable labour.

When questioned as to who she is, the hag replies

> I am the Disconsolate of Burren, and my lineage is of the Tuatha de Danan race, and the heads and members of you, royal prince, and of your people, are the carnage before me.[22]

Ferguson makes of this one of his most effective passages, and expands the woman's answer as follows:

> 'I am the Washer of the Ford,' she answered; 'and my race
> Is of the Tuath de Danaan line of Magi; and my place
> For toil is the running streams of Erin; and my cave
> For sleep is in the middle of the shell-heaped Cairn of Maev,
> High up on haunted Knocknarea; and this fine carnage-heap
> Before me, and these silken vests and mantles which I steep
> Thus in the running water, are the severed heads and hands
> And spear-torn scarfs and tunics of these gay-dressed, gallant bands
> Whom thou, oh Congal, leadest to death.'

(III, pp. 57–8)

The ominous prelude to the battle ends as it had started , in another scene with Lafinda. Accompanied by her nurse Lavarcam she arrives to tell Congal of a dream she has had foreboding ill to his enterprise; when he dismisses her fears the nurse changes into the figure of Brigid and leaves the scene with Lafinda.

All these incidents are of Ferguson's introduction. The supernatural beings and the women characters are akin in that both groups represent values which, in different ways, are opposed to what is implied by "manliness", a key word in Ferguson's vocabulary. Congal, embodying the heroic strengths of manhood, is set apart from the feminine tenderness of Lafinda from the outset. The poem's opening lines have shown him taking leave of her, and every meeting with her subsequently is an explanation or prolongation of his absence. Although Ferguson introduces her as an object of romantic interest, it is an area of experience which is repeatedly rejected in the poem. In the Arthurian tales Guinevere, Enid, Elaine, and the others are integral to the world of Camelot as presented by, say, Tennyson; Lafinda is little more than a cypher in the circumstances surrounding Congal.

The supernatural beings and apparitions around Congal are also opposed to his "manliness". In some respects they provide divine encouragement and opposition to his enterprise, elevating his stature by association. Supernatural intervention is a distinguishing feature of epic, but in *Congal* the gods and other supernatural manifestations are not depicted independently of human perceptions of them. They exist only as seen or heard. Ferguson hedges his bets, introducing supernatural beings but giving them a part in the structure of the story which is subordinate to the mortal characters.

Following the cluster of supernatural warning signs, the remainder of Book III is taken up by speeches from the various leaders as they debate whether to persist or not in the attack on Domnal. After a vigorous and dramatic start the pace of this central book slows appreciably, but there is a crucial speech by Conan Rodd, the true son of the King of Britain identified by Congal in his judgment at the British court. Conan Rodd speaks of himself as a youthful quester who has journeyed the world in search of heroic combat against more than mortal antagonists, but who so far has found only human opponents drawn, like himself, "from dust of vulgar earth".

> And, for their mighty miracles and prodigies sublime,
> Of antique Gods, and holy Saints, these from the olden time
> Had, as they said, ceased utterly; and now were only known
> In lays and legends of their Clerks, as idle as our own.
> Wherefore with glory-thirsting heart, that still insatiate burned,
> I from their barren battle-fields and empty camps returned,
> Resolved amid my native woods, and in the sacred gloom
> Of Stones of power, to seek again some conqueror of the tomb;
> Great Arthur, with the apple-bloom of green Avallon's bowers
> Still redolent; or Uther's self from Caer Sidi's towers;
> But sought in vain.

(III, pp. 68–9)

Now, arrived in Ireland, he finds "Immortal beings visibly commingling, as of old,/In mortal struggles". Congal's fight does have something to offer a Briton; it affords a locus for youth and dreams to engage with an older world.

> Here at length I find my youthful dream
> Made real. Here the mighty deeds of antique heroes seem
> No longer all inimitable. Here Hercul's self might own
> Fit labour for another Toil, nor ask the task alone.
> Wherefore with awful joy elate, I stand; and bid thee hail,
> Last hero-stage of all the world, illustrious Inisfail!
> Land of the lingering Gods! green land, still sparkling fresh and fair
> With morning dew of heroism dried up and gone elsewhere!

(III, p. 69)

Conan Rodd's speech is followed by three others: the Norse king expresses his joy at the prospect of war, and Ardan and Congal also speak before the army moves off to the battleground at Moyra. But it is Conan Rodd who articulates Ferguson's own justification for exploring the old Irish legends. Their primitivism can restore to the modern age something of the lost epic world. The remote lands of the western Gael, the "last hero-stage of all the world", provide a refuge for unregenerate antiquity which, as an object for contemplation, is of value to a society which can regard them with detached sympathy.

Book IV

The fourth book begins with an abrupt change of scene to Domnal's camp. Garrad Gann, the envoy of Domnal who had figured so prominently in the opening section of the poem as he escorted Congal to the feast at Dunangay, reports on the disposition of the insurgent forces. Then follow Domnal's preparations for battle and his addresses to the different sections of his united forces. His magisterial tone is in striking contrast to the doubt and debate which has marked the equivalent episode in Congal's camp. The shift of focus is a reminder of how different had been Ferguson's first conception of the poem, which would have concentrated not on Congal but on the figure of Domnal dealing with a threat posed by forces made up from within and outside his kingdom.

The twenty-two lines written in 1844 had commenced:

> The battle of red Moyra, and praise of Erin's king
> In mighty-worded numbers I take in hand to sing.[23]

Here he announced to himself, if to no one else, a poem about the battle which will take Domnal as its hero. Just four years later, in a review of the *Ecclesiastical History of Down, Connor, and Dromore* by his friend and fellow antiquarian William Reeves, he wrote about the battle of Moyra in a way which evinces a far greater interest in "the proud, unhappy Congal Claen".[24] Much had happened in the intervening four years: there had been the year abroad on the continent, followed by the meeting with his future wife. More pertinently, after the death of Davis and the ravages of the famine he had been stung into a brief involvement with public politics. Something of the turmoil of that time found its way into his revised conception of *Congal*. For instance, among the passages from O'Donovan he omitted was the section describing the peace and prosperity enjoyed in Ireland during Domhnall's reign.[25] This was a commonplace attribute of a good king, and was to be introduced effectively into "Conary". But in *Congal* Ferguson wants to diminish the authority of Domnal and his role in the story, and he sets out to show a troubled state rather than a tranquil one.

The area covered by Reeves's book, Ferguson notes, "is probably the most interesting portion of all Ireland for historical investigation"; it is also, of course, Ferguson's native region. After mentioning Patrick's first preaching, and the prolongation of bardic influence even after Dromceat, he goes on: "Here the final struggle between the old and the new systems was determined, on the field of Moyra".[26] His summary of events leading to the battle shows the changed emphasis he was to give them, with Kellach emerging as the presiding genius:

We may picture to ourselves old Ceallagh Mac Fiachna, carried out on his brazen *Tolg*, to meet his nephew returning from the disastrous feast of Dun-na-n'gedh; and as Congal enumerates the indignities put upon him at the royal banquet, handling under his gown the sword, which none till then suspected the bedridden old senior of carrying; we may imagine its walls resounding to the songs of bards, enumerating the former possessions of the kings of Ulster, and the former privileges of the poets, before the statutes of Dromceat transferred their rents and honours to the Christian clergy, and sent twelve hundred of them adrift on Ulster, with nothing but their harps and burning words to depend on for life or vengeance; till Congal, at length maddened by a sense of his own wrongs, and by the instigations of outraged poets, undertakes the fatal expedition which terminated in his defeat and death at Moyra.[27]

It is clear that Ferguson had formulated his basic conception of the poem by this stage; when he set to to write *Congal* in earnest four years later in 1852, it was to expand on the particulars of this account without altering any of them. From now on, whenever he speaks of the battle of Moyra it is in terms of the struggle between two orders.

Most of Book IV is taken up with describing the progress of the battle. From the dates attached to various parts of the PRO manuscript, it is evident that this part was written relatively late, while Ferguson was in France during the summer of 1858. It therefore post-dates the draft of what is now the fifth and final book.

In the course of the battle there is the incident of the flight of Sweeny from the battlefield as he is impelled by some supernatural force. Sweeny has become a richly emblematic figure in modern Anglo-Irish writing; it fell to Ferguson to be the first to write of him. In the original Irish story Sweeny's fit comes upon him as the result of being cursed by St Ronan, but here Erc of Slane is the outraged saint who thus punishes him with flight. Ferguson's Sweeny is a man torn by conflicting impulses, anxious to fly the danger of battle yet conscious of the shame consequent on such an action. He becomes a man caught in a moral dilemma because of his failure to live up to the heroic values which govern his world. As "the terror in his soul at length to madness grew", his departure from these norms of behaviour becomes characterised as "madness". Ardan recognizes what has happened:

> No coward's flight is here,
> But sacred frenzy sent from Heaven. The wings of vulgar fear

Ne'er lifted weight-sustaining feet along the airy ways
In leaps like these; but ecstasies there be of soul, that raise
Men's bodies out of Earth's constraint, and, so exalted, he
Acquires the sacred Omad's name, and gains immunity
From every earthly violence. 'Twas thus Wood Merlin gained
His seership on Arderidd field, else Britain had remained
Still unenriched of half her lore.

                                                          (IV, p. 103)

Even this fugitive figure is integrated into the story of *Congal*,
where he figures as the brother of Lafinda. Ardan's speech allies
Sweeny at once with sacred powers (although it is difficult to tell
whether the Heaven he mentions is Ferguson's Christian one or
a pagan concept of his own) and with the Arthurian Merlin.
Sweeny is rehabilitated and placed in the larger scheme of
things.

The impulse towards integration is again apparent a little
further on when the description of the battle's progress is
interrupted to trace the descendants of Domnal Brec (Freckled
Domnal). He is captured by the Irish King's forces, and released;
afterwards he becomes king of Scotland,

A famous sovereign: and his race in Yellow Eochaid's hall
Reigned after him; till Selvach, son of Fercar, named the Tall,
To proud Dunolly's new-built burg transferred the royal chair.
. . . . .
And after Selvach, once again to shift the wandering throne
Came conquering Kenneth Alpinson, the first who sat at Scone,
Full King of Scotland, Gael and Pict, whose seat to-day we see
A third time moved, there permanent and glorious to be,
Where, in Westminster's sacred aisles, the Three-Joined-Realm
    awards
Its meed of solemn sepulture to Captains and to Bards;
And to the hands pre-designate of awful right, confides
The Sceptre that confers the sway o'er half of ocean's sides.

                                                          (IV, p. 107)

Bounding over thirteen centuries, Ferguson has brought the
course of the poem briefly into line with Victoria's heritage,
combining – not altogether effortlessly – cultural nationalism
with monarchical unionism. The drafting of these lines can be
dated to the latter end of 1858, which makes them contemporary
with "Westminster Abbey" in *Lays of the Western Gael and Other
Poems*. As in that poem, the Abbey is seen as a locus of unity
encompassing the grandeur of the centre and the simplicity of

the Celtic fringes. To this, the passage from *Congal* adds a temporal dimension, linking back to the age of the battle of Moyra where

> Domnal's brothers in one grave on Irish Moyra lie;
> And to this day the place from them is called Cairn-Albany.
> The hardy Saxon little recks what bones beneath decay,
> But sees the cross-signed pillar-stone, and turns his plough away.
>
> (IV, p. 107)

The mention here of the cultivation of Ulster by the Saxon is yet another insistence on the unified diversity which Ferguson seeks to assimilate within the compass of *Congal*.

Book V

In a prefatory couplet to the poem Ferguson suggests a theme for each of the five books:

> Ambition, Anger, Terror, Strife and Death,
> Each, here, its Book in Congal's story hath.

These indicate the various thematic stages of the poem, and in the fifth and last book it remains to treat of Congal's death. Ferguson was left considerable freedom by his source. In the Irish text Congal is described receiving a wound from Cuanna the idiot, and engaging in fierce combat with Maelduin and losing his right hand. Then comes a confrontation with Cellach, the King of Leinster (an ally of Domhnall's, not to be confused with his namesake, Congal's uncle). Congal recites a poem rehearsing his many battles, and then just fades out of the historical text. His forces are routed, Domhnall is victorious, but on Congal's end the source is silent.

Ferguson adjusts for this; his poem follows Congal from the battlefield and absolves him from the charge of fleeing the combat. Congal is hurried away from the scene of his defeat by an apparently supernatural intervention, when he is hidden from view by a sudden squall. The imagery recalls the earlier descriptions of Borcha and Manannan:

> And thunderous clamors filled the sky, it seemed, with such a sound
> As though to giant herdman's call there barked a giant hound
> Within the cloud above their heads; and loud-resounding strokes
> They also heard, or seemed to hear, and claps of flapping cloaks
> Within the bosom of the cloud.
>
> (V, p. 132–3)

It seems as if an apotheosis into the Celtic pantheon is being prepared for Congal, but his fate is to be very different. It transpires that the poet Ardan has accompanied him in the rush from the battlefield, as they were borne away by stampeding horses. His chariot does not halt until back at Rath-Keltar, Congal's fortress. In the final moments of his life a number of characters gather around him: Lafinda, Sweeny, Ardan, and, most impressively of all, the god Manannan Mac Lir. All have seen a change in their world: Lafinda has foregone the prospect of being Congal's bride and queen to join Brigid's nuns; Sweeny will live out his days as an archetypal fugitive; Ardan the bard has been cast adrift by the new social order; and Manannan and the other Celtic gods have been deposed.

But Ferguson handles the final vision of change with some tact. The giant 'Shape' that appears to the the dying Domnal is obviously Manannan. The Christian Lafinda deems the sight 'unholy' and averts her eyes, but Domnal derives solace from the passage of the god. His huge presence is described in terms of a rich autumnal scene; the lines have been extracted for quotation on a number of occasions, but their full effectiveness lies not only in the lushness of the imagery but also in the momentary identification of Congal's story with the physical landscape of Ireland. And the 'Shape' which passes in silence brings simultaneously a reminder of its power and a sense of spiritual regeneration, so that after its departure Congal speaks of his past 'sins' and 'deeds' as being somehow apart from him. Lafinda is led to hope for his entry into heaven as Congal dies, but Ferguson refrains from any explicit statement. Congal ends his life uncertainly poised between possibilities.

Of those around him, Sweeny departs with the 'Shape', Lafinda returns to the convent, and Ardan is left, 'Last wreck remaining of a Power and Order overthrown' (V, p. 147). Alone, he is brought to the admission that he finds solace neither in 'the lore/Of Bard or Druid' nor 'in the chaunts of those/Who claim our Druids' vacant place'. The poet is left as the true outsider, unable to accept either the old order or the new; he refuses the offer of sanctuary, and yields himself to God's will. But the earthly powers will have their way first, as the last lines of the poem make clear.

> 'Servants of Brigid,' Ardan said. 'To God be thankful praise,
> Who turns the hearts of men like you towards me in tender ways:

Yet, since my King has found the peace I seek to share, outside
Your Saint's enclosure, here will I the will of Heaven abide.
'On his own head, Lord, not on ours,' they said, 'let lie the blame.'
And closed the gate; while up the hill the hosts of Domnal came.

(V, p. 148)

The uncertainties are about to be resolved.

An Irish Epic?

During the 1860s, with *Congal* more or less complete, Ferguson
had offered a number of the lays which he had mined from old
Irish sources to *Blackwood's*; he had also tried to interest that
magazine in the longer poem before publication, and to get it
reviewed afterwards. But the stars in the *Blackwood's* firmament at
that time were novelists such as Trollope, Bulwer-Lytton, and
George Eliot. Its most prominent Irish contributor was Charles
Lever. Irish epic poetry was not the sort of material for its pages.

There had been one notable attempt to combine social realism
and long poetic narrative: Elizabeth Barrett Browning's *Aurora
Leigh* (1856). In its Fifth Book she takes up Tennyson's discussion
of the epic: 'The critics say that epics have died out/With
Agamemnon and the goat-nursed gods;/I'll not believe it'. She
continues

                    every age,
    Heroic in proportions, double-faced,
    Looks backward and before, expects a morn
    And claims an epos.

For her the question is one of perspective. She warns poets
strongly against antiquarianism; they do not need to delve into
history for epic values.

    Their sole work is to represent the age,
    Their age, not Charlemagne's, – this live, throbbing age,
    That brawls, cheats, maddens, calculates, aspires,
    And spends more passion, more heroic heat
    Betwixt the mirrors of its drawing-rooms,
    Than Roland with his knights at Roncesvalles.

The debate on epic was to be decided forcefully in 1872, the
year of *Congal*'s much delayed publication. That year also saw the
publication of *Middlemarch*, and in the 'Prelude' to that novel
George Eliot asserts the unlikelihood of epic fulfilment and the
inappropriateness of epic ambition. Saint Theresa 'found her

epos in the reform of a religious order – many Theresas have been born who found for themselves no epic life wherein there was a constant unfolding of far-resonant action'. In broaching the epic as he did in *Congal*, Ferguson confronted a form and material which were, to say the least, suspect to his contemporaries. The slow development of the poem over three decades, and the finished work, must be evaluated in the light of his having to contend with this factor. Coupled with it was the resistance to Irish subject-matter among English readers, a resistance which became more pronounced during the 1860s. Not only among English readers, indeed; there is a letter from Edward Dowden persuading Aubrey de Vere to write about Beckett rather than about any Irish subject:

> The choice of an Irish mythical or early historical subject confines the full enjoyment of the poem to a little circle. I admire 'Congal' very truly; nevertheless, I feel that I shall never more than half enter into it.[28]

One gets a clear sense of *Congal* the poem being as embattled on all sides as Congal the man. It took Yeats to try to rescue the poem and its author, in an obituary essay which is the starting point for any modern assessment of Ferguson. Having seen the background against which *Congal* was written, we can appreciate the force of his comment that Professor Dowden might have done better had he 'devoted some of those elaborate pages which he has spent on the much bewritten George Eliot' to Samuel Ferguson instead, and so spared him from the comment in *The Academy*, in 1880, that he 'should have published his poems only for his friends'. Yeats continued: 'If Sir Samuel Ferguson had written of Arthur and Guinevere, they [Irish readers] would have received him gladly; that he chose rather to tell of Congal and of desolate and queenly Deirdre, we give him full-hearted thanks; he has restored to our hills and rivers their epic interest'. Ferguson had indeed tried to include something of the world of Arthur and Guinevere alongside Congal; as always, his was an inclusive vision.

We can only speculate on what might have been the course of the Anglo-Irish literary renaissance had Ferguson published his first apparently completed treatment of the battle of Magh Rath in the early 1840s. As it was, in *Congal* and in his other poems dealing with like material, he had two principal concerns. One of them he shared with *The Nation* poets: the culturally nationalist endeavour to bring his readership to an awareness of the 'history' in its possession. The other, in common with his British contemporaries, was to find an appropriate style or *genre* in which to present heroic narrative in an age of social realism. For *The Nation* poets, form was not a problem, while the English poets could take their past confidently for granted. It must be a measure of Ferguson's ambition, if not of his achievement, that he confronted both together.

The Letter to Blackie

In Book III of *Congal* Ferguson had put into the mouth of Conan Rodd a speech which emphasised the value of the lost epic world for the modern age; due weight should be given to the fact that the argument is put into the mouth of one of the British characters. Ferguson was to express this attitude again more directly and fully in his letter of 5th May, 1875, to John Stuart Blackie. Blackie (1809–95) was Professor of Greek at Edinburgh University; he published his *Lays of the Highlands and Islands* in the same year as *Congal* appeared. During the 1870s he actively urged the establishment of a chair of Celtic Literature at Edinburgh, and raised some £14,000 pounds by public subscription. Among the many who responded to his appeal was Ferguson; his contribution was accompanied by a letter which, from its length and the unwonted clarity of the handwriting, was obviously meant to be more than a mere covering note. It is a considered statement of his position on Celtic literature generally, addressed to one whom he regarded as a kindred spirit, and is one of Ferguson's most important critical statements, touching on the complex of racial, intellectual and literary factors which conspire against a full and true appreciation of the Celtic literatures. Written three years after the rather wan reception accorded to the publication of *Congal*, it gives an insight into his perception of the difficulties against which he laboured.

> I enclose a contribution to your Celtic Chair. If my means were larger, my support would be more substantial. We have done our endeavour to found such a chair here: but all things Celtic are regarded by our educated classes as of questionable *ton*, and an idea exists that it is inexpedient to encourage anything tending to foster Irish sentiment. The repugnance to the subject amongst English men of letters – from whom our upper classes have borrowed all they know or feel in the matter – is not unnatural. A man who fancies his education finished,

does not like to learn a new language and a new Classical Dictionary, with a view merely to the expression of critical opinion for an audience at present very limited in number, and probably better read in the subject than himself. Then there is a very prevalent feeling of mingled arrogance and apprehension which causes the common sort of editors and reviewers to revolt from the subject with a kind of loathing. The arrogance has been bred by an assiduous inculcation of the idea that there is a distinct population in these islands who are ethnologically superior to the old native races; and (what is still less probable) that the bulk of the British population is of that blood. The apprehension, so far as it is not, in truth, an unconscious jealousy, springs, I imagine, from a dread lest the free people of these countries should be brought again under their old bondage of foreign ecclesiastical authority, a result to which the restoration of the Irish to any sphere of literary influence has been – in my mind, thoughtlessly – thought likely to conduce.[29]

One can see, in this alleged mix of ignorance, arrogance and confessional mistrust at work in the community of editors, reviewers, and readers, Ferguson's frustration at the lack of success in weaning his contemporaries into an acceptance of his verse treatments of Irish legend. What we have already seen of attitudes to *Lays of the Western Gael and Other Poems* indicates that his grievance was not without foundation. The hope now is that academic detachment will open a window of opportunity for the introduction of this new material which has much to offer the over-exploited resources of literature.

He then takes up obliquely the terms of the *Saturday Review*-er of his *Lays of the Western Gael*, who had remarked that it 'would require a great genius indeed to make us care in the least for tales which we know are not history and which have acquired no fame or interest as legends. The inherent beauty of an Irish legend may be as great as that of a Greek or Teutonic legend, but it has external difficulties to struggle with that they have not'.[30]

It is no answer to say that these things are intrinsically jejune or ugly, or barbarous. You will probably agree with me that much of the best material of the best classic literature is as crude and revolting as anything in Irish or in Welsh story. Raw material, however, to be converted to the uses of cultivated genius, is not all that we might reasonably hope for from such sources. There are ways of looking at things, and even of expressing thought, in these deposits of old experience, not to be lightly rejected by a generation whose minds are restless with unsatisfied speculation, and the very clothing of whose ideas begins to show the polish of threadbareness as much as of culture.

Ferguson looks to the old literature to provide a basic text to be 'converted' to the uses of civilisation. 'Conversion', with its religious undertones, is a term rich in meaning here in the light of the earlier comments on sectarian tensions affecting the reception of Irish writing. That topic was much on Ferguson's mind at this time. Two months after the letter to Blackie, he was writing to his friend Aubrey de Vere, himself a notable convert to Catholicism. Expressing appreciation of de Vere's poetic drama, 'Mary Tudor', he voiced his reservations about the religious conflicts associated with the protagonist: 'I do not like the subject nor the reflections the subject excites at the present time. But this is not the fault of the author, who probably little thought that the subject would so soon be taken out of the sphere of retrospect and made subservient to present politics'.[31] Ferguson is quite content that literature, his own works included, should be seen as a historical exercise, without explicit reference to politics or the development of ideas in his own society; such historical exercises feed only into literature and, perhaps, philosophy which exists somehow on a separate and parallel track.

Even when lifted free of these associations, the term 'conversion' sheds some light on how Ferguson regarded his own literary activity. In one of his copious notes to *Congal* he had already used the term to salute de Vere who had, 'more than any other converter of Irish traditionary material to the cultured uses of modern literature, given sweetness, elegance, and the dignity of a high religious philosophy to his subject' (p. 208).

'To convert' implies a change of purpose or direction; it involves a more radical operation on the source material than does 'to translate'. Ferguson almost invariably worked from an English source text, starting at the point where the translator or redactor, O'Donovan or O'Curry, left off. His working texts were already translated; the need to be faithful to a prior original was but one of a number of requirements to be weighed in the process of writing. The predominant requirement was to enable something of the older vision, not necessarily all of it, to feed into the modern mind. The resultant federalisation of literatures of different ages and cultures would contribute inexorably to the proper adjustment of relations between Britain and Ireland.

Ferguson concludes his letter to Blackie with a clear expression of trust in cultural affirmation which, through a gradualist approach, would end not in nationalist separation but in a pan-Celtic 'Britannicizing' which will discover shared origins and aspirations, if only the best can hold firm and not lack all conviction:

> Our upper classes in this part of the kingdom, if they would not see themselves entirely excluded from local power and consideration, must place themselves, to some – I wish I could say to some further, – extent, in sympathy with the bulk of the people, and it is easier and more probable that this conformity should take place in the direction of literary and intellectual harmony.

This more or less reverses the argument of "Head" in the "Dialogue" published forty years before, which urged that the Protestant elite should give an intellectual lead to their country. The letter ends:

> Next, if I rightly apprehend the course of ethnological and philological enquiry, it goes, with an accelerated progress, towards the Britannicizing of our theories of origin in race, language and institutions. Thirdly, the dread of a re-action in religious thought no longer looks for coming mischief from the solid-minded Irish peasant, but from the inconstant leaders, themselves, of the Anglo-Saxon world of fashion and refinement. There remain then only the latent sentiment referred to, and the aversion from the trouble of learning; and these are minor obstacles, which, if left unsupported, must vanish before such a measure of success as will probably, in any case, attend the project undertaken by a man of your capacity.[32]

The letter to Blackie stands as the clearest critical manifesto we have from the later Ferguson, the Ferguson who wrote the "Lays of the Western Gael" and *Congal*. While not explicitly about his own poetry, it shows a clear awareness of what he was setting out to do, and of the difficulties facing him. As such, it must be seen as one of the key documents which can aid us to understand his later work.

8

Poems

Congal ends on a note of imminence, as Domnal's forces arrive to impose a new order. The first words of the poem had been 'The Hosting here of Congal Claen'; its final moment, set in the same location outside Congal's fort, echoes the opening while marking the change of power which has occurred: 'while up the hill the hosts of Domnal came'. That final word leaves an impression of a new beginning, a coming into power, which is characteristic of Ferguson's treatment of Irish themes; it is implicit in the endings of many of his 1864 'Lays of the Western Gael', which look forward to the refining sensibility of modern Christianity.

In the poems written after 1864 which continue this group of lays, the feature is even more noticeable, and variations of the notion of 'coming' abound in the various final lines. 'Mesgedra' ends with a reminder that it has told of the 'old expectancy of Christ to come'; 'The Twins of Macha' narrates the events which gave Emain Macha the name by which it has since been known: 'So came / Of Emain Macha, Macha's Twins, the name'; in 'Deirdre' the last words are spoken by Fergus, who swears such terrible vengeance that it will ring through Ireland, 'And poets in ages yet to come / Make tales of wonder of it for the world'. Similarly, 'The Naming of Cuchullin' ends with his announcing the new name which he takes on in exchange for 'Setanta', and 'Fergus Wry-Mouth' goes to his death victorious and proclaiming himself the 'survivor' of his combat with the monster Muirdris. Together with the anticipation of an established authority and stability, it is implied that something of the actions and values of these characters will outlast their own age and endure into the present.

These later poems are collected in *Poems* (1880). Ferguson had begun contemplating publication of this volume a couple of years before, and mentioned in a letter to John Blackwood that he hoped it would appear in the autumn of 1878.[1] In the same letter there are comments which indicate something of how he saw his own place in literature at the time. Enclosing a copy of his poem

'The Gascon O'Driscoll', drawn from the Book of Lecan, he remarks: 'This kind of subject has suffered sadly by the vulgarity & vainglory of the popular Irish school. I have a fixed resolve to lift it, if I can, out of their Donnybrook latitudes; & believing I can better do this at home, mean to publish here'. The phrase about 'Donnybrook latitudes' echoes part of his concluding paragraph on translation in the review of Hardiman forty-four years before, where he discussed the problem of finding a suitable language for translations from Irish: 'The classic language of Pope will not answer to the homely phrase of Carolan; but the slang of Donnybrook is equally inconsistent with the Bard's Legacy. Here again the translator's judgment must guide him in the adoption of a characteristic style'.[2] The sense of being caught between the sophistication of English and the directness of Irish persists, and Ferguson, while not naming names, dissociates himself from the posturings of younger Irish contemporaries. But if he felt obliged to stand apart from writers in his own country, he also knew that his poetry would have difficulty finding readers in England. As he wrote to *Blackwood's*, 'I know you have no liking for our barbarian rudiments'.[3]

Ferguson found a Dublin publisher and printer for his *Poems*; William McGee brought out the book, with Ferguson's previous publisher George Bell providing a London connection. The layout of this volume is very different to that of *Lays of the Western Gael and Other Poems*. The various headings which divided up the material of that book are not used here; instead the twenty-five poems included are printed in a run. At the beginning and end of the collection is a number of occasional pieces, often on personal or domestic themes. But in the centre, taking up over 120 of the book's 167 pages, are seven poems, some of them of considerable length, which revisit the matter of the earlier book: 'Mesgedra', 'Fergus Wry-Mouth', 'The Twins of Macha', 'The Naming of Cuchullin', 'Conary', 'Deirdre' and 'The Gascon O'Driscoll'. All of these except 'Conary' and 'Deirdre' are subtitled 'A Lay of the Western Gael', thus continuing the range of poems commenced in Ferguson's first collection, and bringing the original eight up to thirteen in number. 'Conary' and 'Deirdre' are not so subtitled, presumably because their style and length distinguish them from the shorter narrative form of the lay as understood by Ferguson.

Four of the five new additional lays were written soon after the publication of *Lays of the Western Gael and Other Poems* and so spring from the period of creativity during the 1860s; nor was their inclusion in *Poems* the first appearance for three of them: 'The Twins of Macha', 'The Naming of Cuchullin' and 'Fergus Wry-Mouth' (under the title 'The Legend of Fergus Leidesen') had all appeared among the lengthy annotations affixed to the text of *Congal* in 1872. There, together with 'The Origin of the Scythians' reprinted from *Lays of the Western Gael and Other Poems* and some other pieces of poetry, they served to give a legendary heroic background against which to see the action of a later history. 'Mesgedra', perhaps the best of this second group of lays, was complete by Easter 1867 when he offered it (unsuccessfully) to *Blackwood's*.[4] The remaining lay, 'The Gascon O'Driscoll' is set, like 'The Welshmen of Tirawley' and 'Grace O'Maly', in a much later historical period, and was apparently not written until shortly before its appearance in the May 1878 edition of *Blackwood's*.

Ferguson's labelling of these poems is an indication of his desire to group them together so as to constitute a body of work rather greater than merely the sum of its parts. The tendency with *Congal* had been to move towards a larger canvas of epic action, and here in the shorter pieces the individual narratives are presented as part of a corpus of legend and history. This has been a recurrent tendency in Ferguson's writing since the series of *Hibernian Nights' Entertainments* at the start of his career. The poems in the 'Lays of the Western Gael' section of the 1864 collection are arranged in chronological order, suggesting a national progress from legend to history.

A more explicit juxtaposition of some of the poems with history occurs in Mary Ferguson's *Story of the Irish Before the Conquest*, which outlined what was known of Irish history and legend, from the time of the first mythical colonists of the island up to the arrival of Strongbow and the Normans. It is a book in which Ferguson's presence looms large. At the end he contributed a 'Note on the Sources and Nomenclature'. The sources indicated are not just a background for his wife's book but a valuable indication of the material which he himself was using during this period. These include Eugene O'Curry's unpublished translation of the *Táin*, and a manuscript translation of the 'Siege of Howth' from the Book of Leinster made by William Hennessy, as well as printed works by O'Donovan, Petrie, Todd and others, all representing the high level of activity in the editing and translating of Irish texts over the previous twenty-five years. And in dealing with Irish proper names, Ferguson offers a list of Anglicised equivalents for the original forms as found in the manuscripts. In this he is not always consistent with himself: he suggests that the most suitable forms of 'Conaire', 'Domhnall' and 'Magh-rath' are 'Conari', 'Donall' and 'Moyrath', although in his poems he uses 'Conary', 'Domnal' and 'Moyra'.

Ferguson's comments on the handling of names in general are of interest, especially for a readership sensitised to the issue by Brian Friel's play *Translations*. The difficulty with the Irish names for an English reader is threefold: 'Their strangeness, their want of association with anything previously known, and their singular difficulty of pronunciation, constitute, in truth, a very great obstacle to any popular treatment of the subject'. The first two of these difficulties reflect the problem which confronted Ferguson as a poet of the old Irish material. Starting in what was almost a cultural vacuum, as far as knowledge of and sympathy for Irish legend and history were concerned, he sets out to furnish its names and places with an accessible past. With regard to pronunciation, Ferguson suggests that

> in primitive times, when men were sparing of their words, they thought to give increased consideration to all they uttered, and specially to the names of individuals, by magnifying the forms of expression. In more modern times, men have had more to say, and seem to have studied how best to abbreviate and smooth down the old stately but cumbrous forms of expression.

Whether or not one chooses to accept the idea that early man was more lavish with phonemes in order to fill the gaps in conversation, it offers an illustration of what Ferguson in his letter to Blackie was later to speak of as 'raw material . . . . converted to the uses of cultivated genius'.[5] 'Conversion' of the original material to suit the requirements of the later age takes precedence over any concept of fidelity to the earlier.

The 1880 'lays of the western Gael' not only continued one exploration of history in poetic narrative; some of them also formed part of a legendary cycle which Ferguson outlines in introductory notes to 'Mesgedra' and 'Deirdre'. This alternative grouping he refers to as 'the Conorian cycle', after Conor Mac Nessa, the most notable monarch of the age in which the poems are set, although Conor has only an oblique connection with most of the poems. The suggested ordering allows a place for the *Táin*, which remains as an absence in the reconstruction of an Irish heroic literature:

'The Twins of Macha'
'The Naming of Cuchullin'
'The Abdication of Fergus Mac Roy'
'Mesgedra'
'Deirdre'
[The *Táin*]
'Conary'
'The Healing of Conall Carnach'
'The Tain-Quest'

This is the arrangement followed by Lady Ferguson when she edited the poems under the title *Lays of the Red Branch* in 1897 with the two lyrics 'Deirdre's Farewell to Alba' and 'Deirdre's Lament for the Sons of Usnach' inserted after 'Deirdre'. As with her edition of the *Hibernian Nights' Entertainments* ten years before, she availed of the opportunity to present her husband's writing in a framework which suggested the intended historical resonance. *Lays of the Red Branch* appeared as a volume in the 'New Irish Library' series which was under the general editorship of Sir Charles Gavan Duffy; it was fitting that this final authorised arrangement of the poems should have appeared under the aegis of the man who had given such an impetus to Ferguson's career and reputation by including so much of his work in *The Ballad Poetry of Ireland* over fifty years earlier.

It was during the eighteen-forties that Ferguson had first formulated an idea of the past and developed an attitude on the recording and interpretation of it as history. It was a decade which brought important passages in Ferguson's personal life and in the life of Ireland. As he commenced work on the versification of *The Banquet of Dun na n-Gedh and The Battle of Magh Rath*, protested in the national press against the cessation of work on the ordnance survey, and visited some of the great historical sites on the continent, on all sides he became increasingly conscious of the need to recover, assimilate and exhibit the past. Under the pressure of the times, and especially of Davis's influence, the past became a possession which might be seen to have political uses. In a June 1847 review of Thomas Mulvany's biography of Gandon he protested against the destruction of architectural remains by the Ecclesiastical Commissioners, calling it 'an attempt to reconcile men to the notion that they are "a people without a history", who ought, of right, to occupy an inferior position and learn contentedly the lesson of dependence'.[6]

This concern to acquire 'history' was a characteristically Victorian trait. It is, as Seamus Deane has observed, 'already a convention to say that Ireland has no continuity of cultural experience comparable to that of the nation states of France and England';[7] that lack was never more keenly felt than during the nineteenth-century, when genuine traditions were cultivated and spurious ones invented in the attempt 'to establish continuity with a suitable historic past'.[8] Anxiety concerning tradition was a pan-European phenomenon, but whereas in France or England it centred on the *means* of linking back to the historical past, in Ireland it focussed first on identifying and supplying an indigenous past. The impetus for Ferguson's work arose directly from his recognising just such a suitable past for Ireland in the texts which he set out to render into poetry; it was a past individual to Ireland which nevertheless seemed to offer the rudiments of a national myth equivalent to that of Britain.

The nineteenth century was the first so to style itself numerically.[9] This use of the number as identification may indicate a vision of history as a sequential process, organic, evolutionary or dialectic: each possibility had its proponents. But such a vision, seeing the present age as an end product of all that had gone before, did not fully reflect Ferguson's attitude. To him, 'history' was a resource; a nation was rich in its possession, and poor when deprived of it. The numerical epithet was not so much for ordering as for reckoning up amounts. This is to be seen clearly in his essay on Thomas Davis when, stung by some recent remarks in the London *Spectator*, he retorted:

> It is true, we cannot contend in historic dignity with England; . . . but we possess enough of history, and that not ignoble, nor wanting in what the *Spectator* calls picturesque series of events, to support a temperate self-assertion and national spirit.[10]

Twelve months later, reviewing William Reeves' *Ecclesiastical History of Down, Connor, and Dromore*, he returns to the same theme. He begins with Cicero's encomium on the value of history, which is

> that men may feel they are not come into the world strangers, but members of a family long planted in the land before them, owing reverence to the place and institutions of their forefathers, and by that common sentiment strengthening the social bond among one another. . . . It is for this reason we less regret that, for the present, Ireland is without a general history, for in each new accumulation of materials still necessary before a general history can be undertaken,

we have a new store of agencies for the creation and propagation of just national feeling.[11]

Such were the beliefs which were to underlie his poetry during the four decades after the death of Davis, through the various 'lays of the Western Gael', *Congal*, and 'Conary'. They are nowhere more explicitly stated than in 'Mesgedra'.

'Mesgedra'

'Mesgedra' tells of the single-handed combat by the ford at Clane in County Kildare, in which Mesgedra was killed by Conall Carnach. After describing the fight and its aftermath, the last third of this sixty-four stanza poem turns to hymn the 'Delicious Liffey' and the delights of the Kildare and Dublin countryside through which it flows.

> To ride the race, to hunt, to fowl, to fish,
> To do and dare whate'er brave youth would do,
> A fair fine country as the heart could wish,
> And fair the brown-clear river running through.

> Such seemest thou to Dublin's youth to-day,
> Oh clear-dark Liffey, mid the pleasant land;
> With life's delights abounding, brave and gay,
> The song, the dance, the softly-yielded hand.

The one attribute in which the Liffey seems deficient is that of historical associations; as Ferguson says, in a stanza which is sometimes quoted as embodying his poetic credo,

> For thou, for them, alas! nor History hast
> Nor even Tradition; and the Man aspires
> To link his present with his Country's past,
> And live anew in knowledge of his sires.

But the Liffey and the plain through which it flows can furnish a 'loving mind' with the substance of 'many a gracious lay/And many a tale not unheroic', as Ferguson himself had already shown in 'The Rebellion of Silken Thomas'. Now he has supplemented that 'tale not unheroic' with the 'gracious lay' of 'Mesgedra'. It ends:

> I, from the twilight waste
> Where pale Tradition sits by Memory's grave,
> Gather this wreath, and, ere the nightfall, haste
> To fling my votive garland on thy wave.

Wave, waft it softly: and when lovers stray
At summer eve by stream and dimpling pool,
Gather thy murmurs into voice and say,
With liquid utterance passionate and full,

Scorn not, sweet maiden, scorn not, vigorous youth,
The lay, though breathing of an Irish home,
That tells of woman-love and warrior-ruth
And old expectancy of Christ to come.

In encompassing those subjects 'Mesgedra' moves over a greater range than any of the other lays. The introductory note to the poem discusses the differences between the heroic tradition preserved in the 'Conorian cycle' and that in the tales centred on Cormac Mac Art and the Fenian heroes some two-and-a-half centuries later.

> In the second cycle . . . the dawn of the coming change to Christianity tinges all the characters with a greater softness and humanity, as in the romance of Dermid and Grania, and in many of the Ossianic fragments. But the better defined and more characteristic forms of grandeur, with the stronger accompaniments of pity and terror, must be sought for in the earlier story. There, we are amongst the *rudera* of such a barbaric kind of literature as the great tragedians turned to immortal drama in Greece, and Ovid converted into beautiful legends in Italy. (p.32)

Ferguson makes a distinction between the source literature, primitive and anonymous, and the derivative texts which are the product of cultivated and civilised individual minds. This distinction between the 'raw' and the 'cooked' is, of course, directly applicable to Ferguson's own conversion of the Irish material. Although 'Mesgedra' attaches to the earlier Conorian cycle, the poem is imbued with an anticipation of Christian temperateness and looks forward to the needs of nineteenth-century Ireland.

The opening of the poem is set in the pagan Ireland of Atharna, the Ulster bard who has exacted an exorbitant tribute from the kingdom of Leinster. Once Atharna has crossed the Liffey and left the kingdom, the king Mesgedra deems himself free to raid the baggage train and to recover the goods and slaves taken from him. The outraged bard invokes a curse on Leinster, and his fulminations are so loud that they are heard by the Ulster champion Conall Carnach who arrives to take up Atharna's cause. In the ensuing battle Ulster's forces are victorious and Mesgedra, who has lost a hand in the fighting, flees into Kildare pursued by

Conall Carnach; his predicament is remarkably akin to that of Congal after the battle of Moyra. He is overtaken by Conall Carnach at Clane on the river Liffey, and agrees to a single combat if Conall will also fight one-handed. The struggle between the two is equal until Mesgedra accidentally cuts through the bonds securing his opponent's arm, whereupon Conall feels justified in using both hands; he swiftly puts an end to Mesgedra and cuts off his head as a trophy. The middle part of the poem tells of the immediately subsequent meeting between Conall Carnach and Buana, Mesgedra's wife; when he flings down the severed head at her feet she dies on the spot of shock and grief. This example of loving fidelity causes Conall to receive some intimations of the possibility of a God more forgiving than the 'dread Deities' of Celtic worship:

> Some mightier Druid of our race may rise;
> Some milder Messenger from Heaven descend;
> And Earth, with nearer Knowledge of the Skies,
>
> See, past your sacrificers' grisly bands,
> Past all the shapes that servile souls appal,
> With fearless vision, from a thousand lands,
> One great, good God behind and over all.

This glimmering of a new dispensation leads into the poem's praise of the timeless Liffey, together with a reaching back towards the past which the river encompasses.

The commerce between the past and the present which is the overt theme of the poem's closing stanzas is also reflected in the more dramatic narrative of the combat. Conall is described arriving at the battlefield on the site of what was to become Dublin,

> where the city now sends up her vows
> From holy Patrick's renovated fane,
> (Small surmise then that one of Conall's house
> Should there, thereafter, such a work ordain).

Not only does Ferguson look forward to the conversion of Ireland, he also manages to insert a compliment to his relation by marriage, Benjamin Lee Guinness, who paid for the restoration of St Patrick's Cathedral during the mid-sixties. (Although 'Guinness' is an Ulster name, we may suspect that the lineage from Conall Carnach is a bit of genealogical licence worthy of an old Irish bard.) This reference immediately establishes a connection with contemporary affairs, and also links into Conall's final action; struck by the devotion of Buana he orders that a tumulus be erected over her grave by the Liffey as a witness 'of Pity and of Love'. Each building recalls the other as a tangible expression of spiritual impulse. Mention of the grave also connects with later time, for there is a prominent mound known as 'Buana's Grave' still to be seen at Clane. In fact it seems to be a motte from Norman times, but while Ferguson the antiquarian would have deplored the inaccuracy, Ferguson the poet appreciated the intersection of myth with history.

'Fergus Wry-Mouth'

For 'Mesgedra', O'Curry's *Manuscript Materials of Ancient Irish History* had once again provided an outline of the story, which is taken from the Book of Leinster.[12] The next 'lay of the Western Gael' in the 1880 volume, 'Fergus Wry-Mouth', has as its source a gloss attached to the *Senchas Már*, the compilation of tracts preserving the archaic Brehon laws which have their origin in pre-Christian Irish society. O'Donovan and O'Curry had been engaged on the transcription and translation of the Brehon laws during most of the decade preceding their deaths in the early 1860s. Their work was published posthumously in volumes entitled *Hiberniae Leges et Institutiones Antiquae or Ancient Laws and Institutes of Ireland*; the first volumes appeared in 1865, and two years later Ferguson read a paper to the Royal Irish Academy discussing the published portions of the *Senchas Már*. The poem probably dates from that time, which makes it roughly contemporary with 'Mesgedra'.

'Fergus Wry-Mouth' tells a story of Fergus Mac Lete, a character distinct from the later and better known Fergus Mac Roy. One day, when asleep by Loch Rury – probably Dundrum Bay, although Ferguson was anxious to identify it with his native Belfast Lough (*Congal*, p. 192) – Fergus is about to be borne away by a troop of water-fairies when suddenly he wakes up and manages to catch three of them. They earn their release by granting Fergus the power to walk underwater at will, warning him at the same time never to venture into Loch Rury. But of course Fergus cannot resist the temptation of the Loch, and exploring there he encounters the horrid *muirdris*, the mere sight of which so frightens him that when he regains dry land his face is distorted. As such deformity would automatically disqualify him for kingship, his disfigurement is kept a secret from him for years until, one morning, his handmaid Dorn angrily taunts him with his 'wry mouth'. Fergus re-enters Loch Rury. His subjects, assembled on the bank, see the water stir and redden with blood. After a day and a night Fergus emerges briefly with the head of the monster in his hand and his own face restored to normality. He dies, proclaiming himself the victor.

Ferguson's telling of the story, while omitting the preliminary material, sticks closely to the final part of the eighth-century version as given by O'Donovan. The doubt in the original text as to whether Fergus was enabled to walk underwater by means of a herbal preparation in his ears or by wearing some sort of hood is reproduced, as are the comparison of the *muirdris* to a black-smith's bellows and Fergus's final triumphant description of himself as 'Survivor'.

'The Twins of Macha' and 'The Naming of Cuchullin'

'The Twins of Macha' and 'The Naming of Cuchullin' are both based on pre-tales attached to the *Táin Bó Cuailgne*. The former gives the story of how Emain Macha got its name from the outcome of the ill-fated race between Conor's horses and Macha, pregnant by Crunn. The story was given by Ferguson's friend William Reeves, in a pamphlet published in 1860. Reeves quotes an extract on the origin of the name of Armagh as given in the *Dinnsennchus* in the Book of Lecan, with a translation furnished by Eugene O'Curry.[13]

O'Curry is probably also the immediate source for 'The Naming of Cuchullin', as his manuscript translation of the *Táin* and its pre-tales is at the head of the list of references appended by Ferguson to his wife's *Story of the Irish Before the Conquest* (1868). This poem is the longer and more interesting of the two lays, in that Ferguson turns to the form of a poetic drama, with the lines spoken by Conor, Setanta/Cuchullin, Cullan, the bard Cathbad and – in a very minor role – Fergus the step-father of Conor. He also uses the blank iambic pentameter, previously used by him in 'The Death of Dermid', for most of the poem. This allows him to break into rhymed verse for the lines in which Cathbad, inspired, foretells the destiny which awaits Cuchullin as the champion of Ulster. The vision which Cathbad proffers looks ahead to the glory which Cuchullin will bring to his people; the final passage elides the tribal future of Ulster and the national future of Ireland in lines that suggest the condition which Ferguson wishes for his country:

The extern tribes look up with wondering awe
And own the central law.
Fair show the fields, and fair the friendly faces
Of men in all their places.
With song and chosen story,
With game and dance, with revelries and races,
Life glides on joyous wing.

These lines match with those at the end of 'Mesgedra' in which
Ferguson surveys the Ireland of his own time. They paint a lyrical
picture of cultural independence in a pastoral setting, where
song, story, dance and sport are allowed to flourish under the
stability of a unifying rule.

'Conary'

It was a condition devoutly to be wished, but the two longest
poems in the volume, 'Conary' and 'Deirdre', show internal
strife and dissent striking at the well-being of a state. 'Conary'
starts from a condition of stability; it was a commonplace of the
old Irish material to represent the land flourishing under a
favoured king. The collapse into strife comes not as a result of any
internal flaw or transgression but because the code of law is
infringed. The process starts within three lines of the opening:

Full peace was Erin's under Conary,
Till – though his brethren by the tender tie
Of fosterage – Don Dessa's lawless sons,
Fer-ger, Fer-gel, and vengeful Fergobar,
For crimes that justly had demanded death,
By judgment mild he sent in banishment.

At the root of the tragic events in the poem is a double derogation
from the rule of law: added to the unspecified lawlessness of Don
Dessa's sons is Conary's own failure to apply the proper punishment as required by the code of justice. These infringements at
the outset are compounded by Conary's wittingly or unwittingly
going against a number of *gesa* or taboos, urged on by the
influence of the supernatural *sidh*. Setting aside at once the
dictates of jurisprudence and religion, Conary is bound upon a
course to heroic death in Da Derga's hall. While 'Conary', like
Congal, tells of an attack launched against the rightful king by an
alliance of disaffected subjects and foreign enemies, and the
focus of sympathy is again with the defeated, here the loser in

battle is the king who, like Fergus Wry-Mouth, goes to his doom with a regal integrity. Like Congal, Conary is doomed, but his transgressions are more absolute than mere rebellion against a temporal lord; he has the stature of a tragic hero, confronting at once invisible spiritual powers and betrayal by his own foster-brothers.

'Conary' is the longest of Ferguson's poems after *Congal*, comprising nearly a thousand lines of blank verse. The first two-thirds of the poem is concerned with events preliminary to the final conflict, as scouts report back to the invading foster-brothers and their allies on the state and strength of Conary's force; as a result a great part of the poem, including many of the descriptive passages, is in direct speech. In this it resembles the verse monodramas 'The Naming of Cuchullin' and 'Deirdre'.

'Conary' is based on the ninth-century Irish tale *Togail Bruidne Da Derga* ('The Destruction of Da Derga's Hostel'); the text is preserved in a number of Irish manuscripts, of which the earliest is the twelfth-century *Lebor na hUidre* where it is placed immediately after the Táin Bo Cuailgne; Ferguson accords it a similar position in the 'Conorian cycle' of his poems which he drew up in the preamble to 'Deirdre'.

The *Togail* was not edited until 1901, but Ferguson was provided with a manuscript translation by William Hennessy;[14] this enabled him to begin work on a version sometime before 1872, as a passage describing the sword of Keltar is included among the notes to *Congal*. This first attempt, while recognisably an early version of the lines in 'Conary' (*Poems* pp. 75–76), is closer to the original Irish text. Ferguson's treatment of the story as he found it in the original encompassed several alterations and rearrangements in source material. His opening line, 'Full peace was Erin's under Conary', is a close rendition of a line at the start of the *Lebor na hUidre* text, '*Lansid i nErind hi flaith Conaire*', and there is a number of lines in the poem which render pieces of the Irish prose quite accurately in blank verse. But generally, as regards characterisation, imagery and narrative development, Ferguson uses the original story as a point of departure. For instance, here is the description of the wealth of Conaire's reign as given in Whitley Stokes's literal translation:

> Since he assumed kingship, no cloud has veiled the sun for a space of a day from the middle of spring to the middle of autumn. And not a dewdrop fell from grass till midday, and wind would not touch a beast's tail until nones. And in his reign, from year's end to year's end,

no wolf has attacked aught save one bullcalf of each byre; and to maintain this rule there are seven wolves in hostageship at the sidewall in his house, and behind this a further security, even Maclocc, and 'tis he that pleads (for them) in Conaire's house. In Conaire's reign are the three crowns on Erin, namely, crown of corn-ears, and crown of flowers, and crown of oak-mast. . . .

The equivalent passage in 'Conary' runs as follows:

Since he has reigned there has not fallen a year
Of dearth, or plague, or murrain on the land:
The dew has never left the blade of grass
One day of Conary's time, before the noon;
Nor harsh wind ruffled upon the side
Of grazing beast. Since he began his reign
From mid-spring to mid-autumn cloud nor storm
Has dimm'd the daily-shining, bounteous sun;
But each good year has seen its harvests three,
Of blade, of ear, of fruit, apple and nut.
Peace until now in all his realm has reigned,
And terror of just laws kept men secure.
What though, by love constrained, in passion's hour,
I joined my fortunes to the desperate fates
Of hapless kinsmen, I repent it now,
And wish that rigorous law had had its course
Sooner than this good king should now be slain.

(*Poems* pp. 79–80)

Ferguson makes Lomna Druth the speaker of these lines, rather than Ferragon; the switch is insignificant, in that both are originally innocent brothers who chose exile with the three offenders out of kinship. The marvellous change in climate under Conary is easily altered to conventional pastoralism, with 'the side / Of grazing beast' delicately substituted for 'beast's tail'. The picture of a golden age in the kingdom is elaborated in preference to reproducing the more fanciful pact with the wolves, and Conary's qualities are made apparent through his application of the laws.

Much of the Irish text is concerned with listing the warriors accompanying Conaire and with describing their prowess in a series of reports to the invading party. Ferguson reproduces this feature to good effect, in that the successive accounts build up to an impressive indication of the king's authority over those around him. In addition, it is apparent that Ferguson is glad of the opportunity to portray the richness and complexity of an old Irish society ordered according to a hierarchy of functions. At times that hierarchy seems to approximate more to a town-house in Victorian Dublin (in North Great George's Street, perhaps) than to pre-Christian Ireland: Conary is

> Followed by a household numerous and strong,
> Cooks, butlers, door-wards, cup-bearers and grooms.

Ferguson develops the doubts expressed by Lomna Druth and Ferragon regarding the rightness of attacking Conary; these two, allied with the pirates out of fidelity to their criminal brothers, are the focus of the narrative throughout the first part of the poem. When it is decided to launch the attack, first Lomna and then Ferragon kill themselves rather than be party to the assault. This is Ferguson's invention, and he invests a great deal of feeling in these two characters. The speech given to Lomna Druth in which he protests against the destruction of Erin's legal, cultural and defensive resources by an outside power, is very much in line with Ferguson's own arguments against Britain's administrative policy in Ireland as expressed in his prose writings.

> we gave thee not
> Licence to take the life, the soul itself
> Of our whole nation, as you now would do.
> For, slay our reverend sages of the law,
> Slay him who puts the law they teach in act;
> Slay our sweet poets, and our sacred bards
> Who keep the continuity of time
> By fame perpetual of renowned deeds;
> Slay our experienced captains who prepare
> The youth for martial manhood, and the charge
> Of public freedom, as befits a state
> Self-governed, self-sufficing, self-contained;
> Slay all that minister our loftier life,
> Now by this evil chance assembled here,
> You leave us but the carcass of a state,
> A rabble ripe to rot, and yield the land
> To foreign masters and perpetual shame.
> (*Poems* p. 81)

While the analogy must not be pressed too closely, these lines can be read as a statement in heroic terms of Ferguson's more moderately felt cultural nationalism. Two fears of his are amalgamated in the passage: first, the removal of social and administrative institutions from Dublin under a policy of centralisation, and, accompanying this threat from above, the one from

below which menaced the position of the enlightened
ascendancy, the element best equipped to 'minister our loftier
life'.

The final part of 'Conary' is the story of the attack on the
hostel, Conary's resistance, his request for a drink to assuage the
the supernatural thirst inflicted on him by the opposing druids,
and the attempt by Cecht and the child Ferflath to procure water
for their king. Again Ferguson refines the Irish material.
According to the original, Cecht arrives back with the drink after
Conaire has died from his exertions and been beheaded; Cecht
fulfils his mission faithfully by pouring the water down his king's
gullet, whereupon the severed head speaks a poem in praise of
his henchman. Furthermore, to obtain the drink Cecht has had to
travel all over Ireland, for the rivers refuse to yield him water until
eventually he gets some from Uaran Garad in Roscommon.
Ferguson brings this marvellous errand within the compass of a
more familiar convention by repeating the triple attempt of Finn
to bring water to the dying Dermid: twice Cecht and Ferflath try
to return to the hostel with water from a nearby well, but each
time the water spills; on the third occasion they succeed, but find
the king about to die.

> 'Thou, Ferflath, take the cup
> And hold it to thy father's lips,' said Cecht.
> The child approached the cup; the dying king
> Felt the soft touch and smiled, and drew a sigh;
> Ana, as they raised him in the chariot, died.
>
> (*Poems* p.94)

And so Conary dies, in an altogether more composed fashion
than does Conaire.

It is left to Conall Carnach to have the last words in the poem,
as in the Irish text. There, Conall after the battle returns to his
father and gives a succinct account of what has happened and
shows his own wounds. But in 'Conary' Conall speaks to Cecht
and Ferflath of their release from the power of the *sidh* and other
supernatural influences which have brought about the destruction of their forces and, in a conclusion typical of Ferguson's
poetry, he appeals to the 'Great Unknown Being' to take 'compassion on the race of men'. He ends

> And I have heard
> There come the tidings yet may make us glad

Of such a one new born, or soon to be.
Now, mount beside me, that with solemn rites
We give the king, at Tara, burial.

(*Poems* p. 96)

'Conary' begins with the consequences of a departure from
those temporal laws which, no matter how great the king's
inclination towards mercy, it was his duty to uphold; it ends in
anticipation of a new and greater rule which will allow both
freedom and 'comfort'.

Ferguson breaks new ground in 'Conary', in that it moves
away from a strictly Ulster theme and setting to write about a
Leinster legend, although the presence of Conall Carnach connects with his more usual material. The story of *Togail Bruidne Da
Derga* seems to have more than usual significance in the chronicles of Ireland, perhaps referring to a historical event which
caused a sudden overthrow in the ancient order of things.[15] In so
far as the story exhibits such a character, it is of a kind with the
other epochs of Irish legend and history which attracted Ferguson the writer: the impact of Christianity in *Lays of the Western
Gael*, the establishment of a new social order in *Congal*, the
consolidation of English power in the *Hibernian Nights' Entertainments*. The theme is imminent change, represented as a crisis
of anticipation but set retrospectively in a lost Ireland.

'Deirdre'

'Deirdre', which stands as his final treatment of early Irish
material, is different from the preceding work in a number of
respects even though it returns to to the story of the Sons of
Usnach which he had taken as the theme for the first of his
Hibernian Nights' Entertainments in the *Dublin University Magazine*
nearly fifty years previously. As Ferguson remarked in an introductory note to the poem, the story was now well-known to
readers thanks to the prose translations of O'Flanagan and
O'Curry, and to the poetic treatments by Macpherson in
'Darthula' and most recently by Robert Dwyer Joyce, who had
published his *Deirdre* in 1876 (*Poems* p. 97). Ferguson revisits the
theme with a greater freedom than he had when he reproduced
O'Flanagan's translation almost sentence for sentence, but he
persists in preferring O'Flanagan's edition as a source even
though its reliability had been called into question by O'Curry
and by Robert Atkinson.[16] He was still of this opinion in 1882

when he wrote to Aubrey de Vere on the publication of the latter's *Foray of Queen Maeve*: 'You have been more conscientious than I in your treatment of the Sons of Usnach. I always thought the version in the Iberno-Celtic Society's *'Proceedings'* [sic] better than that in the *Atlantis*, and am glad that you work on the former'.[17]

Ferguson suggests that his 'Deirdre' is a 'monodrame'; the notion of such a poetic form had recently been made current by Tennyson when, some two decades after the original publication of his *Maud*, he had given it the sub-title 'A Monodrama'. As Ferguson notes, 'Deirdre' does not really adhere to the form as it presents a number of different speakers, but on the other hand 'the action is unbroken, the principal figures remain in sight throughout, moving in a progressive scene' (*Poems* p. 97). Certainly Deirdre and the three brothers are present from the beginning until their deaths at the end, and changes of scene are swiftly indicated by speeches briefly describing the country or setting through which the characters move as they return from exile in Scotland to Emain Macha. Another feature of Tennysonian monodrama is the range of mental states and emotions experienced by the central character; while 'Deirdre' is by no means an exploration of the psyche of its characters, the heroic largeness of the other poems is here replaced by a much more human scale. The poem begins in Glen Etive, the lovers' refuge in Scotland. Deirdre is happy there, but Naisi chafes at the constraints:

> Love makes the woman's life
> Within-doors and without; but, out of doors,
> Action and glory make the life of man.
> Here I have room for neither: here there's room
> Only for solitude interminable,
> For desert vastness and vacuity.
> *(Poems* p. 100)

The story here is not so much one of romantic exile and codes of honour as of the growing certainty of Deirdre's forebodings and her unavailing attempts to convince Naisi of the dangers in wait for him.

The contrast with the heroic mode of treatment is nowhere more apparent than at the end when, with Naisi and his two brothers dead, Deirdre sings a dirge over their grave. 'Deirdre's Lament', which Ferguson composed for 'The Death of The

Children of Usnach', images the three dead as lions, falcons, dragons, warriors, and hunters, 'sweet companions' among the glens and mountains of Glen Etive. The death-song in 'Deirdre', while not totally excluding the wild life experienced in exile, focuses on on more domestic qualities:

> Naisi, my husband, O my slaughtered lord,
> O pierced by cruel swords that pierced not me,
> Thou Honor's Sanctuary, thou Tower of Justice,
> By sacrilegious treason beaten down! –
> ......
> Thou wast the one, with prudent-generous sway,
> That kept thy household and thy festive hall, –
> The one, with mildness and with manly patience,
> That kept thy wilful helpmate, ordered well.
> ......
> A day shall come, the May-day of Mankind,
> When, when through thy quickening clods and teeming pores,
> The sunward-mounting, vernal effluences
> Shall rise of buried Loves and Joys re-born.
>
> (*Poems* p. 143–4)

As a poem, it is palpably inferior to the earlier lament, but this should not obscure the fact that part of Ferguson's difficulty springs from his attempt to have Deirdre celebrate the sons of Usnach under a new guise. In the lays of the Western Gael, in *Congal* and in 'Conary' we have seen Ferguson struggle to reconcile the heroic dimension of his material with the spiritual values professed in his own age. Of all the aspects of his acts of translation or conversion, this was the most radical, and in 'Deirdre' he carried it to its fullest extent. It is Naisi who voices the new vision most comprehensively when he attempts to counter Deirdre's misgivings which are based on intuitions and omens:

> Man lives by mutual trust. The commonwealth
> Falls into chaos if man trust not man.
> For then all joint endeavours come to nought,
> And each pursues his separate intent,
> Backed by no other labour than his own.
> Which confidence, which bond of social life,
> Is bred in some of just experience,
> Of oaths and terror of the Gods in some,
> But, in the most, of natural honesty
> That God has planted in the breast of man,
> Thereby distinguishing him from the beasts.

And where I find it, ground it as it may,
In use, religion, or mere manliness,
There do I love, revere, and cherish it.
                                        (*Poems* p. 129)

It would not be a bad creed to live by; Naisi and his companions
die by it, betrayed by the treacherous casuistry of Conor, but
there is no doubt where the moral weight of the poem rests.
When at the end Fergus hastens to the scene, conscious that
those to whom he guaranteed safety have been killed, he rages
about 'Confusion, horror, blood, and treachery', but the temper
of events has been more ordered and thoughtful than his description of them would indicate. That is the inappropriate language
of heroic action; more fitting is his final threat to pull down and
burn the palace of Conor, dismantling the edifice which is at the
centre of such ruinous mistrust.

In the final lines of 'Deirdre' Ferguson takes leave of that
particular story, looking forward to when 'poets in the ages yet to
come/[will] Make tales of wonder of it for the world'. Indeed,
Ferguson is at the end of his long engagement with early Irish
legend and history generally, and when 'poets' are mentioned
he would surely be permitted to have one particular poet especially in mind. And, by an altogether proper dispensation, Ferguson has it that these lines which look forward to future generations are spoken by Fergus.

Other Poems

'Deirdre' is followed by the last poem to be described as 'A Lay
of the Western Gael'. This is 'The Gascon O'Driscoll' which tells
of an incident drawn, like 'The Welshmen of Tirawley', from the
period of Anglo-Norman domination in the early thirteenth
century. Ferguson had found the hint for the subject matter in a
passage from the Book of Lecan which had been included in the
Miscellany of the Celtic Society (1849), and which Ferguson reproduces in his introductory note to the poem. He does not give the
English, but O'Donovan's translation of the relevant lines is as
follows:

> The reason he was called the Gascon was this: he was given as a
> pledge for wine to the crew of a merchant's ship from Gascony in his
> twelfth year and he remained in the East (in Gascony), until he was set
> to care of vines, when it was proved that he was of noble blood, for the

vines grew without defect during his time, and he was conveyed back to his own country.[18]

The story turns on the belief that nature thrives under a noble and just ruler, a theme also present in 'Conary'. When Ferguson had offered 'The Gascon O'Driscoll' successfully to *Blackwood's* two years before, he had remarked on the succinctness of the Irish account.[19] His treatment expands it into a poem of twenty-six stanzas; the poem displays a vigour which makes it more akin to his early ballads such as 'Willy Gilliland' or 'Young Dobbs' than to the 'lays of the Western Gael'.

Another poem from the collection which, like 'The Gascon O'Driscoll', had been published previously in *Blackwood's* was 'The Widow's Cloak', expressing a loyal admiration for Queen Victoria. He had forwarded it to the magazine during the summer of 1877, and when it had still not appeared by the November issue he wrote to the editor:

> I have a reason for desiring that the 'Cloak' appear this autumn. Its omission from succesive numbers has disappointed me. It is now almost too late for my purposes; so, if you cannot make it convenient to publish in your Dec. issue, it will be better to return it to me.[20]

The poem duly appeared in the December issue. The reason for Ferguson's concern regarding this poem in praise of his sovereign probably became clear to Blackwood when Ferguson wrote to him early the following year saying that he was about to receive a knighthood.[21] The honour was duly conferred on March 18th, for literary and official services. 'The Widow's Cloak' is a suitably elliptical title for a poem which fastens more on the attributes of the monarchy than on the character of Victoria herself; Ferguson indicates her majesty by listing the castles, military strength, and territories under her sway. While Ferguson's fondness for writing about armed might is here enlisted in the service of his queen, there is, as in the unpublished stanzas added to 'Grace O'Maly', a momentary note of reproach on the infrequency of her visits to Ireland although she graces Scotland on her annual visits to Balmoral:

> She loves the Highland nature; and, the Dalriad deeps beyond,
> To every pressure of her palm the Irish hearts respond.
> What though we seldom see her St. Patrick's Hall within,
> The Gael her presence yearly cheers
>   Are kith and kin.
>
> > *(Poems* p. 25)

Even in this most loyal of his poems, Ferguson finds space to hint at his continuing concern about the apparent neglect of Ireland within the United Kingdom as a result of unthinking centralisation.

The volume ends with a number of other occasional poems addressed to friends: a sonnet to Isaac Butt, following his failure to win election to the Royal Irish Academy in 1876, three sonnets on the artist Veronese, lyrics 'To a Lady' and 'The Little Maiden'. All these appear to have been written between 1875 and 1878, as the collection was being assembled. The most notable of them is the elegy 'Dear Wilde'. Sir William Wilde died on the 19th of April 1876. Ferguson was in Oxford at the time, but three days later he had completed seventy lines of rhymed couplets in memory of his friend. They were published in the next number of the fortnightly *Irish Builder* on May 1st.

It is difficult not be struck by the difference between this elegy and Ferguson's other essay in the genre, written thirty years before on Thomas Davis. Here Ferguson is able to concentrate more evenly on the achievements of the dead one, conscious that he too is nearing the time of his own death; there is none of the bursting energy of life which marks the early stanzas of 'Thomas Davis'. Wilde is remembered as an antiquarian and academician; his work as a surgeon is not mentioned. But as well as honouring his deceased friend Ferguson takes the opportunity to comment on a current controversy in the Royal Irish Academy; the rich collection of archaeological finds which Wilde had catalogued for the Academy was about to be moved, at Government insistence, to the museum where they may still be seen today. Ferguson was foremost among those resisting this encroachment on the resources of the Academy, and he used the poem's publication in the *Irish Builder* as an occasion to swipe at the proposal. The rich artefacts are

> products of progressive man
> Since civil life in Erin first began,
> Described by thee, where'er their destined place,
> Whether, still sharing Academic grace
> And Cyclopaediac union, they retain
> Their portion in the high clear-aired domain
> Of arc and sine and critic-judgment heard
> Alternate with the searcher's symbol-word,
> Historic aids, to little arts unknown,
> Heirlooms of all our Past, and all our own,

Or whether, at despotic power's command,
They bow their beauty to a stranger's hand,
Mid various wares in halls remore display'd
To swell a programme or promote a trade.

(Poems pp. 166-7)

By 1880, when the collection *Poems* appeared, the removal of the pieces was a *fait accompli* and the elegy had to be prefaced with a short note explaining the background against which it had been written.

Most of the other poems in the volume are short occasional lyrics of little weight, often touching on personal faith or piety. There is one piece which has the same lively narrative as is apparent in 'The Gascon O'Driscoll', and that is 'The Sinking of the Monitor', a curious poem which takes an event of the American Civil War twenty years for its subject. The *Monitor* was noteworthy as one of the earliest ironclad warships, and distinguished itself in an engagement against the *Merrimack*, a former Union battleship which had been captured by the Federal side and named *Virginia*. Although it fought well the *Monitor* was not very seaworthy, and in December of that same year it sank in a storm off the North Carolina coast. Ferguson's poem is about an attempted rescue on the occasion of the shipwreck. However, the poem musters more energy than elegance in its story of the valiant but doomed efforts by Rodney Brown and his anonymous crew. Its most notable feature is the abandon with which Ferguson pairs off such words as 'petrel' and 'Federal', 'hurricane' and 'American', 'janitor' and 'Monitor', in rhymes which wallow and pitch like the ship itself.

The pieces at the beginning of *Poems* show Ferguson writing in a manner more personal and intimate than anywhere else in his work. They concentrate mainly on matters of faith, grappling with the problem of human unworthiness when faced with the compassion of God. Ferguson, who in practically all of his poetry and fiction hitherto had adopted characters and stories from independent sources, is here writing directly of himself. It would be impertinent to comment on his spirituality as displayed in these poems, but there is no doubt that the verses make for difficult reading. A stanza in 'The Morning's Hinges' is probably the worst he ever permitted into print:

What! does all, then, end in this,
That, amid a world amiss,
Man must ever be but parcel–

Imperfection? and the soul
Ever thus in poise between
Things contrarient, rest, a mean
Averaged of the universal
Good and ill that make the whole?

(*Poems* p. 3)

One feature of these personal poems exploring matters of faith and doubt is the multiple viewpoint which they often embody. 'Three Thoughts', 'Three Seasons', 'Bird and Brook' and 'Two Voices' are all structured on dialogue or internal debate. The first two of these, together with another piece in *Poems*, 'The Hymn of the Fisherman', had been included in an anthology of religious verse *Lyra Hibernica Sacra* in 1878, along with some of Oscar Wilde's earliest poems. 'Two Voices' enacts a discussion between 'Conscience' and 'Soul', in which the persistent interrogation of Conscience brings Soul to an admission of God's compassion. The title suggests an imitation of Tennyson's early poem 'The Two Voices' which, although a much longer work, has a similar subject matter, with the poet arguing against 'a still small voice' that prompts him to despair.

In these most intimate writings Ferguson uses a structure of internal dialectic to allow different viewpoints find their expression. Writing about personal themes, he returns to the device he had employed in 'A Dialogue between the Head and Heart of an Irish Protestant'. But when engaging with an objectified body of Gaelic material, the idea of struggle could be seen in remote dynastic terms: Congal against Domnal, Conary against the outlaws. The real dialectic there, carried on in the principal body of Ferguson's writing, lay in the negotiation between an urgent cultural need to forge a vernacular English poetry for nineteenth-century Ireland and a legendary history which proved recalcitrant to the dominant sensibility of that Ireland.

The most noteworthy feature of these spiritual pieces is that they attracted the scorn of a reviewer in *The Academy*, and so called forth the rebuke which Yeats was to direct at Dowden a few years later in his obituary essay on Ferguson's poetry.

A few pages from him would have made it impossible for a journal like *The Academy* to write in 1880, that Sir Samuel Ferguson should have published his poetry only for his intimate friends, and that it did not even 'rise to the low-water mark of poetry'. . . . If Sir Samuel Ferguson had written to the glory of that, from a moral point of view, more than dubious achievement, British civilization, the critics, probably including Professor Dowden, would have taken care of his reputation.[22]

The offending, indeed offensive, notice is brief:

> Sir Samuel Ferguson's verse may possibly give pleasure to a few intimate friends, but it would have been much better to have printed it privately, and issue copies as presents only. There is absolutely nothing in it that reaches even to the low-water mark of poetry, The first verse of 'The Hymn of the Fishermen' may be quoted as a fair specimen of the book: –
>
> > To God give foremost praises,
> > Who, 'neath the rolling tides,
> > In ocean's secret places,
> > Our daily bread provides;
> > Who in His pasture grazes
> > The flat fish and the round,
> > And makes the herring 'maces'
> > In shoaling heaps abound.
>
> We would suggest that it would be more reverent if persons who have not the gifts necessary for composing poetry would confine themselves entirely to secular subjects.[23]

It can still make one wince at this distance. Of course, the young Ferguson had established himself as an Irish poet by reacting virulently in print to Hardiman, but that review had at least paid Hardiman the compliment of giving the book serious and sustained attention.

Even *Blackwood's* failed him. His last letters to the magazine are peppered with reproaches at the lack of a review in its pages.

> I do not know whether you are aware that I have published some volumes of verse in no way inferior to The Forging of the Anchor, but which so far have received little or no recognition either here or with you across the channel. It may be that the fact of my being a Protestant & Conservative, on the one hand, & of my publishing in Dublin & and taking Irish matter to so great an extent for my text, on the other, may account for this state of affairs.[24]

In the eyes of his English readers he remained essentially the poet of "The Forging of the Anchor". *The Academy* in its dismissive brevity had noticed only the spiritual poems; of the poems on Irish themes which make up four-fifths of *Poems* there was not a mention. As in *The Athenaeum* notice of *Lays of the Western Gael and Other Poems* fifteen years before, the Irish narrative poems which were at the centre of Ferguson's poetic achievement are erased. It was as if they did not exist for English critics.

9

Passing On

During Ferguson's last sojourns at Howth, in his seventies, he was a neighbour of the Yeats family who lived there from 1881 to 1884. Whether he ever had occasion to exchange words with the teenage William and pass on words of advice or encouragement to the aspirant poet remains a topic for an imaginary conversation, but it is recorded that gifts of freshly caught fish from the bay were left outside Ferguson's door by William's younger sister Lily.[1] Yeats was later to pay his own tributes to the elder poet, in articles written during the decade following Ferguson's death in 1886; it seems reasonable to speculate that his championing of Ferguson may have sprung not just from a real admiration of the work but also from an early awareness of him as a fellow-inhabitant of Howth.

The intervention of Yeats is inextricably bound up with Ferguson's posthumous reputation, but his last poems of these years held little to attract the younger writer. After *Poems* in 1880, Ferguson published only *Shakespearian Breviates* (1882), a curious little book in which he sets out to make Shakespeare's plays suitable for drawing-room performances or readings. His principal object was to cut them down to manageable length, while at the same time skirting those passages which might offend propriety; how changed from the Ferguson of 'Father Tom and the Pope'! The book consists of rhymed verses summarising the action of scenes and acts which are to be omitted, with directions as to where the standard dramatic text is to be followed. Its main interest is the sidelight which it affords on the social activities of ascendancy Dublin in the later Victorian age. Lady Ferguson gives a list of those gathered for a performance of *Cymbeline* in 1869: it includes one of the foremost Shakespearean scholars of the time, Edward Dowden, as well as J. P. Mahaffy and his wife, John Kells Ingram, the Provost of Trinity, R. P. Graves, and Dr Stokes and his daughter Margaret.[2] The tercentenary of Shakespeare's birth in 1864 had given rise to a flurry of celebratory initiatives, and the readings were found to have a social usefulness which made them part of the North Great George's Street scene for a couple of decades following.

The book furnishes further evidence, if more were needed, that Ferguson preferred to write in a derivative mode. Once again, there is a definite text antecedent to Ferguson's own work; here it is Shakespeare's plays, in the past he had used Hardiman's *Irish Minstrelsy* for the lyric translations, historical sources for the *Hibernian Nights' Entertainments*, or the Irish Archaeological Society's publications for the lays and *Congal*. The only original and personal poem of his which has a power of its own is the lament for Thomas Davis, a piece which he did not include in either of his collections.

But in the six years of life remaining him after the publication of *Poems* Ferguson continued to write occasional poems, among which the most remarkable are the three printed by Lady Ferguson in her biography, and which do not have a source text behind them: 'In Carey's Footsteps', 'At The Polo Ground' and 'The Curse of the Joyces'. They do, however, have a specific contemporary event standing behind each of them, and so fit into the pattern evident in pieces such as the early sonnet 'Athens', the lament for Davis, and 'Inheritor and Economist'.

'At The Polo-Ground' is a blank verse poem which enters into the mind of James Carey, the Fenian who gave the signal to those who stabbed to death Lord Frederick Cavendish, the newly-arrived viceroy, and T. H. Burke the under-secretary, in the Phoenix Park on 6th May 1882. 'In Carey's Footsteps' is a companion-piece, supposedly giving the thoughts of a Catholic priest who visits the scene of the killings some time afterwards while trying to reconcile the claims of nationalism with the teachings of religion.

Both poems are meditative excursions into an alien ideology. Lady Ferguson, in a genteel attempt to depoliticise the poetry she prints, describes these blank verse monologues as a type of exercise in imitation of Robert Browning.[3] For here was Ferguson, by now senior establishment figure, buttressed by a knighthood and other honours, setting out to anatomise and portray the minds of an accessory to a political murder and of a covert sympathiser. Various motives are suggested to be at work on Carey as he steels himself to action in 'At the Polo-Ground': class resentment, personal advancement, fear of his accomplices. Ferguson does not offer a clear indication as to which predominates, being more concerned in conveying the hesitancy of Carey as the

moment to give the signal approaches. This hesitancy is
attributed to Carey in the light of his turning Queen's evidence at
the subsequent trial; it allows Ferguson to glance at the state of
Ireland as it might be presumed to impinge on one of the Catholic
majority, and to admit that a nationalist may have a very different
image of what Ireland might be in the medium-term future.
Carey finds a spur to his intent in the sight of the polo-players,

Young fops and lordlings of the garrison
Kept up by England here to keep us down;
All rich young fellows not content to own
Their chargers, hacks, and hunters for the field,
But also special ponies for their game;
And doubtless, as they dash along, regard
Us who stand outside a beggarly crew.[4]

His mind runs further on the distribution of wealth and property,
but mentally he rejects Davitt for Parnell, and then in practice
rejects both these constitutional politicians by facilitating the
violent act which follows. The last hesitation to cross his mind
before singling out the victims is of more general nature, and
recurs to the theme of an ordered polity which Ferguson had
already raised in 'Conary':

Is it worth while – the crime itself apart –
To pull this settled civil state of life
To pieces, for another just the same,
Only with rawer actors for the posts
Of Judges, Landlords, Masters, Capitalists?[5]

As Yeats was to put it in an epigram some fifty years later, having
the benefit of hindsight where Ferguson had to rely on conjecture:

Hurrah for revolution and more cannon shot;
A beggar upon horseback lashes a beggar upon foot;
Hurrah for revolution and cannon come again,
The beggars have changed places but the lash goes on.

The quatrain is as raw as the Horatian version on the 'Birmingham mob' which Ferguson had sent as his first contribution to
Blackwood's in 1832, but 'At the Polo-Ground' is much more
reflective both in its method of presentation and in its content.
    While Lady Ferguson had offered to depoliticise this type of
poetry by calling it an exercise in imitation of Browning, Ferguson
himself was more concerned to deny its subject any possibility of

the epic stature which attaches to deeds of violence in the lays or *Congal*. The self-questioning of Carey does not so much open up a psychological insight into the individual as call into doubt his aims and those of his associates, and the emphasis on the petty mechanics of the deed – blowing his nose to give the signal, wondering whether to feign a twisted ankle in order to avoid implication – undercut any possibility of the heroic.

In a letter to *Blackwood's* written in early 1882, just three months before the event dramatised in the poem, Ferguson had given his considered opinion of the country at the time:

> You ask me what I think of the condition of things here. It seems to me that the tendency is to some form of Irish independence. The desire to be their own master pervades almost all classes. The classes especially benefited by the transfer of property, and, so, strengthened in making their opinions operative, are deeply imbued with this feeling. It is hoped however that this very transfer & other measures of a like kind, will work a complete alteration in their sentiments, & under the sense of business & the stimulus of self-interest, bring about permanent contentment & industry. I do not think that will be the result. Work, even for the sake of larger returns, is not agreeable to that class; at home, where in truth they regard themselves, through at least three of the provinces, as a royal race, like the Jews in Canaan, & would think it only their right to have their servile work performed by others. I believe this proud spirit is inherent in the race, and underlies all the varying forms of their discontent.[6]

He goes on to anticipate gloomily the concession of some form of self-government to Ireland. The racial taxonomy of his early writings on Ireland fifty years before is now overlain with a sense of class tension. (This was given expression the next month in a general context in 'A Word with John Bright', the last poem to be printed in *Blackwood's* during his lifetime.) That 'proud spirit', which Ferguson himself had made the matter for his narrative poetry, is now seen as an obstacle to accommodation with English rule and with the property-owning classes in Ireland. In his earlier poetry he had been able to convert that spirit to the service of an imperial and heroic vision, with its violent energy on display in a ritualised primitivism; in the Ireland of his day it remained obdurate and recalcitrant, refusing assimilation into the plurality reigned over by Victoria in her widow's cloak. For preference, Ferguson's Irishry would not be indomitable.

'In Carey's Footsteps' is a longer poem than 'At The Polo-Ground', and even less conclusive in its thought. It commences with the speaker, a priest, thinking on some words he has recently uttered which might give comfort and encouragement to nationalist proponents of physical force. Finding himself in Phoenix Park, surrounded by the monuments and other tangible reminders of British rule, he arrives eventually at the scene of Carey's deed and is led to speculate on the effects of violence and his own role in relation to it. At the end he is left 'still free to choose'.

The degree of suggestiveness in Ferguson's title is not clear; certainly, the priest follows physically in the trail of Carey on that fateful day, but is Ferguson also implying that the priest might emulate him in active opposition? or in eventual collaboration? Like Carey, the priest has his own vision of a future Ireland, with a Cardinal or Archbishop in residence in the Park and religious processions through the grounds. There was something prophetic in this, with the vision having been given some substance since by the presence there of the Papal Nuncio to Ireland, and the huge religious gatherings on the occasion of the Holy Year and the Papal visit to Ireland.

While they may aim at the impersonality of the dramatic monologue, these two poems are more imbued with a sense of Ferguson's own feelings than any of his other pieces. And they are poems of failure, poems which cede ground to alternative and stronger energies; this is accomplished a little more easily, perhaps, when a guise or mask is adopted.

The two poems move abruptly away from the retrospection of the preceding work and fasten on the contemporary world. However, the effort at projection into an unfamiliar cultural tradition which has been a consistent feature of Ferguson's poetry, from the Hardiman translations through the *Lays of the Western Gael* to *Congal*, is again apparent here. This he does through the eyes of Carey and the priest in lines which, while written in despondency, still preserve that generous openness which marks so much of his poetry. But where the earlier work had been exploratory, and prepared to appropriate the material on behalf of an ideally eclectic mainstream of literature in English, here there is only a sad fascination at difference.

At the end there is perfection neither of the life nor of the work. Ireland under the Union, which he had hoped would provide an enabling arena for the enlightened wealth and scholarship of his country, had dwindled on the periphery of the British administration until Ferguson was at last forced to confront the inchoate diversity of possibilities ranged ahead.

If we try to identify the nature of Ferguson's achievement, then it must be seen as resting primarily with his heroic narrative poems. In these, figures are conjured up in contexts which lend voice and action to an Irish past which might then be assimilated into the nineteenth-century consciousness. In doing this he extended the historical perspectives of his country's literature, he provided it with a set of symbolic gestures, and he rehabilitated, to some extent, the primitive values of Gaelic civilization – although he himself would not have used that last term.

Ferguson wrote not about himself but about Ireland. Ireland, as an abstract ideal, had long been a theme of poetry in Irish during the seventeenth and eighteenth centuries; the preferred method of presenting this abstraction was to give it a name, so that Ireland appears variously as *Banba*, or the *Sean Bhean Bhocht*, or Cathleen Ny Houlihan; but in 1834, Ferguson had explicitly rejected one instance such of personification, when quarrelling with Hardiman's reading of *Róisín Dubh* as a veiled naming of the country. Ferguson's interest was directed more towards the parts and places of the physical landscape. The allegorical names were generated by the imagination in poetic texts and songs; he fastened more on to those places which had, or ought to have had, a history.

He had announced the need for such a theme in 1834 in the sonnet 'Athens'. In 'Deirdre', his last poem of any length to mine the material of Irish legendary history, he could look about with some satisfaction in a spirit of poetic recapitulation. When Deirdre and her companions return from Scotland to the shore of north-east Ulster and progress through Antrim, places and features of what was Ferguson's native countryside are named and described: Knocklayd mountain, Lurgeden, Glenariff, the River Bann, Lough Neagh, Dalwhinny, Crevilly and Rathmore. As Deirdre remarks, the lore of these places is enriched by the legendary stories attached to them – stories of the type which Ferguson had embodied in his verse. As if to make the point more forcefully, there are several allusions to the matter of his other poems scattered through 'Deirdre': the legend of Fergus Wry-Mouth is mentioned in connection with Rathmore, the other Fergus refers to his abdication for love of Nessa which allowed Conor to assume the throne, and the absence of Conall Carnach is accounted for by his having departed to do battle with Mesgedra in Leinster. Ferguson has almost arrived at the stage where he has chronicled and peopled a poetic landscape.

John Wilson Foster has written about the importance of place in
the Irish literary revival, and how its links with Gaelic literature
are perceived.

In its preoccupation with place as an unseverable aspect of self, revival
literature is a descendant of the Irish myth and hero tales. Certainly
'setting' is an inadequate word to describe the attention Irish writers
from the adapter of the romances to our contemporaries lavish upon
topography. What was sacred to the community in the old literature is
sacred to the individual writer of modern literature, who tends to have
almost totemic relations with one or more places. Yet one suspects
that the revival passion for place – a passion that serves to limit
freedom of self – derived not only from the example of custom and
tradition but also from the fact that the Anglo-Irish leaders of the
revival felt some unease about how profoundly they belonged to the
places they chose to celebrate, and they to them.[7]

Foster's pages on this feature of the revival are among the most
succinct and authoritative, but his focus is on the latter decades of
the century, and on prose rather than poetry; Ferguson's role in
moulding this uneasy passion is not dealt with.

Yeats had noticed it, however, writing in the immediate
aftermath of Ferguson's death: 'he has restored to our hills and
rivers their epic interest'.[8] Seventy years on, looking back on the
revival, Austin Clarke could take the importance of a native
mythology exultantly for granted; it was intimated to Irish poets
through the landscape in whuch they lived.

They were not exploring a borrowed mythology, but one which
belonged to their country, survived in its oral tradition, and in the very
name of its hills, rivers, and plains. When Keats turned to Greek
mythology, he went to Lempriere's Classical Dictionary; our poets
went out of doors.[9]

Clarke was pleased with this observation, and repeated it elsewhere,[10] but he was overlooking the fact that, at the very time
Keats was rifling through Lempriere, the Irish hills, rivers, and
plains had little to offer Irish writers in English. Ferguson had
found the duns 'nameless' in 1834; it had taken him the next fifty
years or so to reinscribe the Irish landscape with a poetic
toponymy.

That it was possible for Clarke to take the toponymy for
granted was a fundamental but unobtrusive legacy of Ferguson's
work. When a later poet, John Montague, revisits the theme he
does so in terms which echo Ferguson's 'Athens' but with a
confidence that naming history does exist, even if it is occluded:

Scattered over the hills, tribal
And placenamse, uncultivated pearls.
No rock or ruin, dun or dolmen
But showed memory defying cruelty
Through an image-encrusted name.
. . . .
The whole landscape was a manuscript
We had lost the skill to read,
A part of our past disinherited.[11]

A more immediately noticeable legacy from Ferguson's writing
were the forms which he made available to Irish writers. Clarke
himself has pointed out how he began by emulating the legendary
narrative verse of Ferguson;[12] his first book, *The Vengeance of Fionn*
(1917), is a long poem which expands on events around those
which Ferguson had dramatised in 'The Death of Dermid'. Yeats
too made the true start to his career as a poet with an Irish narrative
poem, *The Wandering of Oisin* (1889). In selecting such subject
matter, and in treating it as they did, they were following along a
path which Ferguson had been the first to open up.

Ferguson's achievement in the conversion of the heroic sagas
invites judgment a mode of imitation epic which, as was suggested in the chapter on *Congal*, posed particular problems for his
age. All too often a present-day reader of his work is unsure how to
react to it; one is left respectful at the sheer doggedness with which
he persisted in hacking out the monumental figures buried in an
ancient literature. The rhythms and language regularly collapse
with the effort, leading to passages like the following from
'Conary', where the sense of the reply extricates itself only with
difficulty from the leadenly 'antique' speech and the tangle of
negatives and conditionals:

'What means this concourse, think'st thou, Ferragon?'
'I know not if it be not that a host
Resorting, it may be, to games or fair
At Tara or at Taltin, rest to-night
In a great guest-house. 'Twill be heavier cost
Of blows and blood to win it than it seem'd.'

(*Poems*, p. 71)

But a major significance of Ferguson's long poems lies not in
their momentary effects, nor indeed in any particular qualities as
poetry, but in their managing to give a modern narrative shape to
unfamiliar ancient material. The lays of 'The Healing of Conall
Carnach', 'The Tain-Quest' and 'The Burial of King Cormac'

succeed as stories; when *Congal* fails it does so because the narrative impulse of its plot loses power. His successes are as much
those of a fabulator and redactor as of a poet, and he was foremost
in opening up Irish history and legends to novelists, dramatists
and popularizers as well as to poets: *Old Celtic Romance* by P. W.
Joyce, *Bardic Stories of Ireland* by Patrick Kennedy, and *Legend Lays
of Ireland* by Canon John O'Hanlon ('Laganiensis') were all produced at the start of the 1870s, to be followed by the books of
Jeremiah Curtin, Eleanor Hull, Standish O'Grady and others.

The work of Lady Gregory, Douglas Hyde, Yeats and the collec-
tors and anthologisers of the later generation diverged from that
of Ferguson in one important respect: they saw themselves as
presenting what were essentially oral and folk tales, whereas he
had based his material on what he perceived as being written
sources. His stratagem had been to align his stories with the
values and methods of Homeric myth, which might be more
readily recognised by an educated readership.

The narrative lays published between 1860 and 1880 form one
of the strands which Ferguson fed into the course of Irish poetry,
but by no means the only one. A second aspect of his influence on
subsequent writing stems from the distinctive lyrical pace of a few
– very few – early poems, most notably 'The Fairy Thorn' and the
translated 'Cashel of Munster'. One of the more remarkable
features of Ferguson's poetry is the fact that, although capable of
the delicacy in these pieces, he never struck the same subtle note
again. 'The Fairy Thorn' has all the restrained vagueness of the
Celtic Twilight poetry sixty years later; both AE and Yeats
admired and imitated its language,[13] and Yeats's 'The Stolen
Child' is on a similar theme. Yeats also used another, very different, metre which Ferguson had tried: 'Red Hanrahan's Song
About Ireland' is written in fourteener couplets, the same measure that Ferguson had used for both 'The Forging of the Anchor'
and *Congal*. Yeats's choice of this infrequently used metre may be
coincidental, as might be the faint echo from *Congal* in the lines,

> The wind has bundled up the clouds high over Knocknarea,
> And thrown the thunder on the stones for all that Maeve can say.

Congal, meeting the Washer of the Ford, is told that her place

> For sleep is in the middle of the shell-heaped Cairn of Maev,
> High up on haunted Knocknarea.
>
> (*Congal* p. 58)

(Ferguson had actually written 'skill-heaped'.[14]) A rather more definite instance of Ferguson's words entering into the stock of later poetry occurs in one of Joseph Campbell's lyrics from his 1906 collection *The Rushlight*, 'The Sea-Field', which uses a refrain identical to that in the second stanza of 'The Fairy Well': 'Mournfully, sing mournfully'. Although 'The Fairy Well' did not achieve the prominence of 'The Fairy Thorn', it was apparently known as a ballad in County Antrim by the 1860s[15] and may have been transmitted to the Belfast-born Campbell as a folk poem.

As a translator, his influence was almost immediately evident in the work of Mangan, whose 'Dark Rosaleen' and 'Timoleague Abbey' derive from his work. The emphasis which he gave to versions from the Irish finds its proper aftermath not so much in the output of subsequent specialised translators such as George Sigerson and Douglas Hyde, but in more recent writing by Irish poets such as Clarke, Kinsella, Montague and others, who have accorded the translation of Irish material an important place in their work. The thirty or so songs that he translated, in verse or prose, have defined a core of pieces for treatment. These almost constitute a set of test pieces, many of them to be translated again, not necessarily because of any inadequacy in his versions but because Ferguson had given them currency.

It is a feature of literary translation that it is time-bound; the end-result belongs very much to its age. The writer of an original poem may console himself by entertaining the pleasant convention that he is writing for posterity. The translator has no such recourse; indeed, working on texts from history, he or she *is* the posterity. Engaged in more than a simple linguistic exercise, the translator aims at idioms and images which are faithful at once both to the original text and to the sensibility of his readers. As a result, it is scarcely to be wondered at if the work appears particularly dated to subsequent generations. When a translation endures beyond its own time and shapes the perceptions of a later age, it is a real poetic accomplishment in serving two masters. A number of Ferguson's lyric translations do retain their vitality.

His conversions of the old Irish sagas have survived less well, as the original hard-edged and spare vision is compromised by accommodation to the values of Victorian world. In the lays he had to show men living out their destiny through action. Their narrative progress immediately suggests a teleology, which Ferguson expressed either spiritually, in a movement towards nineteenth-century faith, or historically, moving towards the imperial moment in which he lived. For us, that shaping is inappropriate; our reading of him today is inseparable from the particular narrative shapes we have since put on our own history. It is part of the paradox of his achievement that he passed on a set of myths which took on values radically different to those which governed his own assembly of them.

Perhaps the most significant aspect of Ferguson's achievement was simply that he had persisted. Although his poetry failed to find its intended audience during his own lifetime, the simple fact of his presence as a precursor who had aimed at a definably Irish body of literature in full seriousness allowed later poets such as Yeats and Clarke to trace a lineage for themselves at a time when the need for one was keenly felt. Writing against a background of tension between an almost lost Irish tradition and an imperious English one, Ferguson established himself as a precedent. His constant use of textual sources may have been more than simple antiquarianism; it also compensated for the absence of any pattern or literary frame of reference in the Ireland of his day.

His presence, if only as a name to reached for, ensured that later generations of writers would never be in the same predicament so acutely. But, recognizing the presence which he has supplied to Irish writing, it is not too much to ask that we should go to encounter his work with as much openness and commitment as he displayed when taking up the unknown and neglected literature of Ireland.

Notes

Chapter 1

1. OED. A writer in the *Dublin University Magazine* in 1837 complained that walking through College Park had become hazardous, so many and various were the types of boomerang being experimented with there, and Charles Graves later maintained that the only two things he learned at school around this time were how to draw a longbow and how to throw a boomerang (A. P. Graves, *To Return to All That*, 1930, p. 15).
2. See, for instance, Robert Welch, *Irish Poetry from Moore to Yeats*, p. 123, and Seamus Deane, *A Short History of Irish Literature*, p. 69; Robert O'Driscoll, refers to the article obliquely, and tips the scale, in the title of his monograph *An Ascendancy of the Heart: Sir Samuel Ferguson and Irish Literature*, although the phrase which provides his main title is actually taken from Ferguson's review of Hardiman's *Irish Minstrelsy*.
3. Desmond Bowen, *The Protestant Crusade in Ireland, 1800–70* p. 174.
4. *Dublin University Magazine* IV, August 1834, p. 158.

Chapter 2.

1. 'An Irish Patriot', *The Bookman* X, May 1896, pp 49–50.
2. *Life* I, p.275.
3. NLS 4032 f 249, 2 February 1832.
4. NLS 4032 f 261, 29 June 1832.
5. NLS 4032 f 265, 6 August 1832.
6. NLS 4032 f 259, 11 June 1832.
7. *Life* I, pp. 25–26.
8. M. Oliphant, *Annals of a Publishing House* II, p. 102
9. NLS 4032 f 259, 11 June 1832.
10. NLS 4035 f 208, 29 March 1833.
11. In *The Poets and Poetry of Ireland* (Boston 1881), edited by Ferguson's American friend A. M. Williams, both poems were included among a generous selection of Ferguson's work but without the link between them being made explicit.

12. James Macpherson, *The Poems of Ossian, to which are prefixed A Preliminary Discourse, and dissertations on the aera and poems of Ossian*, pp. 130–137.
13. NLS 4035 f 211, 3 June 1833.
14. NLS 4038 f 239, 11 March 1834.
15. NLS 4032 ff 255, 257, 8 14 May 1832.
16. Jeanne Cooper Foster, *Ulster Folklore*, p. 110.
17. NLS 4035 f 211, 31 May 1833.
18. *Blackwood's Edinburgh Magazine* XIII, pp. 209–213.
19. *Life* I, p. 42.
20. NLS 4035 f 213, 5 November 1833.
21. NLS 4035 f 215, 15 November 1833.
22. NLS 4038 f 235, 7 January 1834.
23. NLS 4038 f 239, 11 March 1834.
24. Malcolm Brown, *Sir Samuel Ferguson*, p. 51
25. O'Driscoll, *op. cit.* p. 24.
26. James Hardiman, *Irish Minstrelsy* I, p. 351.
27. Seán Ó Tuama and Thomas Kinsella (edd.), *An Duanaire 1600–1900: Poems of the Dispossessed*, p. 308.
28. RIA 12 N 20.
29. Hardiman, *op. cit.* I, p. 300.
30. NLS 4035 f 211, 31 May 1833.
31. Joseph R. Fisher and John H. Robb, *Royal Belfast Academical Institution: Centenary Volume 1810–1910*, p. 106.
32. Hardiman, *op. cit.* I, p. 224.
33. Hardiman, *op. cit.* I, p. 238.
34. Charles Gavan Duffy, ed. *The Ballad Poetry of Ireland*, p. 29.

Chapter 3

1. *Life* I, p. 50; *LRB*, p. xxiv.
2. *Life* I, p. 43.
3. Fisher and Robb, *op. cit.*, p. 250.
4. *Life* I, p. 45.
5. NLI 2976.
6. *Dublin University Magazine*, February 1834, p. 158.
7. Frederic Madden, *Archaeologia* XXII [(1829)] pp. 307–314.
8. NLS 4045 f 155, 28 March 1838.
9. Poe, *Collected Works* II, p 340.
10. *Catholic Registry*, p. 158.
11. *Authenticated Report of a Discussion which took place between the Rev. Richard T. D. Pope and the Rev. Thomas Maguire . . . .*

12. NLS 4045 f 157, 9 April 1838.
13. *A Report of the Trial of the Action in which Bartholomew McGahan was Plaintiff and the Rev. Thomas Maguire Defendant* . . .
14. *Life* I, pp 274–5.
15. NLS 4045 f 155, 28 March 1838.
16. See, for example, James M. Cahalan, *The Irish Novel: A Critical History*; John Cronin, *The Anglo-Irish Novel, Volume I: The Nineteenth Century*; Thomas Flanagan, *The Irish Novelists, 1800–1850*; John Wilson Foster, *Fictions of the Irish Literary Revival: A Changeling Art*; Barry Sloan, *The Pioneers of Anglo-Irish Fiction, 1800–1850*.

Chapter 4

1. NLS 4056 f 15, 29 January 1841.
2. *Dublin University Magazine* XXX, p. 128.
3. NLI 463, 1 August 1845.
4. 7 September 1844, p. 762.
5. NLI 5756 f 197, 16 September 1845.
6. In *The Life and Labours in Art and Archaeology of George Petrie, LL.D, M.R.I.A.*, William Stokes lists Ferguson as a contributor to the *Irish Penny Journal*.
7. NLI MS 2644.
8. 14 September 1844, p 778.
9. NLI MS 2644.
10. *Life* I, pp. 139–40.
11. *Ibid.*, p. 134.
12. *Dublin University Magazine* XXIX (February 1847), pp. 190–99.
13. Seán Ó Tuama (ed.), *Caoineadh Airt Uí Laoghaire*, p. 23.
14. D. F. MacCarthy (ed.), *The Book of Irish Ballads*, p. 13.
15. Reported in *The Nation*, 1 July 1848, pp. 422–3.

Chapter 5

1. William Allingham, *A Diary*, pp. 113–114.
2. *Life* I, p. 344.
3. Breandán Ó Buachalla suggests that they are original compositions (Brown and Hayley (edd.) *Samuel Ferguson: A Centenary Tribute*, p. 47n).
4. W. H. Drummond, *Ancient Irish Minstrelsy*, pp. xxiv-xxv.

5. *Dublin Evening Mail*, 5 November 1838, p. 3. That Ferguson wrote this piece is evident from its praise of 'Archaeus', a contributor to *Blackwood's*; in a letter to Blackwood he mentions that he has written such a notice in the *Mail* (NLS 4046 f 163, 2 November 1838).
6. William Maginn, *Homeric Ballads*, p. xii.
7. Matthew Arnold, *Essays Literary and Critical*, p. 241.
8. *Dublin Evening Mail*, 27 June 1836.
9. Eugene O'Curry, *Lectures on Manuscript Materials of Ancient Irish History*, p. 30.
10. Standish O'Grady, *Early Bardic Literature, Ireland*, p. 37.
11. O'Curry, *op. cit.*, p. 274.
12. NLS 4160 f 148, 11 November 1861.
13. LHL, Ferguson Manuscripts.
14. NLI 8403 f 69.
15. *Dublin University Magazine* XXV (April 1845), pp. 379–396. This was one part of what turned out to be a two-pronged attack in the RIA controversy between Petrie and Sir William Betham; in the same month Ferguson published a hostile review of Betham's *Etruria Celtica* in *Blackwood's*.

Chapter 6

1. D. F. MacCarthy, *A Book of Irish Ballads* (1874), p. 13.
2. Standish Hayes O'Grady, *Toruigheacht Dhiarmuda agus Ghrainne*, pp. 185–95.
3. *Dublin University Magazine* XXXIX, March 1852, p. 288.
4. 'Hardiman's Irish Minstrelsy – No. III', *Dublin University Magazine* IV, October 1834, p. 448.
5. *Saturday Review* XIX, 28 January 1865, p. 116–117.
6. Matthew Arnold, *On the Study of Celtic Literaure and Other Essays*, p. 72.
7. *ibid.*, p. 85.
8. *ibid.*, p. 82.
9. 'Recent Irish Poetry', *Dublin Review* VIII, April 1865, p. 315.
10. *The Athenaeum*, 3 December 1864, pp. 739–740.

Chapter 7

1. NLS 4160 f 148, 11 November 1861; *Congal* (1872) p. 218.
2. 7 September 1844, p. 762.
3. *Congal*(1872), p. 232.

4. NLS 4065 f 249, 8 July 1843.
5. PRO M 6055.
6. *Congal*, p. vii.
7. NLS 4032 f 249, 2 February 1832.
8. John O'Donovan (ed.), *The Banquet of Dun na n-Gedh and The Battle of Magh Rath*, p. xxii.
9. *Dublin University Magazine* XXIX, February 1847, p. 191.
10. NLS 4138 ff 139–140, 30 November 1859.
11. NLS 4148 f 155, 10 February 1860.
12. NLS 4160 f 148, 11 November 1861.
13. LHL Ferguson Manuscripts, 2.
14. Geoffrey Keating, *The History of Ireland*, pp. 118–120.
15. *ibid.*, p. 118.
16. PRO M 6055.
17. *Congal*, pp. 183–184.
18. PRO M 6055, p. 10.
19. *Congal*, p. 207.
20. W. P. Ker, *Epic and Romance*, p. 37.
21. John O'Donovan (ed.), *op. cit.*, pp. 35–39.
22. *Dublin University Magazine* IV, October 1834, p. 462.
23. PRO M 6055.
24. *Dublin University Magazine* XXXI, February 1848, p. 213.
25. John O'Donovan (ed.), *op. cit.*, pp. 99–107.
26. *Dublin University Magazine* XXXI, February 1848, p. 212.
27. *ibid.*, p. 213.
28. Edward Dowden, *Letters*, p. 68.
29. NLS 2631 ff 281, 282; *Life* II, pp. 220–221.
30. *Saturday Review* XIX, 28 January 1865, p. 116.
31. *Life* II, p. 228.
32. NLS 2631 ff 281, 282; *Life* II, pp. 220–222.

Chapter 8

1. NLS 4374 f 115, 23 Feb 1878.
2. 'Hardiman's Irish Minstrelsy – No. IV' *Dublin University Magazine* IV, November 1834, p. 529.
3. NLS 4374 f 115, 23 February 1878.
4. NLS 4220 f 153, Easter Monday 1867.
5. *Life* I, p. 221.
6. 'Architecture in Ireland', *Dublin University Magazine* XXIX, June 1847, p. 174.
7. Seamus Deane, *Celtic Revivals*, p. 18.

8. Eric Hobsbawm and Terence Ranger (edd.), *The Invention of Tradition*, p. 1 and *passim*.
9. Geoffrey Tillotson, *A View of Victorian Literature*.
10. *Dublin University Magazine* XXIX, February 1847, p. 170.
11. *Dublin University Magazine* XXXI, February 1848, p. 207.
12. O'Curry, *op. cit.*,pp. 268–270.
13. Reeves, William, *The Ancient Churches of Armagh*.
14. Stokes, Whitley, ed. 'The Destruction of Da Derga's Hostel', *Revue Celtique*, XXII (Paris, 1901); Hennessy's translation is referred to in *Poems*, p. 61, and in the notes to *Congal*, p. 157.
15. See the essay on 'Togail Bruidne Da Derga' by Mairin O'Daly in Myles Dillon (ed.), *Irish Sagas*, p. 106.
16. Eugene O'Curry, *Atlantis* pp 377–422; Robert Atkinson, 'Introduction', *The Book of Leinster*, p.59n.
17. *Life* II, p. 232.
18. John O'Donovan (ed.), *Miscellany of the Celtic Society*.
19. NLS 4374 f 119, 16 March 1878.
20. NLS 4358 f 192, 30 October 1877.
21. NLS 4374 f 115, 23 February 1878.
22. John P. Frayne (ed.), *Uncollected Prose by W. B. Yeats*, I, p. 89.
23. *The Academy*, XVIII, 24 July 1880.
24. NLS 4444 f 59, 20 December 1883.

Chapter 9

1. William M. Murphy, *Prodigal Father: The Life of John Butler Yeats (1839–1922)*, p. 135.
2. *Life* I, p. 201.
3. *Life* I, p. 258.
4. *Life* I, p. 259.
5. *Life* I, p. 261.
6. NLS 4431 f 150, 8 February 1882.
7. John Wilson Foster, *Fictions of the Irish Literary Revival: A Changeling Art*, p. 16.
8. John P. Frayne (ed.), *Uncollected Prose by W. B. Yeats*, I, p. 90
9. Austin Clarke, *Poetry in Modern Ireland*, p. 8.
10. J. E. Caerwyn Williams (ed.), *Literature in Celtic Countries*, p. 155.
11. John Montague, *The Rough Field*, p. 30.
12. Williams *op. cit.*, p. 168.
13. *ibid,*, pp. 156–7.
14. PRO M 6055.
15. *Life* II, p. 196.

Samuel Ferguson: A Chronology

1810:	10 Mar	SF, youngest of six children of John Ferguson,born High Street, Belfast, in house of maternal grandparents. His childhood spent between Belfast and Antrim.
1823:	Aug	Enrolled at Belfast Academical Institution; friends there include John Maclean, Thomas O'Hagan, George Fox.
1828:	28 Sept	Death of eldest brother William in Bolivia.
1830:	Mar	First published poem, 'Sir Kenneth Kerr', in *Ulster Magazine*, followed by others at intervals over next twelve months. Ulster Gaelic Society founded.
1832:	Feb	'The Forging of the Anchor' and two translations in *Blackwood's*; frequent contributions over next two years.
	Spring	Visits the Blackwood family in Edinburgh, and is given letters of introduction to various figures in London.
	May-June	Law student at Lincoln's Inn, London.
	Aug-Oct	In Belfast.
	Dec	At Lincoln's Inn.
1833:	Jan	*Dublin University Magazine* (DUM) commences publication.
	Jan-June	At Lincoln's Inn, London.
	Aug	Isaac Butt takes over editorship of DUM; SF makes his first contribution, the poem 'Don Gomez and the Cid'; he continues as a contributor, with occasional interruptions, until 1853.
	Sept-Nov	In Belfast.

	10 Sept	Tells Petrie he is learning Irish.
1834	7 Feb	Enrolled at Trinity College, Dublin, as Pensioner.
	Feb-Mar	In Belfast; illness.
	Mar	Joins Royal Irish Academy; 'The Fairy Thorn' in DUM.
	Apr-Nov	Review of 'Hardiman's Irish Minstrelsy' in DUM.
	Sept	Death of William Blackwood.
	Sept–Oct	Tour through Kildare, Carlow, Kilkenny.
	Dec	Hibernian Nights' Entertainments begin in DUM.
1836	June	Walking tour of Wicklow with Carleton.
1837		Living at 38 Eccles Street, Dublin.
	Oct	'The Involuntary Experimentalist' is first contribution to Blackwood's since Feb 1834.
1838	22 Jan	Reads first paper to RIA.
	May	'Father Tom and the Pope' in Blackwood's.
	June	Called to the bar.
	Aug	Commences legal practice on North-Eastern Circuit; this will take him back to his native east Ulster several times a year. During this year writes for Dublin Evening Mail.
1839	Autumn	In Belfast helping Bunting to prepare Ancient Music of Ireland III for press; some illness.
1840	Nov	Elected to Council of RIA on Committee of Antiquities Bunting's Ancient Music of Ireland III published. Irish Archaeological Society founded.
1840		Living at 92 Talbot Street, Dublin.
	29 Jan	Tells Blackwood's that he has had nothing to do with DUM for some time past.

1842	Mar	Moves to 56 Dominick Street.
	Apr	Lever becomes editor of *DUM*.
	Summer	SF in Sligo. During this year O'Donovan's edition of *The Banquet of Dun na n-Gedh and The Battle of Magh Rath* is published; SF visits site of battle at Moyra.
	Dec	Writes an attacking review of William Betham's *Etruria Celtica* which he sends to *Blackwood's*.
1843	3 June	Incensed at Thackeray's *Irish Sketch Book*.
	7 Jul	Writes to William Smith O'Brien M.P. about importance of RIA.
	8 Jul	'Celtic epic' completed.
	28 Aug	Writes to Hardiman, expressing regret at tone of 1834 review.
	21 Dec	Death of Bunting
1844		Living at 11 Henrietta Street.
	Mar	Purchases notebook for draft of *Congal*.
	Sept	Patches up quarrel with *DUM* and publishes a review of Carleton, his first contribution for four years; frequent reviews in ensuing months.
	Dec	New Year poem to Robert Gordon ('Coul Goppagh') offered to *Blackwood's* then withdrawn.
1845	Jan	Lever quits editorship of *DUM*.
	Apr	*Etruria Celtica* review at last appears in Blackwood's, simultaneously with SF's review of Petrie's *Ecclesiastical History* in *DUM*; SF in Belfast attending to 'severe domestic afflictions'.
	Jun	Death of father.
	Aug	SF at Howth; Gavan Duffy's *Ballad Poetry of Ireland* published, with ten poems by SF.
	16 Sept	Death of Thomas Davis; SF ill.

1846	Jan	Leaves for continent via London, where he is described as looking very ill; then on through Boulogne, Arras, Amiens, Douay, Rouen.
	Feb-Mar	In Paris.
	Apr	In Eastern France, passing through Lagny, Metz, Luxueil; Nancy, the Vosges, 'in the footsteps of St Columbanus'.
	July-Aug	In Rome, then to Bobbio. Other places visited while in Italy include Pavia, Trento and Ravenna.
	Autumn	Returns to Dublin.
1847	Jan	Pamphlet *On the Expediency of Taking Stock*; becomes active on Reproductive Employment Committee, later renamed Irish Council. Meets Thomas D'Arcy McGee Meets his future wife, Mary Catherine Guinness.
1848	Apr	Founder member of Protestant Repeal Association.
	10 May	Engaged to Mary Guinness.
	27 June	Speech to Protestant Repeal Association.
	Summer	At Howth, when not on circuit.
	16 Aug	Marriage to Mary Guinness, followed by honeymoon in County Meath; takes house at 9 Upper Gloucester Street.
	2 Nov	Successfully defends Richard D'Alton Williams.
1849	20 Jun	Death of Mangan.
	Jul	SF and Mary entertain Charles Knight and Douglas Jerrold in Dublin, then accompany them on a visit to Killarney.
1850		Acquires 20 North Great George's Street, his home for the rest of his life.
1851	25 Mar	Mentions possibility of publishing a collection.

1852	Sept	Visits Clonmacnoise, Clare and Aran Islands; at work on draft of *Congal*. RIA moves to Dawson Street premises.
1853	June	Review of A. H. Layard's *Discoveries in the Ruins of Nineveh and Babylon* is his last contribution to *DUM*.
	20 Nov	SF tells Blackwood that he is 'for the present almost out of the literary world'. Applies unsuccessfully for appointment as Keeper of Irish Records.
1854	Feb	Irish Archaeological Society and Celtic Society merge.
1855		Edward Hayes' *Ballads of Ireland* includes a number of poems by SF. Charles Gavan Duffy emigrates to Australia.
1856	Feb-Mar	At Howth, working on Book V of *Congal* while recovering from illness.
	Sept	Attends weekday service at Westminster Abbey, London.
1857		SF joins British Association.
	3-21 Sept	To Aran Islands with party including Petrie, Stokes, O'Donovan, Wilde, following meeting of British Association in Dublin. Death of friend Robert Gordon. *The Hibernian Nights' Entertainments* published in New York.
1858	Aug-Sept	To Vichy.
	Sept-Oct	At work on Book IV of *Congal*. 'Aideen's Grave' ('The Cromlech on Howth') written.
1859	Autumn	To Vichy.
	10 Nov	Writes of *Congal* as being 'nearly complete'. Called to Inner Bar; makes speech at Mansion House on occasion of centenary of Robert Burns.

1860	10 Feb	Wants to revise *Congal*.
	Summer	At Marine Cottage, Howth.
1861	June	*Congal* more or less completed.
	Autumn	Visit to Kerry; writes 'The Healing of Conall Carnach'.
	10 Dec	Death of John O'Donovan. 'The Cromlech on Howth' published, with illustrations by Margaret Stokes; death of mother.
1862	30 July	Death of Eugene O'Curry.
	Autumn	To Netherlands, Ardennes, Moselle and Homburg.
1863	Aug-Sept	To Brittany, via Paris and Loire valley; tours megalithic remains; meets Villemarqué; writes 'Adieu to Brittany'; returns to Dublin via London and Stonehenge.
	9 Nov	Reads paper on Breton megaliths to RIA.
1864	4 Jan	Active on Shakespeare Committee.
	Apr	Afternoon lecture on 'Our Architecture' in Museum of Art and Industry, St Stephen's Green.
	Aug-Sept	Visits Sligo, Donegal, Roscommon, with Mary Ferguson, Stokes, Petrie, J. H. Todd and others.
	Oct-Nov	*Lays of the Western Gael* published; meets Boucicault, in Dublin for premiere of *Arrah-na-Pogue*.
	14 Nov	First paper on Ogham to RIA.
	31 Dec	Returns to Dublin after visit to Stonehenge and Avebury.
1865	24 Feb	St Patrick's Cathedral reopened after restoration.
	Spring	Visits megaliths at Killeen Cormac, Co. Wicklow.
	12-19 May	Allingham is SF's guest.
	23 May	Dines at Petrie's, in company with Allingham and others.

	June	At a dinner for Duffy, on visit from Australia, in company with D. F. McCarthy, Dillon, John O'Hagan and others.
	Summer	Honorary LL.D. conferred by University of Dublin.
	Aug	Visits Killeen Cormac again. First draft of 'Mesgedra'.
1866	17 Jan	Death of Petrie.
	Autumn	To Paris and Vichy.
1867	August	Appointed Deputy Keeper of the Public Records; visits London.
1868	Spring	To Clare; visits Mount Callan.
	Aug-Sept	Abroad to Germany and the Hague.
1869	19 Jan	Reading of Shakespeare's *Cymbeline* at SF's house, with Stokes, R. P. Graves, Edward Dowden, J. P. Mahaffy, A. P. Graves.
	Spring	Examines megaliths in Wales.
	Early Apr	Visits sites in Ardmore and Dungarvan, Co. Waterford; then to Kilkenny.
	21 Apr	Becomes member of Kilkenny Archaeological Society.
	16 May	Whit Monday visit to Castletimon, Co. Wicklow
	28 June	Death of J. H. Todd. Makes second visit to Mount Callan in course of year.
1870	Apr	Another visit to Mount Callan.
	July	To Dingle and west Kerry, making ogham casts.
1871	5 Mar	SF writes he has been 'ailing a long while'.
1872	Spring	*Congal* published.
	8 July	Fourth visit to Mount Callan.

SAMUEL FERGUSON: A CHRONOLOGY   193

	Aug	In Wales. Official duties entail extensive travelling through Ireland in course of year, overseeing transfer of various documentary records to Dublin.
1873	Spring	Inspects cromlechs in Monaghan and Tyrone.
	Aug	In Devon with Mary.
1874	13 Apr	Elected Honorary Member of Society of Antiquaries of Scotland.
	16-18 May	Spends Whit Weekend near Killala, Co. Mayo.
	Autumn	In South Wales.
	26 Dec	Makes cast of ogham at Mullagh, Co. Cavan.
1875	5 May	Sends letter and subscription towards Chair of Celtic at Edinburgh University to John Blackie.
1876	19 Apr	Death of William Wilde; SF in Oxford.
	Spring	Visit to South Wales.
	1 May	'Dear Wilde' published in *Irish Builder*.
	Autumn	Alone at home while alterations made to house. Made a Vice-President of RIA.
1877	July	In Galway, early part of month.
	Dec	'The Widow's Cloak' in *Blackwood's*.
1878	7 Jan	Death of Stokes.
	18 Mar	Knighted for literary and official services.
	May	'The Gascon O'Driscoll' in *Blackwood's*.
	14-21 Aug	British Association meets in Dublin.
1879	May	Death of Isaac Butt.
	25 Jun	Gives inaugural lecture to Meath Antiquarian Society at Trim.
1880	May	*Poems* published.
1881		Elected President of RIA; remains President until his death in 1886.

	Autumn	Yeats family, including seventeen-year-old W. B., take up residence at Howth, where they live for the next two-and-a-half years, neighbours of SF during his visits there.
1882	Mar	Presidential address to RIA.
	7 Apr	Death of D.F. McCarthy. *Shakespearean Breviates* published,
1883	Aug	In London to secure Stowe manuscripts for RIA. Illustrated edition of *The Forging of the Anchor* published.
1884	Apr	To Edinburgh as President of RIA for tercentenary of university; receives honorary degree.
	July	In South Wales
1885	1 Feb	Death of Thomas O'Hagan.
	Spring	Completes work on 'Confessio' of St Patrick.
	Summer	Journeys to Scandinavia.
1886	Jan	Ill.
	8 Apr	Last day at Public Record Office.
	May	Unable to attend centenary banquet of RIA.
	Summer	At Howth, in failing health.
	9 Aug	Dies early in the day.

A Checklist of Samuel Ferguson's Published Writings

This checklist has as its foundation the Bibliography which Lady Ferguson appends to Volume II of *Sir Samuel Ferguson in the Ireland of His Day*; it adds to and emends that bibliography and others derived from it. It omits two items which she attributed to her husband, and questions her attribution of a third (No 76); see note at end.

The checklist has four main groupings: (i) Contributions to literary periodicals and newspapers; (ii) Contributions to learned journals (generally of an archaeological or antiquarian nature); (iii) Contributions to books; (iv) Books and pamphlets written wholly by Samuel Ferguson. Section (iii) is restricted to original publications; poems or stories reprinted in anthologies are not listed.

Not included in this checklist are the reports which Ferguson wrote as part of his duties as Deputy Keeper of the Public Records. These were published annually from 1869 to the end of his life.

(i) Periodicals and Newspapers. (The date after each heading indicates the period during which Ferguson contributed.)

Items are briefly identified as follows:
A = Article or Essay; F = Fiction; L = Letter;
P = Poem(s) or Verse; R = Review.

Blackwood's Edinburgh Magazine (1832–1882)

1. 'Roger Goodfellow: A Song, To be sung to all sorry rascals' XXI (February 1832) p. 276 [P]
2. 'The Forging of the Anchor' XXI (February 1832) pp. 281–3 [P]
3. 'Horatian Version (Epodon VII): On Meeting the Birmingham Mob, Dec. 1831' XXI (February 1832) p. 285 [P]
4. 'The Wet Wooing: A Narrative of '98' XXI (April 1832) pp. 624–645 [F]

5. 'Light and Darkness' XXXII (October 1832) pp. 681–3 [P]
6. 'An Irish Garland. I. Ye Gentlemen of Ireland. II. Ye Jack-asses of Ireland. III. Song to be Sung at the Lifting of the Conservative Standard. IV. Song to be Sung at the Lifting of the Revolutionary Standard.' XXXIII (January 1833) pp. 87–8 [P]
7. 'The Forrest-Race Romance (Extracted from Papers Dated 1773)' XXXIII (February 1833) pp. 243–260 [F]
8. 'The Fairy Well' XXXIII (April 1833) p. 667 [P]
9. 'Songs After the French of Beranger. I. The Studies of the Ladies (A La Francaise). II The Little Brown Man. III. My Lisette, She is No More!. IV. The Doctor and the Patient' XXXIII (May 1833) pp. 844–5 [P]
10. 'The Death-Song of Regner Lodbrog' XXXIII (June 1833) pp. 910–23 [P + A]
11. 'Nora Boyle' XXXIV (September 1833) pp. 344–250 [F]
12. 'The Return of Claneboy' XXXIV (December 1833) pp. 928–952 [F]
    Includes poem 'The Parting from Slemish, or the Con's Flight to Tyrone', later printed as 'Owen Bawn' in *Lays of the Western Gael and Other Poems* (178)
13. 'Shane O'Neill's Last Amour' XXXV (February 1834) pp. 249–66 [F]
14. 'The Involuntary Experimentalist' XLII (October 1837) pp. 487–492 [F]
15. 'Father Tom and the Pope; or, A Night at the Vatican' XLIII (May 1838) pp. 607–19 [F]
16. 'Sonnet; Suggested By Mr Wall's Painting of the Falls of Niagara' XLIII (May 1838) p. 647 [P]
17. 'A Vision of Noses' XLIII (May 1838) p. 648–60 [A]
18. 'Betham's Etruria Celtica' LVII (April 1845) pp. 474–488 [R]
19. 'The Siege of Dunbeg; or, The Stratagems of War' LXVII (February 1850) p. 153–174 [F]
20. 'Westminster Abbey' XCIV (September 1863) p. 346 [P]
21. 'The Widow's Cloak' CXXII (December 1877) pp. 742–3 [P]
22. 'The Gascon O'Driscol' CXXIII (May 1878) pp. 545–9 [P]
23. 'A Word with John Bright' CXXXI (March 1882) p. 392 [P]

Dublin Evening Mail (1838)

24. 'Tain Bo Quelgny' (27 June 1838) p. 3 [A]
25. 'Literature' (5 November 1838) p. 3 [A]

These are unsigned, but can be identified as being among a number of Ferguson's pieces for the *Mail*; 24 quotes some lines of verse known to be by him, and 25 is mentioned in one of his letters to *Blackwood's* (2/11/1838, NLS 4045). It seems likely that Ferguson was writing the monthly 'Literature' articles on a regular basis at this time, to judge from the frequent singling out of poems by his friend Robert Gordon ('Coul Goppagh') for praise (3 January 1838; 2 February 1838; 2 March 1838; 4 April 1838). There are also occasional verses contributed by someone terming himself 'Printer's Devil', a description Ferguson had once adopted when writing for the *Ulster Magazine*.

Dublin Penny Journal (1834)

26. 'When My Old Cap Was New – Or Ireland Fifty Years Ago' III, (1 November 1834) p. 143 [P]
    Printed without Ferguson's authorisation, over the initials 'E.N.M.'; see letter to Gavan Duffy, (1/8/1845, NLI 5756)

Dublin University Magazine (1833–1853)

27. 'Don Gomez and the Cid' II (August 1833) p. 143 [P]
28. 'The History of Pierce Bodkin: Extracted from a Mutilated and Antique MS (in Bib. Lunens. FF 1 32); Supposed to have been part of the Lost Annals of Carrickfergus' II (October 1833) pp. 456–64 [F]
29. 'A Dialogue Between the Head and Heart of an Irish Protestant' II (November 1833) pp. 586–93 [A]
30. 'Willie and Pate. A County Down Pastoral' II (November 1833) p. 575 [P]
31. 'The Tale of the Tub, or The Strange Thing That Happened to Bishop M'Hale' II (December 1833) pp. 691–2 [P]
32. 'Inaugural Ode for the New Year' III (January 1834) unnumbered prelims [P]
33. 'Hilloa, Our Fancy. Flight the First' III (January 1834) pp. 25–42 [A]
34. 'Athens' III (February 1834) p. 158 [P]
35. 'Fragments from the History of Grana Weal' III (February 1834) pp. 194–202 [F]

36. 'Captain Bey, or, The Turkish Sack-'Em-Up' III (February 1834) p. 231 [P]
37. 'The Sixpenny Manifesto' III (March 1834) pp. 253–63 [A]
38. 'Grana Weal's Garland: I. Lamentation of Fighting Fitzgerald's Ghost. II. My Nose is at Your Service. III. The Fine Old Irish Gentleman' III (March 1834) pp. 292–5 [P]
39. 'The Fairy Thorn' III (March 1834) p. 331–2 [P]
40. 'The Forester's Complaint' III (April 1834) p. 386 [P]
41. 'Hardiman's Irish Minstrelsy. – No.I' III (April 1834) pp. 455 [misnumbered as 465]-78 [R]
42. 'The Stray Canto' IV (July 1834) pp. 72–78 [P]
43. 'Hardiman's Irish Minstrelsy. – No.II' IV (August 1834) pp. 152–67 [R]
44. 'Irish Storyists – Lover and Carleton' IV (September 1834) pp 298–311 [R]
45. 'Fancy, the Scene Shifter' IV (September 1834) pp. 325 [P]
46. 'Hardiman's Irish Minstrelsy. – No.III' IV (October 1834) pp. 447–67 [R]
47. 'Hardiman's Irish Minstrelsy. – No.IV' IV (November 1834) pp 514–542 [R + P]
    The last thirteen pages are an 'appendix' containing Ferguson's own translations of some of the poems from Hardiman's book.
48. 'Hibernian Nights' Entertainments. The First Night' IV (December 1834) pp. 674–690 [F]
    This contains the story of 'The Death of the Children of Usnach' with the poems 'Deirdra's Farewell to Alba' and 'Deirdra's Lament'.
49. 'Hibernian Nights' Entertainments – Second Night. The Captive of Killeshin' V (January 1835) pp. 58–79 [F]
50. 'Hibernian Nights' Entertainments – Third Night. The Rebellion of Silken Thomas' V (February 1835) pp. 193–215 [F]
51. 'The Hibernian Nights' Entertainments – Fourth Night. The Rebellion of Silken Thomas' V (March 1835) pp. 293–312 [F]
52. 'The Hibernian Nights' Entertainments – The Fifth Night. The Rebellion of Silken Thomas – Part Third' V (April 1835) pp. 438–58 [F]
53. 'The Hibernian Nights' Entertainments – The Sixth Night. The Rebellion of Silken Thomas – Part Fourth' V (June 1835) pp. 705–23 [F]

54. 'The Hibernian Nights' Entertainments – Seventh Night. The Rebellion of Silken Thomas – Part Fifth' VI (July 1835) pp. 50–71 [F]
55. 'Hibernian Nights' Entertainments – Eighth Night. The Rebellion of Silken Thomas – Conclusion' VI (August 1835) pp. 207–23 [F]
56. 'Hibernian Nights' Entertainments – Ninth Night. Corby Mac Gillmore' VI (September 1835) pp. 278–95 [F]
57. 'The Black Monday of the Glens' VI (September 1835) pp. 332–44 [F]
58. 'Hibernian Nights' Entertainments – Tenth Night. Corby Mac Gillmore – Part Second' VI (November 1835) pp. 537–57 [F]
59. 'Hibernian Nights' Entertainments – Eleventh Night. Corby Mac Gillmore – Conclusion' VI (December 1835) pp. 640–61 [F]
60. 'Three Ballads: I. Una Phelimy II. Willy Gilliland. III. Young Dobbs' VII (January 1836) pp. 66–71 [P]
   'Una Phelimy' and 'Willy Gilliland' had already been published in the *Ulster Magazine*, the latter as 'The Rescue of the Mare' (see 122 and 124).
61. 'Hibernian Nights' Entertainments – Twelfth Night. Rosabel of Ross – Part I' VII (January 1836) pp. 96–116 [F]
62. 'Hibernian Nights' Entertainments – Thirteenth Night. Rosabel of Ross – Part II' VII (March 1836) pp. 327–42 [F]
63. 'Hibernian Nights' Entertainments – Fourteenth Night. Rosabel of Ross. Part III' VII (April 1836) pp. 380–400 [F]
64. 'Hibernian Nights' Entertainments. Fifteenth Night; Rosabel of Ross. Concluded' VII (May 1836) pp. 579–96 [F]
65. 'The Sketcher Foiled' VIII (July 1836) p. 16 [P]
66. 'The Attractions of Ireland. – No. I. Scenery' VIII (July 1836) pp. 112–131 [R + A]
67. 'The Attractions of Ireland. – No. II. Scenery and Society' VIII (September 1836) pp. 315–333 [A]
   This includes the poem 'The Pretty Girl of Lough Dan'.
68. 'The Attractions of Ireland. – No. III. Society' VIII (December 1836) pp. 658–75 [A]
69. 'The Capabilities of Ireland. Being a Sequel to The Attractions of Ireland' IX (January 1837) pp. 46–57 [A]
70. 'Curiosities of Irish Literature. The Libraries. The Thaumaturgists' IX (March 1837) pp. 341–59 [A]

71. 'Curiosities of Irish Literature. – No. II. The Mere Irish' IX (May 1837) pp. 546–58 [A]
72. 'The Scotic Controversy and the Highland Society's Prize Essay' IX (June 1837) pp. 710–26 [R]
73. 'More on the Scotic Controversy' X (October 1837) pp. 430–47 [A]
This is a reply to Ferguson's criticisms in 72, with extensive comments by Ferguson.
74. 'Gallery of Illustrious Irishmen – George Petrie' XIV (December 1839) pp. 638–42 [A]
75. 'The *Dublin Penny Journal*' XV (January 1840) pp. 112–28 [A]
76. 'Clarendon on the Horse' XXI (February 1843) pp. 186–89[R]
See note at end.
77. 'Carleton's *Traits and Stories*. – New Edition' XXIV (September 1844) pp. 269–282 [R]
78. 'Mrs Hamilton Gray's Works on Etruria' XXIV (December 1844) pp. 527–43 [R]
79. 'Eugene Sue' XXIV (December 1844) pp. 702–17 [R]
80. 'Robert Burns' XXV (January 1845) pp. 66–81 [A]
81. 'Miss Barrett's Poems' XXV (February 1845) pp. 144–154 [R]
82. 'Robert Burns. Second Article' XXV (March 1845) pp. 289–305 [A]
83. 'Petrie's Round Towers' XXV (April 1845) pp. 379–396 [R]
84. 'O'Connor's History of the Irish Brigade Etc.' XXV (May 1845) pp. 593–608 [R]
85. 'Jerusalem' XXVI (September 1845) pp. 266–82 [R]
86. 'The Welshmen of Tirawley' XXVI (September 1845) pp. 308–14 [P]
87. 'Claims of Archbishop de Londres to a Niche in the New House of Lords, in a Letter to Henry Hallam, Esq.' XXVI (November 1845) pp. 628–34 [A]
88. 'The Didactic Irish Novelists. – Carleton, Mrs Hall' XXVI (December 1845) pp. 737–52 [R]
89. 'Our Portrait Gallery. – No. XLII. Thomas Davis' XXIX (February 1847) pp. 190–99 [A]
This includes sonnet 'To the gentlemen of *The Nation* Newspaper' and the poem on the death of Davis.
90. 'Architecture in Ireland' XXIX (June 1847) pp. 693–708 [R]
91. 'Reeves's Ecclesiastical Antiquities' XXXI (February 1848) pp. 207–27 [R]
92. 'The Annals of the Four Masters' XXXI (March 1848) pp. 359–76 [R]

93. 'The Dome of the Rock' XXXI (April 1848) pp. 411–29 [R]
94. 'The Annals of the Four Masters: Second Article' XXXI (May 1848) pp. 571–84 [R]
95. 'Inheritor and Economist, – A Poem' XXXIII (May 1849) pp. 638–49 [P]
96. 'Ruskin's Seven Lamps of Architecture' XXXIV (July 1849) pp. 1–14 [R]
97. 'Dublin: A Poem. In Imitation of Third Satire of Juvenal' XXXIV (July 1849) pp. 102–9 [P]
98. 'Ferguson on Fortification' XXXIV (August 1849)
99. 'Hungary: A Poem' XXXIV (September 1849) p. 292 [P]
100. 'Physical Geography. – The Air' XXIV (Novemeber 1849) pp. 497–515 [R]
101. 'Fallacies of the "Fallacies"' XXXIV (December 1849) pp. 640–6 [R]
102. 'Irish Tourists. – Giraldus Cambrensis' XXXV (January 1850) pp. 1–16 [A]
103. 'Irish Tourists. – Giraldus Cambrensis: Second Article' XXXV (February 1850) pp. 192–212 [A]
104. 'Irish Tourists. – Giraldus Cambrensis: Conclusion' XXXV (March 1850) pp. 388–401 [A]
105. 'A Rummage Review. Philip James Bailey – W. G. T. Barter – Charles Mackay – Mrs H. R. Sandbach – John Struthers – Nicholas Michell – Francis Du Bourdieu – William Charles Kent – John Alfred Langford – W. Harris – H. Latham – William Allingham – Edward Kenealy' XXXVI (November 1850) pp. 567–83 [R]
106. 'Ruskin's Stones of Venice' XXXVIII (September 1851) pp. 253–271 [R]
107. 'The Celtic-Scythic Progress' XXXIX (March 1852) pp. 277–291 [R]
     Contains poem 'The Origin of the Scythians'.
108. 'Chesney on Artillery and Fire-Arms. – The National Defences' XXXIX (April 1852) pp. 447–57 [R]
109. 'Clonmacnoise, Clare, and Arran: Part I' XLI (January 1853) pp. 79–95 [A]
110. 'Clonmacnoise, Clare, and Arran: Part II' XLI (April 1853) pp. 492–505 [A]
111. 'Archytas and the Mariner: Horat. Od. I, 28' XLI (April 1853) p. 506 [P]
112. 'Nineveh. – Second Article' XLI (June 1853) pp. 740–57 [R] Apparently this follows on from 93

Freeman's Journal (1886)

113. [Letter to the Editor] (29 March 1886) p. 5 [L]
    One of a number of letters solicited from various figures as a
    follow-up to an article 'The Best Irish Hundred Books'
    published 23 March 1886.

Irish Builder (1876)

114. 'Dear Wilde' XVIII (1 May 1876) p. 120 [P]

Penny Cyclopedia (Knight's) (1836)

115. 'Brehon Laws' V (1836) pp. 382–87 [A]

Quarterly Review (1868)

116. 'Lord Romilly's Irish Publications' CXXIV (April 1868) pp.
    423–45 [R]

Revue de Bretagne et de Vendée (1864)

117. 'Adieu to Brittany' XV (January 1864) pp. 5–17 [P]
    With a prose translation into French by the Comte de la
    Villemarqué, who also introduces the poem with a prefatory
    note.

Saunders' News-Letter (1844, 1869)

118. 'Ordnance Memoir of Ireland' (8 March 1844) [p 2] [A]
    Ferguson mentions this in a letter to Thomas Davis (7 March
    1844, NLI 2644); Lady Ferguson lists a similarly entitled
    article which appeared in the *Dublin University Magazine* the
    same month, but her husband was not writing for the
    University then.

119. 'Literature' (22 January 1869) [p 3] [R]
    A review of David Herbison's poetry.

Ulster Magazine (1830–31)

120. 'Sir Kenneth Kerr' I (March 1830) p. 182 [P]
121. 'To the Anti-**** Society' I (March 1830) p. 182 [P]
122. 'Ulster Ballads. No. I "The Rescue of the Mare"' II (January 1831) pp. 37–8 [P]
    This was later retitled 'Willy Gilliland'; see 60
123. 'The Expostulation of Lord Augustus Touchmenot with Earl Grey' II (March 1831) pp. 160–1 [P]
124. 'Ulster Ballads. No. II "Una Phelimy"' II (March 1831) pp. 174–5 [P]
125. 'Two Songs of Horace – To False Sweethearts. I. To Barine; II. To Pyrrha' II (April 1831) pp. 230–1 [P]

(ii) **Contributions to learned journals.**

Journal of the Royal Historical and Archaeological Association of Ireland (1874)

126. 'The Ogham Monuments of Kilkenny, being a Letter from Samuel Ferguson, Esq., Q.C., LL.D. etc. with Some Introductory Observations by John G. A. Prim' 4th series, II (1874) pp. 222–38 [A]
127. [Letter to Rev. James Graves , on Inscribed Cromlechs] 4th series, II (1874) pp. 523–531 [A]

Proceedings of the Royal Irish Academy (1864–1888)

128. 'On the Antiquity of the Kiliee, or Boomerang' I (1837) pp. 130–1, 133 [A]
129. 'Remarks on the late Publication of the Society of Northern Antiquaries' I (1837) pp. 180–2 [A]
130. 'Account of Inscribed Stones in the Sepulchral Monument, called Mare Nelud, at Locmariaker in the Department of Morbihan, Brittany' VIII (1864) pp. 398–405 [A]

County of Cork' 2nd series, I, Polite Literature and Antiquities (1879) pp. 207–10 [A]

159. 'Introductory Remarks to Remarks on an Ogam Monument by the Right Rev. Charles Graves, D.D.' 2nd series, II, Polite Literature and Antiquities (1888) p. 279 [A]
160. 'On the Kenfig Inscription' 2nd series, II, Polite Literature and Antiquities (1888) pp. 347–54 [A]

Transactions of the Royal Irish Academy

161. 'On the Antiquity of the Kiliee, or Boomerang', XIX, Polite Literature and Antiquities (1843) pp. 22–31
162. 'On the Rudiments of the Common Law discoverable in the published Portion of the Senchus Mor', XXIV, Part II – Polite Literature and Antiquities (1867) pp. 83–117
163. 'Fasciculus of prints from Photographs of Casts of Ogham Inscriptions', XXVII, Polite Literature and Antiquities (1881) pp. 47–56
164. 'On Sepulchral Cellae' XXVII, Polite Literature and Antiquities (1882) pp. 57–66
165. 'On the Patrician Documents' XXVII, Polite Literature and Antiquities (1885) pp. 67–134

(iii) Contributions to Books

166. 'Of the Antiquity of the Harp and Bagpipe', Chapter III of *The Ancient Music of Ireland, Arranged for the Piano Forte. To which is prefixed A Dissertation on The Irish Harp and Harpers, Including an Account of the Old Melodies of Ireland* [3rd volume] by Edward Bunting (Dublin: Hodges and Smith, 1840) pp. 37–9
Other parts of the introductory matter contain extensive quotation from 'The Death of the Children of Usnach' in 48 above, and the text of 'To the Harper O'Connellan' taken from 47; Ferguson helped Bunting to prepare this volume for the press – see Fox, *Annals of the Irish Harpers*.
167. 'Our Architecture', *The Afternoon Lectures on Literature and Art. Delivered in the Theatre of the Museum of Industry, St Stephen's Green, Dublin, in April and May 1864* Second Series (London: Bell and Daldy; Dublin: Hodges and Smith, and McGee, 1864) pp. 29–65
168. 'Note on the Sources and Nomenclature', *The Story of the*

Irish Before the Conquest. From the Mythical Period to the Invasion under Strongbow by M. C. Ferguson (London: Bell and Daldy, 1868) pp. 294–303

169. 'Preface', *Leabhar Breac, The Speckled Book, otherwise styled Leabhar Mór Dúna Doighre: A Collection of Pieces in Irish Compiled from Ancient Sources About the Close of the Fourteenth Century* (Dublin: Royal Irish Academy, 1876) pp. vii-vii

170. Drawing of church and tower at St Maurice, Epinal, *Early Christian Architecture in Ireland* by Margaret Stokes, Illustrated with Woodcuts, (London: George Bell and Sons, York Street, Covent Garden, 1878)
As indicated by the drawings preserved among his manuscripts in the RIA and the LHL, and those illustrating some of his antiquarian papers, Ferguson was a competent sketcher.

171. 'Westminster Abbey', 'The Hymn of the Fisherman', 'Three Thoughts', 'Three Seasons', *Lyra Hibernica Sacra* compiled and edited by Rev. W. MacIlwaine, D.D., M.R.I.A. (Belfast: M'Caw, Stevenson and Orr; London: Geo. Bell and Sons; Dublin: Hodges, Foster and Figgis, 1878) pp. 48–53
'Westminster Abbey' had already been published in *Lays of the Western Gael and Other Poems* (176 below).

(iv) Books and Pamphlets

172. *On the Expediency of Taking Stock. A Letter to James Pim, Jun, Esq.* By Samuel Ferguson M.R.I.A. Barrister-at-Law, Dublin: James M'Glashan, MDCCCXLVII [1847]
16pp; the letter is dated 7 January 1847, from 10 Henrietta St, Dublin.

173. *Inheritor and Economist; A Poem* Dublin: James McGlashan, 21 D'Olier St, MDCCCXLIX [1849]
32pp pamphlet of 95 above; text dated May 1849.

174. *The Hibernian Nights' Entertainments*, by Samuel Ferguson, Esq. LL.D., M.R.I.A., Editor of the Dublin University Magazine, Author of the Forging of the Anchor, etc. etc. New York: P. M. Haverty, 110 Fulton St, 1857
This reprints the *Dublin University Magazine* text 48–56, 58, 59, and 61–64 above. It seems to have been an unauthorised edition, judging by the erroneous description of Ferguson as editor of the *Dublin University Magazine* and his wife's omission of it from her bibliography.

175. *Father Tom and the Pope; or A Night at the Vatican*. As related by
Mr. Michael Heffernan, master of the national school at
Tallymactaggart, in the County of Leitrim, to a friend during
his official visit to Dublin, for the purpose of studying
political economy, in the spring of 1838. Baltimore: Printed
by Jos. Robinson, 1858
The first of a number of unauthorised U.S. editions.

176. *The Cromlech on Howth, A Poem*, by Samuel Ferguson, Q.C.,
M.R.I.A., With Illuminations from the Books of Kells and
Durrow, and Drawings from Nature by M.S.. With Notes on
Celtic Ornamental Art, Revised by George Petrie, LL.D.
London: Day and Son, Lithographers to the Queen, and to
H.R.H. the Prince of Wales, 6 Gate Street, Lincolns Inn
Fields, W.C., [1861]
This poem was reprinted in 178 under the title 'Aideen's
Grave'. 300 copies of this lavishly ornamented large-format
book were for sale at £2.2.0 each. 'M.S.' was Margaret
Stokes. The date 'mdccclxi' appears on the ornamental
title-page of the book.

177. *Father Tom and the Pope; or, A Night at the Vatican*, Philadelphia: C. Sherman and Son, 1861

178. *Lays of the Western Gael, and Other Poems*, by Samuel Ferguson, London: Bell and Daldy, 186 Fleet Street, 1865 [1864]
This includes 2, the poem in 12, 20, 39, 40, most of the
poems in 47, the poems in 48, 60 [I and II only], 67, 86, 98,
106, 110, 117 and 175, as well as previously unpublished
pieces.

179. *Father Tom and the Pope, or A Night in the Vatican*, New York:
A. Simpson and Co., 1867
An anonymous preface speculates on the identity of the
author, mentioning attributions to Lord Brougham and the
Duke of Wellington; the writer suggests Maginn. This is a
well-produced book.

180. *Father Tom and the Pope; or, A Night at the Vatican*, Philadelphia: John Penington and Son, MDCCCLXVII [1867]

181. *Father Tom and the Pope; or, A Night in the Vatican*, New York;
Moorhead, Simpson and Bond, publishers, 1868.
An 'ante-preface' corrects the misattributions in 179.

182. *Congal: A Poem, in Five Books* by Samuel Ferguson, Dublin:
Edward Ponsonby, Grafton-Street. London: Bell and Daldy,
York Street, Covent Garden, 1872

In the 'Notes' at the end of the book the poems 'The Naming of Cuchullin', 'The Twins of Macha' and 'The Legend of Fergus Leidesen' ('Fergus Wry-Mouth') are printed for the first time.

183. *Inaugural Lecture of the Meath Antiquarian Society* delivered by Sir Samuel Ferguson, Q.C., LL.D., Vice-President of the Royal Irish Academy, Deputy Keeper of the Records, etc. at the County Court House, Trim, on Wednesday 25th June 1879. Trim: Joseph Moore, Market St, 1879
24 pp; not listed in Lady Ferguson's bibliography.

184. *Father Tom and the Pope; or, A Night at the Vatican*. By the late John Fisher Murray [sic]. With Illustrative Engravings. Philadelphia: T. B. Peterson and Brothers, 306 Chestnut Street [1879 ?]

185. *Poems* by Sir Samuel Ferguson, Dublin: William McGee, Nassau Street. London: George Bell and Sons, York Street, Covent Garden, 1880
This collection includes 21, 22, 114, the three pieces first printed in 171, and the three poems given in the 'Notes' to 182, as well as a number of previously unpublished pieces.

186. *Deirdre*. A One-Act Drama of Old Irish Story. By Sir Samuel Ferguson, Dublin (for private Circulation) 1880

187. *Shakespearean Breviates: An Adjustment of Twenty-Four of the Longer Plays of Shakespeare to Convenient Reading Limit* by Samuel Ferguson Knt., LL.D. P.R.I.A. Dublin: Hodges, Figgis and Co., Grafton Street, London: Belland Sons, York Street, Covent Garden, 1882

188. *The Forging of the Anchor*. A Poem. By Sir Samuel Ferguson, LL.D. Illustrated by A. Barraud, H. C. Glindoni, G. W. Harvey, W. Hotherell, Seymour Lucas, Hal Ludlow, J. Nash, W. H. Overend, C. J. Staniland, and W. L. Wyllie, Cassell and Company, London, Paris and New York, 1883 24pp.

189. *Ogham Inscriptions in Ireland, Wales, and Scotland* by the late Sir Samuel Ferguson, President of the Royal Irish Academy; Deputy Keeper of the Records of Ireland; LL.D Dublin and Edinburgh; etc etc. Edinburgh: David Douglas, 1887
Preface by Lady Ferguson.

190a. *Hibernian Nights' Entertainments*. By Sir Samuel Ferguson. Contents, First Series: The Death of the Children of Usnach. The Return of Claneboy. The Captive of Killeshin. Dublin: Sealy, Bryers and Walker, 94, 95 and 96 Middle Abbey Street, London: George Bell and Sons, 5 York Street, Covent Garden, 1887

190b. *Hibernian Nights' Entertainments.* By Sir Samuel Ferguson. Contents, Second Series: An Adventure of Shane O'Neill's. Corby Mac Gillmore. Dublin: Sealy, Bryers and Walker, 94, 95 and 96 Middle Abbey Street, London: George Bell and Sons, 5 York Street, Covent Garden, 1887

190c. *Hibernian Nights' Entertainments.* By Sir Samuel Ferguson. Contents, Third Series: The Rebellion of Silken Thomas. Dublin: Sealy, Bryers and Walker, 94, 95 and 96 Middle Abbey Street, London: George Bell and Sons, 5 York Street, Covent Garden, 1887
These volumes collect 12, 13, 48 – 56, 58, 59.

191. *Congal:* A Poem, in Five Books. By Sir Samuel Ferguson. Second Edition, Dublin: Sealy, Bryers and Walker, 94, 95 and 96 Middle Abbey Street, London: G. Bell and Sons, 5 York Street, Covent Garden, 1887
This has an 'Editor's Preface' by Mary Ferguson, and detailed prose summaries prefixed to each book; Ferguson's 'Notes' provided in 177 are omitted. Uniform with 190.

192. *Lays of the Western Gael, and Other Poems.* By Sir Samuel Ferguson. Dublin: Sealy, Bryers and Walker, 94, 95 and 96 Middle Abbey Street; London: George Bell and Sons, 5 York Street, Covent Garden, 1888
This cheap edition, uniform with 190, has an introduction by Alfred M. Williams, written to protect American copyright (see *Life* II, p. 282).

193. *The Remains of St Patrick, Apostle of Ireland. The Confessio and Epistle to Coroticus* Translated into English Blank Verse, with a Dissertation on the Patrician Documents Contained in the 'Trias Thaumaturga' and 'Book of Armagh', etc., by Sir Samuel Ferguson, LL.D., President of the Royal Irish Academy, Dublin: Sealy, Bryers and Walker, 94, 95 and 96 Middle Abbey Street; London: George Bell and Sons, 5 York Street, Covent Garden, 1888
This reprints the material in 165, with a lengthy introduction by Lady Ferguson.

194. *Father Tom and the Pope; or, A Night at the Vatican.* As related by Mr. Michael Heffernan, Master of the National School at Tallymactaggart, in the County of Leitrim, to a friend, dur-

ing his official visit to Dublin, for the purpose of studying
Political Economy, in the Spring of 1838. New York: Peter
Eckler, Publishers, No. 35 Fulton Street, [1896]
Bound with *History of the Pope's Mule* by Alphonse Daudet.

195 *Lays of the Red Branch* by Sir Samuel Ferguson, Q.C., LL.D.
Late President of the Royal Irish Academy, and Deputy
Keeper of the Records of Ireland. With an Introduction by
Lady Ferguson, London: T. Fisher Unwin, Paternoster
Square, Dublin: Sealy, Bryers and Walker, Middle Abbey
Street, MDCCCXCVII [1897]
Twelfth volume in 'The New Irish Library' series edited by
Sir Charles Gavan Duffy. This gathers together poems
dealing with Irish history and legend from 178 and 185,
following an arrangement suggested by Ferguson in the
latter.

196. *Father Tom and the Pope* by Samuel Ferguson, New York and
London: G. P. Putnam's Sons: The Knickerbocker Press
[1905 ?]

197a. *Hibernian Nights' Entertainments.* By Sir Samuel Ferguson.
Contents, First Series: The Death of the Children of Usnach.
The Return of Claneboy. The Captive of Killeshin. Dublin:
Sealy, Bryers and Walker, 94, 95 and 96 Middle Abbey
Street, London: George Bell and Sons, 5 York Street, Covent
Garden, 1904

197b. *Hibernian Nights' Entertainments.* By Sir Samuel Ferguson.
Contents, Second Series: An Adventure of Shane O'Neill's.
Corby Mac Gillmore. Dublin: Sealy, Bryers and Walker, 94,
95 and 96 Middle Abbey Street, London: George Bell and
Sons, 5 York Street, Covent Garden, 1906
These are the same as 190a and b with the addition of some
pages of notes at the end on 'Topography 2nd Series *Hibernian Nights' Entertainments*' to 189b and 'Topography 3rd
Series *Hibernian Nights' Entertainments*' [sic] to 189a. Presumably there was a Third Series in this edition but I have not
seen it.

198. *Father Tom and the Pope* by Samuel Ferguson, New York and
London: G. P. Putnam's Sons: The Knickerbocker Press
[1905 ?]

199. *Congal*: A Poem, in Five Books. By Sir Samuel Ferguson.
Third Edition, Dublin: Sealy, Bryers and Walker, 94, 95 and
96 Middle Abbey Street, London: G. Bell and Sons, 5 York
Street, Covent Garden, 1907

This edition is in effect a reprint of 191.

200. *Poems of Sir Samuel Ferguson* with an Introduction by Alfred Perceval Graves, M.A., Every Irishman's Library, Dublin: The Talbot Press, Ltd, 89 Talbot Street; London: T. Fisher Unwin, Ltd, 1 Adelphi Terrace, n.d. [1918]

A very extensive selection of Ferguson's poetry, giving all of *Congal*, the 'Lays of the Red Branch' as in 195, and nearly all of the material in 182 and 185.

201. *Poems of Sir Samuel Ferguson* with an Introduction by Alfred Perceval Graves, M.A., The Irish Library, The Phoenix Publishing Company Limited, Dublin, Cork and Belfast, n.d.

The text is a reprint of 200.

202. *Father Tom and the Pope; or, A Night at the Vatican.* As related by Mr. Michael Heffernan, master of the National School at Tallymactaggart, in the county of Leitrim, to a friend, during his official visit to Dublin, for the purpose of studying political economy, in the Spring of 1838. Library of Liberal Classics, No. 14. New York: P. Eckler, 1920

203. *Samuel Ferguson, Selected Poems*, with Life and Notes, The Educational Series of English Classics, The Educational Company of Ireland, 1931

32 pp; a very brief and partial selection, with only four poems given in full: 'The Burial of King Cormac', 'To the Harper O'Connellan', 'The Hymn of the Fishermen' and 'The Little Maiden'.

203. *The Poems of Samuel Ferguson* Edited with an Introduction by Padraic Colum, An Chomhairle Ealaíon series of Irish Authors, Number Two, Allen Figgis, Dublin, 1963

204. *The Battle of Moira* being the Epic Poem 'Congal' by Samuel Ferguson with a historical introduction by Ian Adamson, no publisher named, Newtownards [Northern Ireland], 1980

This is a photographic reprint of 182, with some additional prefatory material by Adamson.

NOTE

Lady Ferguson assigns the authorship of two other pieces in the *Dublin University Magaine* to her husband: an article on the 'Ordnance Memoir of Ireland', XXIII (March 1844) pp. 494–500, and a poem 'To Clarence Mangan', XXIX (May 1847) p. 622. As Ferguson mentions in his correspondence to Thomas Davis (7 March 1844, NLI 2644), he did not resume writing for the *DUM* until September of that year. He did contribute a similarly entitled article to *Saunders' Newsletter* (118 above) which is probably the source of Lady Ferguson's confusion. The poem 'To Clarence Mangan' was speculatively assigned to Ferguson in a review of *Lays of the Western Gael and Other Poems*, and so listed by Lady Ferguson; her listing was corrected by D. J. O'Donoghue in his biography of Mangan, who states categorically that the piece was written by 'an eminent bishop of the Church of Ireland, the Right Rev. William Fitzgerald' (p. 199). I also question the attribution of 'Clarendon on the Horse' (76 above); Ferguson said he was not a contributor to the *Dublin University Magazine* at that time, and the writer of the review speaks of having been in France and Germany, which does not accord with what we know of Ferguson's life. However, in the absence of more definite evidence, we must accept the authority of Lady Ferguson.

In the biography of George Petrie by William Stokes, Ferguson is named along with O'Curry, Wills, Anster, Mangan, de Vere and Carleton as a contributor to Petrie's *Irish Penny Journal* (1840–1). The others are known to have written for it, and as Ferguson was a friend of both Petrie and Stokes, and assisted the latter in preparing the biography, due weight must be placed on the statement. There are several pieces signed 'F.' in the magazine, all of them on topics of which Ferguson might have written: 'The Professions' I (9 Jan 1841) pp. 222–3; 'The Destitute Poor of Ireland' I (27 Feb 1841) pp. 273–6; 'On Stimulants: Tobacco' I (13 Mar 1841) pp. 295–5; 'Tomb of Curran' I (26 June 1841) pp. 409–10. However, it should be borne in mind that ten years previously there had been a contributor 'F' to the *Dublin Penny Journal* who was certainly not Ferguson, and contributors to both journals generally kept the same acronym.

There are undoubtedly other writings by Ferguson besides those listed above. In the DUM particularly there are several unsigned articles or poems which read as if from his pen (*e.g.* 'Lines Written the Day before the Queen's Arrival in Dublin', DUM XXXIV, Sept. 1849); however, in the absence of corroborating evidence which would take the attribution beyond conjecture, they are not included in this checklist.

Articles and Books About Ferguson
(in chronological order)

——, 'Lays of the Western Gael', Athenaeum, No 1936 (3 December 1864) pp. 739–740

——, 'Lays of the Western Gael', Saturday Review, XIX (28 January 1865) pp. 116–7

[Cashel Hoey], 'Recent Irish Poetry', Dublin Review, VIII (April 1865) pp. 302–327

——, 'Congal', Dublin University Magazine, LXXX (October 1872) pp. 385–400

——, 'Books Received: Congal', Irish Builder, XIV, 317 (1 March 1873) p. 64

'P.W.' ['Patricius Walker', i.e. William Allingham], 'An Old Story of a Feast and a Battle', Fraser's Magazine n.s., XI (May 1875) pp. 642–654

[Alfred M. Williams], 'A Too Rare Voice', Providence Journal (Rhode Island, U.S; 26 December 1877) p. [2]

[William Allingham], 'Ivy Leaves from the Hermitage, Epping Forest', Fraser's Magazine n.s., XVII (April 1878) pp. 535–536

——, 'Congal', The Catholic World, XXIX (New York, July 1879) pp. 530–536

——, 'Poems' [review], The Academy, XVIII (24 July 1880) p. 60

[Aubrey De Vere], 'Poems by Sir Samuel Ferguson', The Spectator (4 September 1880) pp. 1122–1124

J. P. Mahaffy, 'Sir Samuel Ferguson', The Athenaeum, No 3068 (14 August 1886) p. 205

——, 'Sir Samuel Ferguson on The Loyal Orangeman', Freeman's Journal (18 August 1886) p. 2
First printing of the poem 'The Loyal Orangeman'.

Alfred Perceval Graves, 'Sir Samuel Ferguson' [sonnet], The Spectator (21 August 1886) p. 1118

'M.S.' [Margaret Stokes], 'Obituary: Sir Samuel Ferguson', The Academy, XXX (21 August 1886) pp. 120–122

[Rev. Matthew Russell], 'Sir Samuel Ferguson. In Memoriam', Irish Monthly, XIV (October 1886) pp. 529–536

[Margaret Stokes], 'Sir Samuel Ferguson', Blackwood's Edinburgh Magazine, CXL (November 1886) pp. 621–641
Ends with SF's translation of the first ode of Horace, his last poetical work.

W. B. Yeats, 'Irish Poets and Irish Poetry: The Poetry of Sir Samuel Ferguson', *Irish Fireside* (9 October 1886) pp. 81–86

W. B. Yeats, 'Sir Samuel Ferguson', *Dublin University Review*, II (November 1886) pp. 923–941
Reprinted in *Uncollected Prose*. ed. John Frayne.

——, 'Ogham Inscriptions in Ireland, Wales and Scotland' [review], *The Archaeological Journal*, XLIV (March 1887) pp. 96–98

[Rev. Matthew Russell], 'Aubrey De Vere on Sir Samuel Ferguson', *Irish Monthly*, XV (April, 1887) pp. 224–226

Mr Justice [John] O'Hagan, *The Poetry of Sir Samuel Ferguson* (Dublin, 1887)
Reprinted from *Irish Monthly*, XII, XIII (May, August 1884).

Alfred Perceval Graves, 'Has Ireland a National Poet?' *The Reflector* XVI (14 April 1888) pp. 380–383

Aubrey De Vere, *Essays, Chiefly Literary and Ethical* (London, 1889): 'Poems by Sir Samuel Ferguson' pp. 98–128

Alfred M. Williams, *Studies in Folk-Song and Popular Poetry* (Boston, 1894; London, 1895): 'Sir Samuel Ferguson and Celtic Poetry' pp. 131–165

[Mary Catherine] Lady Ferguson, *Sir Samuel Ferguson in the Ireland of his Day*, 2 volumes (Edinburgh and London, 1896)
The most important source-book on Ferguson, which includes a number of his poems printed for the first time.

W. B. Yeats, 'An Irish Patriot', *The Bookman*, X (May 1896) pp. 49–50

L. G., and Eleanor Hull, 'Is Ferguson the Typical Irish Poet', *New Ireland Review*, VII (1897) pp. 302–305, 371–373

Edward Nagle, 'The Muse of Sir Samuel Ferguson' *New Ireland Review*, XXIV (1905) pp. 98–106

——, 'The Ferguson Centenary' *Irish Book Lover*, I (March, 1910) pp. 113–5 (April, 1910) pp. 125–7 (May, 1910) p. 132

Roden Noel, 'The Poetry of Sir Samuel Ferguson', *Irish Monthly*, XXXVIII (March, 1910) pp. 121–137

Centenary Anniversary of Sir Samuel Ferguson: Catalogue of a Loan Exhibition of Pictures, Books and Manuscripts (Belfast, 1910)

Alfred Perceval Graves, 'The Centenary of Sir Samuel Ferguson', *The Bookman*, XXXVII (1910) pp. 266–70

Alfred Perceval Graves, *Irish Literary and Musical Studies* (London, 1913): 'Sir Samuel Ferguson' pp. 36–50

P. McCrait, 'Two omissions to the Ferguson Bibliography', *Irish Book Lover* VI (October 1914) p. 42

Robert M'Cahan, *Life of Sir Samuel Ferguson* (Coleraine, n.d.)

Arthur Deering, *Sir Samuel Ferguson, Poet and Antiquarian* (Philadelphia, 1931)

Robert O'Driscoll, 'Two Voices: One Beginning', *University Review*, III, 8 (1965) pp. 88–100

Robert O'Driscoll, 'Ferguson and the Idea of an Irish National Literature', *Eire-Ireland: A Journal of Irish Studies*, VI, 1 (Spring, 1971) pp. 82–95

Herbert Fackler, 'Sir Samuel Ferguson: "The Death of the Children of Usnach" (1834) and "Deirdre" (1880)', *Eire-Ireland: A Journal of Irish Studies*, VII, 1 (Spring, 1972) pp. 84–95

Terence Brown, *Northern Voices: Poets from Ulster* (Dublin, 1975): 'Samuel Ferguson: Cultural Nationalism' pp. 29–41

Malcolm Brown, *Sir Samuel Ferguson* (Lewisburg, USA, 1976)

Robert O'Driscoll, *An Ascendancy of the Heart: Ferguson and the Beginnings of Modern Irish Literature in English* (Dublin, 1976)

W. J. McCormack, [Review of *An Ascendancy of the Heart* (1976) by Robert O'Driscoll], *Irish University Review: A Journal of Irish Studies*, VII, 1 (Spring 1977) pp. 123–126

Gréagóir Ó Dúill, 'Samuel Ferguson, An Stát agus An Léann Dúchais', *Studia Hibernica* 19 (1979) pp. 102–117

Robert Welch, *Irish Poetry from Moore to Yeats* (Gerrards Cross, 1981): 'Sir Samuel Ferguson: The Two Races of Ireland' pp. 116–155

David Lloyd, 'Arnold, Ferguson, Schiller: Aesthetic Culture and the Politics of Aesthetics', *Cultural Critique*, 2 (1985/6) pp. 137–169

Augustine Martin, 'Anglo-Irish Poetry: Moore to Ferguson', *Canadian Journal of Irish Studies*, XII, 2 (June 1986) pp. 84–104

Peter Denman, 'Ferguson and *Blackwood's*: the Formative Years', *Irish University Review: A Journal of Irish Studies*, XVI, 2 (Autumn 1986) pp. 141–158

Proinseas Ní Chatháin, 'Sir Samuel Ferguson and the Ogham Inscriptions', *Irish University Review: A Journal of Irish Studies*, XVI, 2 (Autumn 1986) pp. 159–169

Gréagóir O Dúill, 'Samuel Ferguson, Administrator and Archivist', *Irish University Review: A Journal of Irish Studies*, XVI, 2 (Autumn 1986) pp. 117–140

Terence Brown and Barbara Hayley, edd. *Samuel Ferguson: A Centenary Tribute* (Dublin, 1987). Contents: 'Introduction', Barbara Hayley; 'Sir Samuel Ferguson – Poet and Ideologue', M. A. G. O Tuathaigh; 'The Gaelic Background', Breandán O Buachalla; 'Ferguson's *Congal* – Claiming an

Epos?', Peter Denman; 'Ferguson: His Literary Sources',
William Hodder; 'Samuel Ferguson and the *Dublin University Magazine*', J. P. McBride; 'Ferguson's *Conary*',
Terence Brown

Robert Welch, *A History of Verse Translation from the Irish 1789–1897* (Gerrards Cross, and Totowa, N.J., 1988): 'Two
Northern Translators: Matthew Moore Graham and Samuel
Ferguson' pp. 85–101

Bibliography

(Items already included in the Checklist above are not given)

[——], *A Report of the Trial of the Action in which Bartholomew McGahan was Plaintiff and the Rev. Thomas Maguire Defendant, on December 13th and 14th 1827* (Dublin 1827)

[——], *Authenticated Report of a Discussion which took place between the Rev. Richard T. D. Pope and the Rev. Thomas Maguire in the Lecture Room of the Dublin Institution on the 19th, 20th, 21st, 23rd, 24th, 25th of April 1827* (Dublin, 1827)

[——], *Authenticated Report of the Discussion between the Rev. T. D. Gregg and the Rev. T. Maguire in the Round Room of the Rotunda* (Dublin, 1839)

[——], *Catholic Registry* (Dublin 1840)

[——], 'Irish Ballad Poetry', *Dublin University Magazine* XXX (August 1847) pp. 127–145

Allen, Michael, *Poe and the British Magazine Tradition* (New York, 1969)

Allingham, H. and D. Radford, edd. *William Allingham: A Diary* (Harmondsworth, 1985)

Arnold, Matthew, *Essays Literary and Critical* (London, 1906)

——, *On the Study of Celtic Literature and Other Essays* (London, 1910)

Atkinson, Robert, 'Introduction', *The Book of Leinster, sometime called the Book of Glendalough* (Dublin, 1880)

Borlase, William C., *The Dolmens of Ireland; Their Distribution, Structural Characteristics, and Affinities in Other Countries; Together with the Folk-Lore Attaching to Them*, 3 volumes (London, 1897)

Bowen, Desmond, *The Protestant Crusade in Ireland, 1800–70* (Dublin, 1978)

Boyne, Patricia, *John O'Donovan (1806–1861): A Biography* (Kilkenny, 1987).

Burtchaell, G. D. and Thomas U. Sadleir (edd), *Alumni Dubliniensis: A Register of the Students, Graduates, Professors and Provosts of Trinity College in the University of Dublin (1593–1860)*, new edition (Dublin, 1935)

Clarke, Austin, *Poetry in Modern Ireland* (Dublin, 1962)

Curtin, Jeremiah, *Hero-Tales of Ireland* (London, 1894)
——, *The Politics of Irish Literature: From Thomas Davis to W. B. Yeats* (London, 1972)
Davis, Thomas, *Literary and Historical Essays* (Dublin, 1865)
Deane, Seamus, *A Short History of Irish Literature* (London 1986)
——, *Celtic Revivals* (London, 1985)
De Vere, Aubrey, *The Legends of Saint Patrick* (London, 1872)
Dillon, Myles, ed. *Irish Sagas* (Cork, 1968)
Dowden, Edward, *Letters of Edward Dowden and His Correspondents* (London, 1914)
Drummond, William Hamilton, *The Giant's Causeway, A Poem* (Belfast, 1811)
——, *Ancient Irish Minstrelsy* (Dublin, 1852)
Duffy, Charles Gavan, *Conversations with Carlyle* (London, 1892)
——,*Four Years of Irish History, 1845–1849. A Sequel to 'Young Ireland'* (London, Paris and New York, 1883)
——, *Short Life of Thomas Davis 1840–1846*, New Irish Library (London and Dublin, 1895)
——, ed. *The Ballad Poetry of Ireland*, fortieth edition (Dublin, 1874)
——, *Young Ireland: A Fragment of Irish History 1840–1845* (Dublin, 1884)
Fisher, Joseph R. and John H. Robb, *Royal Belfast Academical Institution: Centenary Volume 1810–1910* (Belfast, 1913)
Fitzpatrick, W. J., *The Life of Charles Lever*, revised edition (London [1884])
Foster, Jeanne Cooper, *Ulster Folklore* (Belfast, 1951)
Foster, John Wilson, *Fictions of the Irish Literary Revival: A Changeling Art* (Dublin, 1987)
Fox, Charlotte Milligan, *Annals of the Irish Harpers* (London, 1911)
Hardiman, James, ed. *Irish Minstrelsy, or Bardic Remains of Ireland; with English Poetical Translations*, 2 volumes (London, 1831)
Hayes, Edward, ed. *The Ballad Poetry of Ireland*, 2 volumes, fourth edition (London, 1855)
Hewitt, John, *Ancestral Voices: The Selected Prose* ed. Tom Clyde (Belfast, 1987)
Hobsbawm, Eric and Terence Ranger, edd. *The Invention of Tradition* (Cambridge, 1984)
Joyce, P. W., *Old Celtic Romances, Translated from the Gaelic*, second edition, revised and enlarged (London 1894)
Keating, Geoffrey, *The History of Ireland, from the Earliest Period to the English Invasion* ed. John O'Mahony (New York, 1866)
Kennedy, Patrick, *The Bardic Stories of Ireland* (Dublin, 1871)

Knight, Charles, *Passages of a Working Life During Half a Century, with a Prelude of Early Reminiscences*, 3 volumes (London, 1864–65)

'Laganiensis' [Canon John O'Hanlon], *Legend Lays of Ireland* (Dublin, 1870)

Levy, F. J., 'The Founding of the Camden Society', *Victorian Studies* VII, 3 (March, 1964) pp. 295–305

Macaulay, Thomas Babington, *Lays of Ancient Rome* (London, n.d.)

MacCarthy, Denis Florence, ed. *The Book of Irish Ballads*, new edition (Dublin, 1874)

MacMahon, Thornton, ed. *The Casket of Irish Pearls* (Dublin, 1846)

Macpherson, James, *The Poems of Ossian, to which are prefixed A preliminary Discourse, and dissertations on the aera and poems of Ossian* (London, 1819)

Madden, Frederic, 'Ancient Norman-French Poem on the erection of the Walls of New Ross, in Ireland, A.D. 1265' *Archaeologia* XXII (1929) pp. 307–314

Maginn, William, *Homeric Ballads; with Translations and Notes* (London, 1850)

Malory, Sir Thomas, *Le Morte D'Arthur* ed. Janet Cowen, 2 volumes (Harmondsworth, 1969)

Meyer, Kuno, *The Death-Tales of the Ulster Heroes*, Royal Irish Academy Todd Lecture Series, Vol. XIV (Dublin 1906)

Montague, John, *The Rough Field* (Dublin, 1972)

Montgomery, Henry R. [ed.], *Specimens of the Early Native Poetry of Ireland, in English Metrical Translations with Historical and Biographical Notices* (Dublin and London, 1846)

Murphy, William M., *Prodigal Father: The Life of John Butler Yeats (1839–1922)* (Ithaca and London, 1978)

Ó Broin, León, *Charles Gavan Duffy, Patriot and Statesman: The Story of Charles Gavan Duffy (1816–1903)* (Dublin, 1967)

Ó Buachalla, Breandán, *I mBéal Feirste Cois Cuain*, (Dublin, 1968)

O'Curry, Eugene, *Lectures on the Manuscript Materials of Ancient Irish History*, re-issue (Dublin and London, 1873)

——, 'The Exile of the Children of Uisnech', *The Atlantis, or Register of Literature and Science of the Catholic University of Ireland*, III, 6 (London, 1862) pp. 377–422.

O'Donoghue, D. J., *The Life and Writings of James Clarence Mangan* (Edinburgh, 1897)

O'Donovan, John, ed. *The Banquet of Dun na n-Gedh and The Battle of Magh Rath, An Ancient Historical Tale*, Irish Archaeological Society (Dublin, 1842)

——, ed. *The Genealogies, Tribes, and Customs of Hy-Fiachrach, Commonly Called O'Dowda's Country*, Irish Archaeological Society (Dublin, 1844)

——, ed. *Miscellany of the Celtic Society* (Dublin, 1849)

O'Flanagan, Theophilus, ed. *Deirdri, or The Lamentable Fate of the Sons of Usnach, an Ancient Irish Dramatic Tale, One of the Three Tragic Stories of Erin*, Transactions of the Gaelic Society (Dublin 1808).

O'Grady, Standish Hayes, *Toruigheacht Dhiarmuida agus Ghrainne; or, the Pursuit after Diarmuid O'Duibhne, and Grainne the daughter of Cormac Mac Airt*, Transactions of the Ossianic Society, Vol. III (Dublin, 1857)

O'Grady, Standish [James], *Early Bardic Literature* (London, 1879)

Oliphant, M., *Annals of a Publishing House*, 2 vols (New York, 1897–98)

O'Reilly, John Boyle, ed. *The Poetry and Song of Ireland* (New York, 1887)

O Tuama, Seán, ed. *Caoineadh Airt Ui Laoghaire* (Dublin, 1961)

O Tuama, Seán, and Thomas Kinsella, ed. *An Duanaire 1600–1900: Poems of the Dispossessed*, (Dublin, 1981)

Poe, Edgar Allan, *Collected Works* ed Thomas O. Mabbott, 3 vols (Cambridge, Massachusetts, 1978)

Reeves, William, *The Ancient Churches of Armagh* (Lusk, Co. Dublin, 1860)

Ryan, William Patrick, *The Irish Literary Revival: Its History, Pioneers and Possibilities* (New York, 1970)

Sadleir, Michael, *Dublin University Magazine; Its History, Contents and Bibliography*, Bibliographical Society of Ireland (Dublin, 1938)

——, 'Tales From Blackwood', *Edinburgh Bibliographical Society Transactions*, II (Edinburgh 1946)

Sheehy, Jeanne, *The Rediscovery of Ireland's Past: The Celtic Revival 1830–1930* (London, 1980)

Stokes, Whitley, ed. 'The Destruction of Da Derga's Hostel', *Revue Celtique*, XXII (Paris, 1901).

Stokes, William, *The Life and labours in Art and Archaeology of George Petrie, LL.D. M.R.I.A.* (London, 1868)

Tillotson, Geoffrey, *A View of Victorian Literature* (London, 1978)

Todd, James Henthorn with the Hon. Algernon Herbert, edd. *The Irish Version of the Historia Britonum of Nennius*, Irish Archaeological Society, (Dublin, 1848)

Welch, Robert, *Irish Poetry from Moore to Yeats* (Gerrards Cross, 1981)

Wilde, William R., *The Beauties of the Boyne, and its Tributary the Blackwater*, second edition, 1850 (Cork, 1978)

Williams, J. E. Caerwyn, ed., *Literature in Celic Countries*, Taliesin Congress Lectures (Cardiff, 1971)

Yeats, W. B. *Collected Letters* I, edd. John Kelly and Eric Domville (Oxford, 1988)

Yeats, W. B., *Uncollected Prose* I, ed. John Frayne (New York, 1970)

Index

223